READING GEORGES BATAILLE

Michèle H. Richman teaches in the Department of Romance Languages at the University of Pennsylvania.

READING GEORGES BATAILLE
Beyond the Gift

MICHELE H. RICHMAN

THE JOHNS HOPKINS UNIVERSITY PRESS
Baltimore and London

The Johns Hopkins University Press, Baltimore, Maryland 21218
The Johns Hopkins Press Ltd., London

Library of Congress Cataloging in Publication Data

Richman, Michèle H.
Reading Georges Bataille.

Bibliography: p. 168
Includes index.
1.   Bataille, Georges, 1897–1962—Criticism and
interpretation.   I. Title.
PQ2603.A695Z86   848'.91209   81–48179
   ISBN   0–8018–2593–8   AACR2

For my family

CONTENTS

ACKNOWLEDGMENTS

This reading of George Bataille focuses on the relevance of gift-giving for modern society. It would be incomplete without mentioning the many instances of generosity I encountered during its preparation which encouraged such a point of view.

I am grateful to my colleagues at the University of Pennsylvania, Jean Alter, Frank Bowman, Clifton Cherpack, Lance Donaldson-Evans, Lucienne Frappier-Mazur, and Gerald Prince, for recognizing the validity of this research from its earliest stages. Their continued support was crucial at different moments on the way to completion. At Penn, my special appreciation extends to Vartan Gregorian, former dean and provost, whose magnanimous example was remembered throughout the writing process.

One gift that I do not discuss in the book, although essential, is time. I am indebted to the American Council of Learned Societies for a fellowship, and the University of Pennsylvania for added support, both providing the free time needed to complete a manuscript. Jean Baudrillard, Maurice Godelier, and Jacques Leenhardt patiently gave of their time during many conversations. Tom Conley, Rodolphe Gasché, René Girard, Fredric Jameson, and Richard Stamelman offered theirs by reading an earlier version of this manuscript. William Sisler, my editor, met requests for more time with consideration.

In one chapter I discuss the special quality of women and the gift of self. I personally benefited from this reality. In their various ways, Dalia Judovitz, Kathryn McMahon, Phyllis Rackin, Selma Pastor, Magali Sarfatti-Larson, and Michael Young offered me more than I could hope to return.

Throughout the history of this book, Josué Harari has been its most constant, and influential, champion. His patience, enthusiasm, and willingness to reread it have been unlimited. I thank him for an exemplary disinterest, which inspired the best that I have said about the gift.

CHRONOLOGY OF GEORGES BATAILLE

1897 Born in Puy-de-Dome.

1914 Conversion to Catholicism (had been raised without religious instruction).

1916 Drafted; discharged in 1917 owing to illness; considers the priesthood.

1918 *Notre-Dame de Rheims,* first published text, appears in pamphlet form; six pages long, it is never again mentioned by Bataille. Enters Ecole des Chartes.

1920 Renounces faith. Assigned to post in Madrid where he witnesses the death of Granero, one of the most popular matadors.

1922 Becomes librarian at the Bibliothèque Nationale. Reads Nietzsche, Gnostics, Nicholas de Cues, Hegel, Marx, tantrics, and Christian mystics.

1923 Initiation to ethnology by Alfred Métraux, who attended the lectures of Marcel Mauss. Publication of Mauss's "Essai sur le don" in *L'Année Sociologique.* Later, in an intellectual biography, Bataille comments: "It figures at the basis of all understanding of the economy linked to the destruction of the surplus of productive activity" (VII, 359).

1924 Friendship with Michel Leiris; meets the surrealists, enters into conflict with Breton.

1927 *L'Anus Solaire* (eventually published in 1931 with illustrations by Masson). Influence of Freud leads to psychoanalysis with Dr. Adrien Borel.

1928 *Histoire de l'oeil,* first narrative, published (134 copies) under the pseudonym of Lord Auch. Hostility to Breton puts Bataille in touch with others disaffected from the surrealist group, who are then denounced in the second Manifesto. Bataille, in particular, is singled out by Breton. Writes first anthropological text, a review of the Paris exhibition of pre-Colombian artifacts.

1929–30 *Documents;* thirty articles published, including "Figure humaine," "Le Langage des fleurs," "Le Bas matérialisme et la gnose."

1930 Reads Marx and Engels. Participates in *Cercle Communiste Démocratique* and contributes to review *La Critique Sociale* (1931–34), directed by Boris Souvarine.

1931–33 Publishes a dozen articles, including "La Notion de dépense." Develops close ties with Raymond Queneau.

1934–38 Liaison with "Laure" (Colette Peignot). (Cf. her *Ecrits de Laure* [Pauvert, 1977] for striking similarities with Bataille, especially concerning the sacred.)

1933–39 Attends Alexander Kojève's lectures on Hegel. Commenting on this "most important influence," he notes, "I wish to insist that the interpretation of

Alexander Kojève does not, in any way, lose sight of Marxism. Similarly, it is easy to see that the present 'theory' [of religion] is always rigorously founded on an analysis of the economy" (VII, 359).

1935 *Contre-Attaque* (political group) formed with Breton during temporary reconciliation. Goal was to counter rise of Fascism with equal force, prompting accusations of fascistic tendencies in Bataille.

1936–39 Secret society founded with Georges Ambrosino, Pierre Klossowski, Patrick Waldberg, which Bataille attends concurrently with activities of the Collège de Sociologie. Publish review *Acéphale* four times.

1937 Collège de Sociologie disbanded by participants more preoccupied with the war than was Bataille. Extreme emotional distress prompts him to experiment with yoga. He undertakes writing of *Le Coupable,* first volume of *La Somme athéologique.*

1940 Meets Maurice Blanchot.

1941 *L'Expérience intérieure* published.

1942 Leaves the Bibliothèque Nationale owing to tuberculosis.

1943 Sojourn at Vézelay. Sartre publishes critical review of *L'Expérience intérieure,* "Un Nouveau Mystique."

1946 Founds the review *Critique,* remaining editor-in-chief until his death. Assisted by the first team of Pierre Prévost, Maurice Blanchot, Pierre Josserand, Jules Monnerot, and Eric Weil, Bataille prided himself on the "serious" nature of a publication opposed to existentialism and clearly rivaling Sartre's *Les Temps Modernes.* More eclectic than political, its esoterism corresponded to Bataille's ambition to "totalize" modern thought and experience. His particular synthesis or "general economy" is expounded in many important articles later reprinted in book form.

1949 *La Part maudite,* considered by Bataille to be his most important work, published.

1957 *L'Erotisme* published.

1962 Dies in Paris.

1970 Publication of Volume I (ten projected) of complete works of Bataille by Gallimard.

READING GEORGES BATAILLE

INTRODUCTION: SITUATING BATAILLE

> If, as it appears to me, a book is communication, then the author is
> only a link among many different readings.
>
> *Georges Bataille*

Georges Bataille is undoubtedly one of the most elusive figures of French
intellectual life to attain legendary status in this century. Variously termed a
surrealist, an existentialist, a Hegelian, a Marxist, or a Nietzschean, Bataille is
often first identified as the author of erotic novels. Having equated literature
with evil, the librarian-philosopher thus earned the title *écrivain maudit*, and
the implied filiations with Sade and Lautréamont are intended to contain his
excesses within a literary cliché. But to pigeonhole the unwieldy diversity of
this work into traditional classifications perpetuates an ideological bias by
clouding the moral imperative that motivated Bataille.

Since the death of Bataille in 1962, his posthumous reputation has been
even greater than the notoriety of youth. Born in 1897, Bataille published his
earliest erotic narrative, *Histoire de l'oeil,* in a limited edition under a
pseudonym. During the 1930s, the main outlet for his writing was a series of
short-lived journals, some of which he founded and edited, but the central
volume of *La Somme athéologique—L'Expérience intérieure*— did not appear until
the beginning of the war. With Sartre's review of it in 1943, Bataille's visibility
as a major intellectual presence was assured and was further consolidated in
the postwar period with the publication in 1946 of the eclectic review *Critique.*
Although known among intellectuals during the 1950s, Bataille's work
attracted a more general public during the following decade due to its
increased availability. On ideological grounds, the contributors to the review
Tel Quel established the conditions for this greater receptivity.[1] Individually
and collectively, they featured him as a precursor to what Barthes called a
"mutation" in modern epistemology and theories of classification. Specif-

1

ically, this change involves the status of the literary work and a modification of the values attendant upon the act of criticism.

> The change is clearly connected with the current development of (amongst other disciplines) linguistics, anthropology, Marxism and psychoanalysis. . . . Interdisciplinarity is not the calm of an easy security; it begins *effectively* when the solidarity of the old disciplines breaks down in the interests of a new object and a new language neither of which has a place in the field of the sciences that were to be brought peacefully together, this unease in classification being precisely the point from which it is possible to diagnose a certain mutation.[2]

The text, no longer the classical work of literary creation, is now the product of a conscious violation of the hierarchy of discourses on which genre theory, and poetics in general, depend. Barthes assesses Bataille's writing as the exemplar of textuality:

> What constitutes the Text is, on the contrary (or precisely), its subversive force in respect of the old classifications. *How do you classify a writer like Georges Bataille? The answer is so difficult that the literary manuals generally prefer to forget about Bataille who, in fact, wrote texts, perhaps continuously one single text.*[3]

In his own introduction to *La Part maudite* (1949), Bataille declared his writing unclassifiable. Because this essay's ideas are articulated primarily in economic terms, it was regarded as the culmination of a career that had produced poems, erotic narratives, and essays on anthropology, mysticism, eroticism, literature, and sociology. When pressed to elucidate that provocative but uninformative title, Bataille ventured comparisons with a treatise on political economy, hastily adding, however, that "I did not consider facts from the point of view of qualified economists; my approach regarded human sacrifice, the construction of a church, or the gift of a jewel, as bearing no less interest than the sale of wheat" (VII, 19).[4] The result is a theory of "general economy," which looks at excess rather than scarcity, consumption rather than production, for the etiology of social solidarity and conflict. The general economy argues that the evidence of a surplus in every group is but one dimension of the excess energy generated upon the planet; its global approach considers the means by which this onerous part maudite is expended.

Once faced with a completed work, Bataille acknowledged the need to *situate* it since "a book is nothing if criticism has not marked its place within the general movement of ideas" (VII, 19). His unwillingness to validate the essay, itself an exercise beyond conventional disciplines, by means of any single science, reflects his belief in the universal relevance of its topic: "that of excess energy, translated into the effervescence of life" (VII, 20). The fact is, concludes Bataille, being of interest to all, this book could appeal to no one.

   This study responds to the paradox of situating a work that challenges the paradigms of traditional classificatory schemes. To the critical establishment dependent upon such taxonomies, Bataille offers a situating process guided by the categories of the general economy. Wary that the convoluted path opened by his esoterism would often be avoided, Bataille became his most attentive reader, mapping in his texts the subterranean connections severed by discursive and disciplinary boundaries. My reading is guided by the historical fate of the categories in question: indeed, when the first phase of this study was initiated in the early 1970s, *dépense* (expenditure), heterogeneity, transgression, and sovereignty were the signposts of Bataille's influence. Whether their shared reception took place via the primary texts or indirectly through the vehicle of *Tel Quel* is secondary to a widespread endorsement and the circumscription of this approbation within a precise historical juncture: the impressive outpouring of critical thought that distinguished French intellectual life of the 1960s.

   Thus, this study pursues the implications of Bataille's categories as they gauge both the limits of and transgressions against two moments of consciousness: that of the author as historical subject of the period between the world wars,[5] and that of postwar movements that rejected both existentialism and structuralism for surrealist modernism as seen through the eyes of a critic such as Bataille.[6] In order to determine the possibilities of consciousness, Bataille proposed a general economy, whose sum transcends its accumulated parts and is not to be equated with a quantitative expansion of the scope of traditional economics. The general economy must be differentiated from the restricted economy of capitalism, where the automatic reinvestment of surplus into the forces of production eliminates expenditure that is not ultimately acquisitive. Bataille characterizes his enemy as the economizing person whose individualistic ethos is consonant with the pursuit of random ends determined by the criteria of utilitarianism. As the offspring of bourgeois-capitalism, *homo oeconomicus* cannot conceive of dépense as spending of such an extreme nature that it approaches death. The need for dépense is evidenced in the sacrifices formerly satisfied through collective rituals but which today "leads a man in isolation to incomprehensible and sometimes even stupid behavior" (II, 13).[7] Rarely do the monuments erected by a culture in its aspirations to eternity betray the forces that propel individuals toward destruction as the affirmative willingness to lose things, meaning, and even self.

   Therefore, Bataillian anthropology depends on a notion of dépense which encompasses productive and nonproductive modes of spending. In this way it mirrors the "dual solicitation" posited at the basis of human nature, leading in one direction toward stable, constructive goals; in the other to disruptive, sacrificial projections beyond a self immersed in communal encounters. Bataille's immediate project is to compel readers to discern the force of the general economy beyond its presence in those categories used to accommodate it most readily: poetry, madness, and the sacred. To transgress the limits of consciousness so determined is to look beyond the historical and geographical frontiers of Western civilization. The evidence of societies alternating festivals with the daily homogeneity of work life demonstrates the possibility to integrate an experience of dépense within a social rhythm. Recourse to such anthropological data was necessitated by the absence of other means by which to communicate such unstated and perhaps unsayable needs.

An important influence on the outcome of my reading is that the theory of general economy is treated as central to the totality of this work, and not as a self-contained theoretical construct. Fundamental to such an approach is the idea of economy as a *relationship* between parts and a whole, means and their ends, which permeates every domain of experience and social relations, even though in the final analysis it is determined by the status of that autonomous realm of activity and behavior known as *the* economy. Against the meretricious calculations synonymous with contemporary definitions of economy, Bataille sets the dramatically exotic image of the Kwakiutl chief hurling his copper blazons to an indifferent sea, a tableau inspired by Marcel Mauss's "Essai sur le don" (1923–24). This modest work, not unlike the ceremonial shells transferred from one chieftain to another which tie the vast Trobriand archipelago into a symbolic ring, solders a bond among Bataille and his contemporaries (e.g., Roger Caillois, Jacques Lacan, Claude Lévi-Strauss, and Michel Leiris) who shared its insights into the nature of gift-exchange. By demonstrating the quality of the gift as a "total social fact" responsible for integrating the multiple dimensions of archaic culture, the essay preempted nostalgic ideas of gift-giving which would not account for its "economic" significance. Bataille summed up the influence of the essay this way: "[There] I discerned the basis, if not of a new conception of the economy, at least of an introduction to a new point of view" (*L'Erotisme,* 226).

It is my contention that the significance and impact of the point of view announced by the general economy is best appreciated through its own categories. More than a lexicon and less than a complete paradigm intended to exhaust the meaning of the Bataillian text, they are more appropriately compared to Durkheim's notion of collective representations. The ambiguity connoted by Durkheim's formulation applies to Bataille's categories, since they create an *object* of analysis permitting examination of that which is thought or conceived within a culture, as well as being a *mode* of thinking or perceiving. They are anthropological to the extent that they gauge the potential for knowledge, understanding, and communication for a subject within a precise moment of a culture's history. My reading is guided by them in order to appreciate the discontent of a generation Bataille remembers as tumultuous, convinced that the revolutionary potential of literature was suffocating in its limits. This position summarizes the issues attacked by Bataille's peers who attained maturity between the world wars, aspired to redefine revolution while confronting the historical reality of Fascism, and recognized that the term literature no longer conjured an identifiable object. Bataille's categories plot the domain of an expérience intérieure patterned after the primitive Other it may envy but can never imitate. Its modernity resides in the account of anguished oscillations between discursive and non-discursive possibilities for communication by leaving a scriptural transcription of an experience intended to be shared by more than one individual.

Bataille's categories also apply anthropology in its restricted, disciplinary sense. For instance, one must recognize in the primitive a system more complex than the caricatures perpetrated by a nostalgic ideology. Toward that end, Louis Dumont cites the role of non-Western cultures in innovating categories that modify the capacity for self-scrutiny among Western societies: "Unless I am mistaken, in anthropology, scientific categories are only born out of the contradiction between theory and the facts."[8] From this perspective, Bataille's influence can be traced to categories that undermine those consonant with a restricted view of economics determined by the principle of rationality; he thereby avoids the regressive tendencies of previous avant-garde theories of culture elaborated since the romantics. The allegedly innate propensity of *homo oeconomicus* for rational exchange is challenged by a new perception: the need to give as a means of simulating the totality of exchange evidenced in archaic cultures.

That the study of categories should stimulate new directions for research, especially by pointing out hitherto unexplored connections, is explained by Dumont: "I think that it is for this reason that Mauss sought not a philosophy, that is to say, speculation based on inadequate concepts, but an inventory of categories equivalent to the construction of scientific concepts.[9] Thus the assessment of the general economy's categories in light of subsequent developments in anthropology inevitably confronted the question of their scientific validity. Our reading of *La Part maudite*, using results of recent research, touches upon issues tangential to exchange, such as the psychosocial consequences of an economic organization and the meaning of vestigial gift-giving customs observed in industrialized societies. These topics, however, are central to the anthropological literature that uses evidence of the archaic as the basis for social criticism. Thus, whereas the perceived connections between social science and philosophical anthropology are correct, the use of one to evaluate the other is not. The ensuing confusion is partially dispelled by the identification of two virtually inextricable modes of current French anthropology. The first type refers to the theories of "meta-anthropologists," primarily philosophers grounded in social anthropology. The second mode constitutes the descriptive results of anthropologists guided by the theories of the first, producing work qualified as "pretext-anthropology."[10] Yet more important is the larger picture to emerge from the comparison of texts in neighboring disciplines, which confirms the interdependence between research in the sciences of culture and works of a speculative order, including literature and social theory.[11]

The broad spectrum of issues raised by the categories of the general economy has engaged this study in a situating process structured by an examination of dépense, heterogeneity, sovereignty, transgression, and communication as they appear in Bataille's works irrespective of genre or chronology, and complemented by a historical perspective on their impact through a series of diachronic readings. The overall emphasis is on the critical force of the general economy as estimated through the resistance mounted against it by some theoreticians and its appropriation by others. We therefore underscore how Bataille wants the general economy to be seen, and which factors obfuscate such a vision. While this approach claims neither total allegiance to nor immunity from any one critical method, it does try to abide by Bataille's exhortation to seek in his thought not a general principle but how it *differs* from that of others. Thus, chapter 1 proposes an archaeology of the gift, starting with Mauss, in order to examine its connotations for critical thought. Dépense is then situated within the particular materialism of the general economy where Marxism, psychoanalysis, and philosophy are of limited assistance. Chapter 2 locates the heterogeneity of the general economy in relation to Durkheim's sacred and the metaphysical materialism of the surreal. The anthropological reconstruction initiated in chapter 1 is continued here to appreciate the idealism of the "old antinomies" that Breton claims surrealism upset. My purpose is to examine how the general economy disrupts their binary equilibrium. Sovereignty, as a revision of Hegel's master/slave dialectic, is considered in chapter 3, which includes its repercussions for an erotic experience. Bataille's understanding of trans-gression is examined in chapter 4 in order to appreciate its significance for a modern experience of the sacred. The *expérience intérieure* is the focus of Sartre's reading, as detailed in chapter 5, and leads to a confrontation between existentialist philosophy (and psychoanalysis), phenomenology, and the "sciences of man." Moreover, this chapter introduces a series of intertexual dialogues which draw together the surrealists, Bataille's own reading of his work, and the collision with Sartre over their respective readings of Baudelaire and Genet. All are subsumed by a polemic regarding the role of literature in the act of communication. Chapter 6 moves toward closure by considering the historical fate of the general economy within the textual practice of Derrida's deconstruction. It should be noted that no one chapter is conceived as a self-contained unit: issues raised in one often reappear in a later section.

Proust observed the temptation to regard preferred authors as oracles. Indeed, the ambitious program outlined for this study may appear to have succumbed to the Delphic illusion of all wisdom emanating from one source. Yet it is difficult to ignore Bataille's relevance for a culture periodically rocked by a profound discontent with its economism, only to turn for solace to the most conventional, authoritarian religious structures. Many similar dichotomies examined here continue to inform the dominant discourse on culture. Finally, individuals are still terrorized by the most fantastic representations of their needs, wants, and desires as determined within the restricted economy. To the extent that critical thought has displaced economic man with *homo significans*,[12] it cannot do justice to those anguished moments when language fails and communication nonetheless occurs. Intimations of such possibilities arise in the instance of dépense, in that otherness where Bataille wanted his writing to be situated: "If one were to ascribe me a place within the history of ideas, it would be, I believe, for having discerned the effects, within our lives, of the dissipation of discursive reality" (V, 231). Critics today may choose to shirk the experience of limits or to reduce Bataille's many languages to one. The voice to which this study responds enjoins readers to participate in the moral project Bataille assigned to all cultural activity—the creation of values consistent with the categories of the general economy.

CHAPTER

1

FORMULATING CATEGORIES

Above all one must draw up the largest possible index of categories, starting with those we know men have already used. Only then will we see that there are still many dead, pale or darkened moons on the horizon of human thought.

Marcel Mauss

READING MAUSS

With the publication of "La Notion de dépense" in 1933 and, more importantly, *La Part maudite* in 1949, Bataille consolidated his reputation as the architect of "a theory of the gift for modern life."[1] The wave of interest in his work over the last few decades could be attributed to the same impetus Marcel Mauss perceived as the drawing power of his own research into archaic economies: "The theme of the gift, of generosity and self-interest in giving, reappear in our society like the resurrection of a dominant motif long forgotten."[2] While Mauss's celebrated "Essai sur le don" is Bataille's acknowledged ethnological source, it would be a serious misreading of both to equate their respective positions regarding gift-giving. Indeed, the translation of Bataille's idiosyncratic terms *dépense* and *part maudite* by either *don* or *gift* must be questioned, given that such translation involves radical shifts in cultural contexts. To appreciate the issues entailed we propose a reading of Mauss which will be traced through to Bataille's own view of giving within the framework of the general economy. The historical perspective thus gained then leads to an examination of the theory of gift-giving in psychology, economics, and anthropology, and to a revised approach to the economic foundations of culture.

Whereas in 1951 Claude Lefort could lament that the implications of the gift essay had yet to spread beyond the circle of professionals for whom it had immediate relevance, the current dissemination of the ideas of Mauss within a broad spectrum of disciplines attests to its status as one of the great works of social philosophy in our century.[3] Few people, claims Lévi-Strauss, have been able to read the "Essai sur le don" without experiencing the range of emotions so well described by Malebranche upon his first reading of Descartes: "le coeur battant, la tête bouillante, et l'esprit envahi d'une certitude encore indéfinissable, mais impérieuse, d'assister à un évènement décisif de l'évolution scientifique."[4] The scientific claim to be made for Mauss lies in the fact that for the first time in the history of ethnological thought, an effort has been made to transcend empirical observation and reach deeper social realities. For the first time, the social domain is not reduced to anecdotal impressions, and the systematic nature of social reality as the product of multiple factors is apprehended as an organic whole. Moreover, the totality observed possesses a meaning that can be grasped only when the ethnologist has seized the ensemble of social phenomena within the special logic of their underlying unity. Hence we find Mauss's prescription that the "aim and principle of sociology is to observe and understand the group in its total behavior" (79–80).

The primary goal of Mauss's study is to synthesize a general pattern from the vast array of already documented examples of prestations. The exceptional interest of the topic resides in the employment of gift-exchange by archaic cultures to fulfill contracts and distribute goods. Through the system of prestations thus constituted, social solidarity is guaranteed among the various economic subgroups forming the larger network of tribes, clans, and phratries. Studies of gift-exchange prior to that of Mauss were stymied in their endeavor to extricate definitive statements from the "great mass of complex data," Mauss speculates, because in these "early" societies, the exchange mechanism permeates virtually every activity. It thus earns the gift's claim to be a "total social fact" at the heart of a social order in which "each phenomenon contains all the threads of which the social fabric is composed. . . . In these total social phenomena, . . . all kinds of institutions find simultaneous expression: religious, legal, moral, and economic. In addition, the phenomena have their aesthetic aspect and they reveal morphological types" (1). The correlative to the total character of prestations is that groups, rather than individuals, are the fundamental unit of exchange. Here the essay boldly inverts the individual contract theory of classical political economy. By unmasking the mechanism of reciprocity, Mauss shifts responsibility for gift-giving away from personal initiative to collective constraint. When one person does undertake a spectacular offering, as in potlatch, he is recognized as a symbolic figure, the designated representative of a clan or subgroup.

The portrait of prestations so developed is accompanied by an early observation intended to disabuse the contemporary reader of the notion of "gift" as a voluntary offering without any view to remuneration or immediate return. In contrast with this notion of a "free gift," Mauss points to the disparity within prestations between the form of something generously offered and its content: "The accompanying behavior is formal pretence and social deception, while the transaction itself is based on obligation and economic self-interest" (1). Little in Mauss's description is susceptible to conjuring an idealized version of the archaic gift. On the contrary, it seems that Mauss wishes to show how the modern gift finds its origins in the archaic. Moreover, historical differences notwithstanding, he contends that "the same morality and economy are at work, albeit less noticeably, in our societies, and we believe that in them we have discovered one of the bases of social life; and thus we may draw conclusions of a moral nature about some of the problems confronting us in our present economic crisis" (2).

The moral conclusion so promised indeed contends that the gift can be resurrected in today's world to serve as a corrective to the excesses of purely economic transactions. As a collective experience antithetical to the goals of utilitarian practice, the gift will provide a return to the "old and elemental" in such a way that "once again we shall discover those motives of action still remembered by many societies and classes: the joy of giving in public, the delight in generous artistic expenditure, the pleasure of hospitality in the public or private feast" (57). In the antiindividualistic tradition inspired by Durkheim, Mauss concurs with the author of *Les Formes élémentaires de la vie religieuse*, who claims that the desultory condition of contemporary social life constitutes a historical aberration, that the revival of group expenditure will place Western culture back in the mainstream of human experience: "If we find a little difficulty today in imagining what these feasts and ceremonies of the future could consist of, it is because we are going through a stage of transition and moral mediocrity."[5] Within the history of anthropology, Mauss is respected for having enlisted the evidence provided by archaic cultures for heuristic purposes; thus, a further goal of his essay is to challenge the prevailing rationalism of Western societies, which only "recently turned man into an economic animal. *Homo oeconomicus* is not behind us, but before, like the moral man, the man of duty, the scientific man and the reasonable man. For a long time man was something quite different: and it is not so long now since he became a machine" (74).

If such is the case, then further consideration must be granted the gift proposed as a panacea for the maladies afflicting "the calculating machine," but portrayed as something to be given, to be received, and at the same time, "dangerous" to accept. In the reading of the gift essay that follows, we examine the extent to which an appreciation of the individual who was and speculation on the one to be are contingent upon the translation of the "gift" offered by Mauss.

THE GIFT

It is important to recall that Mauss himself never engaged in fieldwork per se, so that his rereading of the data amassed by others relied upon linguistic clues to resolve anthropological enigmas. The idea of the archaic "gift" is particularly elusive as it links the many possible modes of exchange but is never exclusively identified with any single component of the act involved: giving, receiving, or returning. Appropriately labeled a "hybrid" notion, the gift refers to a variety of functions in the language of tribes having "only a single word to cover buy and sell, borrow and lend" (31), even when they actually perform as separate activities the "antithetical" notions subsumed by their one category. Given the universality of gift-exchange, Mauss must necessarily call into question the viability of his own tools and examine the consequences for his analysis of subsuming the diverse experiences under the restricted connotations of the term "gift" in its current usage. Mauss not only concedes the disparity, but seems willing to investigate its causes. "Our terms 'present' and 'gift' do not have precise meanings, but we could find no others. Concepts which we like to put in opposition—freedom and obligation; generosity, liberality, luxury on the one hand and saving, interest, austerity on the other—are not exact and it would be well to put them to the test" (70).

Although similar reflections surface throughout the essay, no evaluation of respective categories is included in the method of "careful comparisons" which is sufficiently rigorous to be considered a serious test of either the categories of anthropology or the cultural biases buttressing their semantic value. The example of the gift is intended to shake the utilitarian prejudices of classical economic theory, but Mauss tends to divert the hard questions from characteristics of Western culture toward the "ambivalence" of archaic concepts instead. For instance, Malinowski is cited for revealing that the gift conflates "many legal principles which we moderns have isolated from one another. It is at the same time property and a possession, a pledge and a loan, an object sold and an object bought, a deposit, a mandate, a trust" (22). The hybrid quality of the gift—confirmed through innumerable examples but perhaps most dramatically by the German *Gabe,* a simultaneous reference to *gift* and *poison*—is imputed by Mauss to "a strange incapacity to abstract and analyse concepts. But this is unnecessary. In these societies groups cannot analyse themselves or their actions, and influential individuals, however comprehending they may be, do not realize that they *have* to oppose each other" (30). The unasked question would consider the causes and effects of splitting the "antithetical" elements of the archaic unit into discrete terms. Moreover, why are they inevitably reorganized into the binary oppositions of Western philosophy, where one term exerts hierarchical preeminence over the other?

How individuals "constrained" to engage in the collective "effervescence" of incessant exchanges actually experience their relation to the overarching whole moves the analysis of gift-giving from structural-functional considerations to its phenomenological reality. Mauss characterizes the person-gift, subject-object relation as one of confusion, the product of an economy where "things have personality and personalities are in some manner the permanent possession of the clan" (44). Thus it follows that to give a thing is tantamount to self-sacrifice since "a man gives himself, and he does so because he owes himself . . . to others" (44). By demonstrating how everything—men, women, children, festivals, ritual, ceremonies and dances, jokes, and injuries are "tied together" (44) in what Bourdieu describes as their state of "original undifferentiation," Mauss touched on the hallmark of non-Western cultures.[6] What anthropologists after Mauss insisted on extricating as an "economic" structure is in fact a mode of exchange "submerged"[7] in social relations, and can be assessed only within the configuration of religious, economic, and kinship systems. In the ironic formula of one observer, "Money is to the West, what kinship is to the Rest."[8]

The methodological question of how to approach total social facts is raised by Mauss, sensitive to the way in which they challenge the ability of modern epistemology to conceive the category of totality. Whereas the sociological imagination strains to assemble a social whole from its fractured parts, the ethnological temptation tends to accommodate its own technically specialized vocabulary by deconstructing the organic unity of the archaic entity into autonomous subsystems: "We are dealing with something more than a set of themes, more than institutional elements, more than institutions, more even than systems of institutions divisible into legal, economic, religious and other parts. We are concerned with 'wholes,' with systems in their entirety" (77). Despite such caveats, Mauss appears to have betrayed his own precepts by an increasing emphasis on the nature of the gift itself. The very question guiding the orientation of his study indicates its dual focus on both the systemic character of prestations and the nature of the gift: "In primitive or archaic types of society what is the principle whereby the gift received has to be repaid? What *force* is there in the *thing* given which compels the recipient to make a return?" (1, emphasis added). By the end of the essay an exact response has not been reached. Thing, force, persona, sign, or symbol: the gift is assigned a variety of hypothetical identities, but the one most consistently favored is provided by native explanations and alternately endows the gift with the supernatural powers of *hau* or the prestige of *mana*. The imputed magic of the object accounts for the spiritual unity it generates within the community and the identification it brings about between person and property.

Lévi-Strauss subsequently reproaches Mauss for allowing the indigenous explanation to sidetrack him from the course of his own genius, which perceived beyond the give-and-take of goods, previously misconstrued as truck or barter, to the significant level of exchange.[9] The deep structures of gift-giving then excavated by Lévi-Strauss constitute the basis for his own magisterial study of incest, where he conclusively demonstrates that exchange in archaic societies is determined by the structure and praxis of the rules governing kinship relations. All circulation of goods is ultimately governed by the laws of the "symbolic order," and the objects within the central categories of exchange—goods, words, and women—are compared to signs whose transmission sustains the total system of culture as communication.[10]

A distortion more serious than the fallacy criticized by Lévi-Strauss is imposed on the gift as a result of Mauss's twofold effort to provide both an objective appraisal of the gift and ethical considerations for modern readers. Intent on satisfying both goals, he produces a version of the gift which will have significant repercussions for the history of the notion.

The moral imperative guiding Mauss's investigation demands that he enlist archaic gift-exchange as a model for a culture in which there exist neither linguistic equivalents nor structural congruence between its own form of exchange and that of the precapitalist formations described. Mauss's archaeology elicits a dormant stratum of social prehistory which assuages the nostalgia haunting the modern psyche to be liberated from the demons of production and accumulation. Regardless of the institutional changes separating the archaic from the modern, the resurgence of interest in gift-giving in our time is testimony to the desire for a return to "noble expenditure," according to Mauss. The study of the gift subsequently fired utopian speculations among readers eager for alternatives to the hegemony of economic rationality: the "new morality" consists of "the happy medium between the ideal and the real" (67) and assumes that "the rich should come once more, freely or by obligation, to consider themselves the treasurers, as it were, of their fellow citizens" (66). Mauss believes they indeed will and that the blueprint for social harmony thus outlined could be realized within the guidelines of Christian charity or the institutions of a capitalist system—a belief implicit in his original assumptions.

While Mauss recognizes that the resurrection of gift-giving in the modern world requires a modification of the archaic version, he claims that the necessary changes have already taken place and credits the Greeks and Romans (possibly in the wake of northern and western Semites) for taking the first major step toward a modern market economy. The endorsement of such progress lauds "the venerable revolution [that] passed beyond that antiquated and dangerous gift economy, encumbered by personal considerations, incompatible with the development of the market, trade and productivity—which was in a word uneconomic" (52). When divested of the irrational customs of archaic exchange, the economy was able to emerge with full autonomy and assert a convenient independence from cumbersome social considerations. Thus the correlative to the continuity thesis follows: the split between economic transactions and social obligations need not pose an obstacle to a return to gift-giving in the old and elemental way. The modern gift is then determined within the restricted sphere of social relations, in such a way as to compensate for the inequities perpetrated by the economy which need not modify its laws of operation.

Mauss's de-emphasis of this "ontological transformation" further assumes that the consolidation of a capitalistic economy made possible by, and consistently rewarding, the possessive individualism of a market mentality need not be inimical to the spirit of gift-giving.[11] Traces of these issues can be detected in the thread of Mauss's analysis pertaining to the disjuncture between the rules of constraint and how they are followed. In question here is the nature of the individual/group dynamic and the extent to which the social subject is significantly affected by the acting out of inducements of the collective will. For instance, how can one speak of individual motive in cultures where one person often assumes a collective identity when exchanging gifts and where the prestige of an entire clan is at stake? Further, what is the cause of the "friendly feeling" observed among participants in gift-exchanges? The circularity of the question produces the sort of compromise response contained in these observations: "Individuals, even the most influential, were less serious, avaricious and selfish than we are; externally at least they were and are generous and more ready to give" (79). Then again, "they had no choice in the matter" (79).

Although no definitive position on the collective will is assumed in the essay, Mauss's stance is best appreciated within his prescriptions for a benign and enlightened welfare state willing to provide more protection for the individual while "limiting the pursuit of speculation and usury."

> Meanwhile the individual must work and be made to rely more upon himself than upon others. From another angle he must defend his group's interest as well as his own. Communism and too much generosity is as harmful to him and society as the selfishness of our contemporaries or the individualism of our laws. [67]

The exposition of the study of the gift, often more suggestive than rigorous, nonetheless derives its coherence from an ethical drive to renew a covergence between morality and economics in contemporary society. Mauss conducts his investigation on three levels, which essentially correspond to the separate orders of Western experience. The first level deals with the gift as the basic constituent of "total prestations" of the social realm, of which it is the most overt yet unexplored manifestation. Turning then to a demonstration of unity between mind and action in the primitive world, Mauss underlines a congruence between moral purpose and economic deed. If dissonance is perceived between motive and gesture, it is because the modern ethnographer, in search of pristine disinterestedness, extrapolates from an individual psychology. Moreover, the ambivalence subsumed by archaic categories is dramatically underscored by the lack of distinction among terms that have subsequently been put into opposition. The third dimension of the essay parallels the first two by documenting the progressive specialization of linguistic categories previously conflated into a single concept. Mauss's partisan goal here is to emphasize the moral imperatives that sustain the vestiges of gift-giving even within modern mores.

The final intersection among these three levels of analysis is announced in one of the concluding passages of the essay where Mauss insists on the need "to observe . . . minds as wholes and not minds divided into faculties" (79–80). The unexamined factor inhibiting the synthesis he advocates, however, relies on the nature of the role played by the "uneconomic," "dangerous," and "antiquated" form of total prestations in promoting the very cohesiveness he consistently praises. Is the reader to infer that there is, in fact, no connection between that "venerable revolution" that passed beyond gift-giving encumbered by "personal considerations" and the unhampered evolution of an autonomous sphere of economic activity?

We will argue that it is possible to read *The Gift* without establishing a causal relationship between the disappearance of the archaic structures of gift-exchange, the sense of wholeness provided by total prestations, and their corresponding linguistic expression as hybrid notions. By providing evidence of a confluence between morality and economics in which the role of the latter is totally subordinate to the former, Mauss avails his readers of a version of social change that is formulated in primarily ethical terms. What Mauss did not consider is that because economic structures are no longer integrated into the ensemble of social structures but have achieved autonomy, it would be virtually impossible for contemporary readers to fulfill the project he devised for regarding social facts as more

> than systems of institutions divisible into legal, economic, religious and other parts. . . . It is only by considering them as wholes that we have been able to see their essence, their operation and their living aspect, and to catch the fleeting moment when the society and its members take emotional stock of themselves and their situation as regards others. Only by making such concrete observation of social life is it possible to come upon facts such as those which our study is beginning to reveal. Nothing in our opinion is more urgent or promising than research into "total" social phenomena. [77]

The weak point in Mauss's reading of archaic exchange invalidates his otherwise moving entreaty for a return to the old and the elemental. Despite his suppositions, the very structure of modern society, with its sharp distinction between the economic and the social, militates against the sense of totality found in the meeting of morality and economics he optimistically pursued. In this sense, Mauss condemns modern man to a purely symbolic reconstruction of a past irretrievably lost.

BATAILLE READING MAUSS

To a great extent Mauss determined the outcome of his investigation by seeking from his study moral conclusions relevant for contemporary readers. By assuming an underlying continuity between the archaic and the modern evidenced in the vestiges of gift-giving, Mauss was able to articulate his position in a paraphrase of the Gallic dictum that equates innovation with illusion, history with repetition: "These pages of social history, theoretical sociology, political economy and morality do no more than lead us to old problems which are constantly turning up under new guises" (2). The determination to translate the ambiguous pluralism of a total social fact into a voluntary gesture on the part of individuals produced a category of limited connotations suitable for modern anthropology. Mauss exhorts his reader to reorient social life with an increased emphasis on the model of gift-exchange observed among cultures having passed beyond the antiquated total prestations. He argues as follows: "We should come out of ourselves and regard the duty of giving as a liberty, for in it there lies no risk" (69). Equilibrium is the desired goal, grounded in the reciprocal give-and-take of gifts of equal value as recommended in the Maori proverb, " 'Give as much as you receive and all is for the best' " (69). Moreover, the feverish intensity of archaic festivities, capable of suddenly veering "from a feast to a battle" (80), has been replaced with the progressive stabilization of contracts and the triumph of reason: "It is by opposing reason to emotion and setting up the will for peace against rash follies of this kind that peoples succeed in substituting alliance, gift and commerce for war, isolation and stagnation" (80).

Clearly the instability of archaic ambivalence has been settled, but to accuse the *traduttore* of betraying its ethnographic difference would be to judge what Mauss himself declared an impossible compromise. According to another reading of the essay, however, the case against Mauss's treatment of the etymology of the gift must be recognized within a broader "appropriation and reductionism of the savage ambiguity" similar to the attempt to formulate the gift as a generic phenomenon subsumable under the category of prestations.[12]

The homogeneity of Mauss's evidence is broken by the existence of potlatch, whose violently agonistic confrontations disrupt the pattern of harmonious reciprocity he clearly admires. This "monster-child"[13] of exchange exposed Bataille to the existence of cultures actively engaged in the pursuit of giving, those which demonstrate that it can be in the interest of societies "to spend rather than save" (I, 103). Armed with evidence that social organizations were structured around the ceremonial expenditure of their *part maudite*—the excess invested into privileged goods destined for destruction—Bataille then proceeded with the formulation of a general economy based on the experience of dépense.

Practiced among the American Indian tribes of the Pacific Northwest, potlatch ceremonies consist in the sacrifice of vast quantities of amassed goods, usually blankets and copper blazons, where one individual representing a clan or phratry must crush a rival by his superior ability to dispose of precious objects. Potlatch is further distinguished from other permutations of the gift phenomenon by the pervasive "effervescence" of the atmosphere of agonistic competition, which impressed upon Bataille the need for collective dramatization of dépense. Although Mauss tries to assimilate potlatch into a generic pattern of prestations ("The potlatch, so unique a phenomenon, . . . is really nothing other than gift-exchange" [53]), he includes as distinctive features its violence, rivalry, and antagonism. Moreover, the collective nature of the contract is more pronounced than usual. Most striking, however, is the value placed on the ritual consumption and destruction of virtually unlimited quantities of goods, tying a man's honor and prestige to expenditure. To give, according to the rules of potlatch, is to destroy. For Mauss, potlatch leads to a veritable "war of wealth," prompting him to assert that the "ideal" would be a potlatch that would not be returned. Echoed by Bataille, this statement reflects the undeniably paradoxical nature of a social phenomenon where rank and honor are "acquired" through the most extravagant expenditures.[14] For even when destruction is mandatory, an implicit accounting system tallies the value of goods involved, thereby compelling the next giver to up the ante. For Mauss, the ideal form of potlatch would annul the mediating dimension of time and free the possibility for disinterestedness from the "interest" of an accounting system. Unlike Mauss in his perception of a decline of ethical integrity brought by the discrepancy between the "air" of pure dépense and the consequent reality of gain, Bataille is disturbed by the escalation of goods among participants. The experiential reality of destruction is supplanted by a quantified representation of sacrifice, and the original sentiment of loss, with its brutal proximity to death, is cushioned.

In his formulation of the general economy Bataille counters the diminished impact of potlatch by reasserting a unilateral gesture of dépense. The sun that figures in *La Part maudite* is the eternal exemplar of a munificent outpouring of energy which gives without demanding a return.

> The source and essence of our riches are given in the effulgence of the sun, who dispenses energy—riches—without a counterpart. The sun gives without receiving: men were aware of this long before astrophysics measured this unceasing prodigality; they observed it ripen harvests and linked the splendor that is his to the gesture of he who gives without receiving. [VII, 35]

Although "clouded by practical reason and Christian morality," the archaic sentiment is still alive: "One sees it in the romantic protest against the bourgeois world: it only loses all effect in the concepts of classical economics" (VII, 35–36). Bataille's revitalization of the sentiment was most systematically attempted in *La Part maudite,* though it constitutes but one segment of a total effort to reconsider a variety of phenomena through the optics of the general economy. The "Copernican revolution" is solar, intended to dispel the blindness, utility, and rationality that obfuscate the need for dépense found in war, mysticism, sacrifice, eroticism, and art. Herein lies Bataille's version of the other—general—economy of surplus which explains why people gamble, dissipate fortunes, and exhaust great reserves of energy and goods while exhibiting equal disdain for the immediate preservation of self and concern for the future. Bataille contends that gift-exchanges (including potlatch) are indeed deceptive manifestations of the most ancient motive of dépense as a total experience, later confused with restricted exchanges, and even more inappropriately subsumed under the rubric of economic activity.

> Exchanges, at least in primitive societies, are not subject to laws other than those of dépense. Even in contemporary societies dépense plays a decisive role. It is true that if "need" were defined as the petty preservation of life, economics could limit itself to the study of modes of acquisition and production. But need, in fact, consists in a continual release of vital forces, in an immense destruction of lives and riches—a juggernaut that suspends life at the limit of anguish and nausea, or carries it to the point of trance and orgiastic excess. [II, 156]

By modifying potlatch as a model for the general economy, Bataille thus underscores the difference between dépense and the don of Mauss's version of gift-exchange in which there is neither loss nor gain. Rid of the "child-like prodigality" of potlatch, the gift exchange envisioned by Mauss is represented by a series of metaphors that must be contrasted with the Aztec sun as a symbol of the gratuitous expenditure of which nature is capable. In his effort to capture the benefits of voluntary gift-giving, especially the peace and order it can regulate, Mauss also enlists the wheel and the ring to buttress his argument. When speaking of the Kula of the Trobriand Islanders, an exceptionally complex variant of the basic exchange model, we find that

> Malinowski does not translate the word, which probably, however, means "ring": and in fact it seems as if all these tribes, the sea journeys, the precious objects, the food and feasts, the economic, ritual and sexual services, the men and the women, *were caught in a ring around which they kept up a regular movement in time and space.* [20, emphasis added]

The controlling power of the circular symbol is even more effectively embodied in the Yuit wheel—an eternally rotating figure, clearly mimetic of the sun and "decorated with all manner of provision . . . Inside the tent it is manoeuvered by means of another wheel and is made to turn clockwise like the sun. It would be hard to find a better expression of this mode of thought" (12–13). The admirable congruence between concept and symbol cited by Mauss raises a host of problems when Bataille confronts the representation of loss during potlatch ceremonies. The final "paradox" of this rite is discerned within the call for "the unreachable, the use-less employment of oneself and one's goods," in tension with the inescapable fact that it also "tries to *capture* that which it denies utility" (VII, 75, emphasis added). The concrete manifestation of this tension is observed in the use of things, albeit meant for destruction, yet deplored by Bataille as the index of a lingering reserve, and in the unwillingness to relinquish a final attachment to the restricted economy of calculated returns.

Blinded by the dominance of practical reason, the need for loss often betrays its transgressive impulse to move beyond the boundaries of utility and tries "to find a way to force this transgression back into those very limits" (VII, 72). By recovering the gesture that defies taboos, by converting loss to acquisition, restricted exchange can integrate the part maudite as a thing. The fluid energy of dépense is appropriated by a logocentric universe, where every object acquires meaning and every act significance. There exists an inner necessity to this process, however, which compels Bataille to reformulate his critique.

> Potlatch cannot be unilaterally interpreted as a consumption of riches. Only recently was I able to reduce this difficulty and give to the principles of a general economy a sufficiently ambiguous basis, which is that a dilapidation of energy is always the opposite of a *thing*, but can only be considered once it has entered an order of things, transformed into a thing. [VII, 71]

Although the nature of this order, including its moments of apparent disorder, is cause for considerable debate among anthropologists, the overriding issue for Bataille is how the "order of things" determines the status of the part maudite. His hypothesis is that potlatch is the means by which the established order is periodically disrupted, and the anguishing confrontations with death symbolized in the destruction of goods ritually dramatized. Behind Bataille's discontent with the concentration of dépense into things, one cannot assume a conventional disparagement of conspicuous consumption, nor the romantic disdain for bourgeois material comforts. At stake is the potential risk of consolidating the social hierarchy through the acquisition of rank (albeit as a result of destroying goods) and, perhaps more importantly, the possibility of acceding to the realm of intimacy, sometimes glimpsed through sacrifice or potlatch as an evanescent shadow. Alternately sought through action (history) or contemplation (thought), the shadow of potlatch is that which "by definition we would not know how to seize and which, in vain, we call poetry or the depth of passion. We are necessarily duped because we wish to capture this shadow" (VII, 76).

To speak of an order of things is to assert the hierarchy of priorities by which value is gauged. All groups, observes Bataille, wage a battle of forces committed to production and conservation against those that would compel them to consume and spend. The particular virtue of the societies described by Mauss is to have conceded only the minimum effort mandated for the survival of the species in order to devote the excess part maudite, supplied by nature and augmented by human effort, to activities whose chief goal is loss. Whereas Mauss feared that the displays of potlatch would spawn a "war of wealth," Bataille detects in them the signs of incipient class warfare, encoded in the distinctions made among the quantity and quality of the goods.

At issue here is Bataille's correct perception that the value ascribed to objects—whether in their production, exchange, or consumption—plays a decisive role in structuring the pattern of social relations exhibited within a culture. Things play a necessary and inevitable role in identity formation as they mediate between man and man, man and nature. In the preoccupation with *les choses* evidenced throughout *La Part maudite* lies the will to explicate the specificity of bourgeois culture not bounded by the limits of existential absolutes, but marked by the ideology of utilitarianism within a capitalist society; hence the necessary counterreference to archaic exchange, where the object circulated is never reduced to inertia, "to the absence of life characteristic of the profane world. The gift offered was a sign of glory, and the object itself had the radiance of glory" (VII, 58). Whether the reference is to the "force" of archaic gifts, the "objects of bright pride" made for potlatch, or the animals or persons deemed sacred, the common denominator among these "things" is their ability to open communication with the realm of intimacy.[15] Moreover, the energy they attract and radiate during ceremonial rituals endows them with a value other than that appraised by the "limited" notion of utility: "The intimate world is opposed to the real as excess to measure, madness to reason, and drunkenness to lucidity" (VII, 63).

The etymology of potlatch, traced from the verbs *to nourish* and *to consume,* inspires a revised theory of consumption where the general economy of death and destruction has usurped the rationality principle of production and accumulation. Commenting on this special trait of potlatch Mauss notes: "To give is to destroy . . . . Destruction seems to be a superior form of expenditure. It is called 'killing property' among the Tsimshian and Tlingit" (102). This displaced ritual slaying extends the motif of organic structure to suggest an ontologic link between person and property.

> As in war, masks, names and privileges of the slain owner may be seized,
> so in the war of property, property is "slain" . . . either one's own so that
> others may not get it, or that of others by means of giving their goods

which they will be obliged, and possibly unable, to repay. The other motif
is that of sacrifice. If property can be "killed" this means it is "alive." [102]

The violence of potlatch is undeniable and must be appreciated as a significant factor in the formulation of Bataille's own ideas. Thus, several points
derived from Mauss's documentation are retained. First, violence for Bataille
is subsumed by the negative connotations of the French sense of *consumation*,
a level of meaning contrasted with the *consumption* of the consumer society.
The archaeology of dépense unearths a substratum of energy activated by the
willed accession to the extremes of expenditure: "And if I consume in this
excessive manner, I reveal to my peers what I am intimately: communication
is the means by which separate individuals communicate. All is transparent,
open, infinite, among those who consume intimately" (VII, 63).

Second, one must consider the effects of an exercise in destruction on
those who ostensibly seek power or prestige from it. Indeed, potlatch is
typical of a widespread pattern of gift-giving among Indians of the New
World, where the chief's noteworthy privilege is distinguished by the license
granted his tribe to submit him to "a permanent pillage."[16] The misleading
scenario of a chief ensconced atop a pyramid of subordinates producing the
goods he alone may consume must be replaced with the drama of archaic
gift-exchange. There, an exemplary character histrionically acts out on the
stage of group life the cycle of incorporation and excretion reproduced daily
by every tribal member through his/her bodily economy: "The chief is said to
'swallow the tribes' to which he distributes his wealth; he 'vomits property.'
Or, in reference to a chief who has given a potlatch, and of his people who
receive but do not give away, 'It is only said he satisfied their hunger. It is only
said he made them vomit' " (103).

Finally, we conclude that the critical issue that subtends the analysis of
the order of "things" is, in fact, the nature of the *order* it presupposes.
Following Mauss's observation of total social facts, French anthropology
developed the concept of the symbolic order to include the ensemble of rules
governing the possible conditions of all exchange. As stated in Bataille's
earliest anthropological essay, this *ethos* is all-pervasive, and it remains to be
seen how the hierarchy of values that determines it is encoded in the law of the
symbolic order.[17] The work ethic of bourgeois capitalism demotes the
noneconomic to a secondary status; nineteenth-century Marxism perpetuates a similar hierarchy with its infra/superstructural distinction; the
general economy illuminates the force of dépense within the totality of a
culture: "My approach regarded human sacrifice, the construction of a
church, or the gift of a jewel, as bearing no less interest than the sale of wheat"
(I, 314).

With the scarcity premise of traditional economics upset by the theory
of general economy, all things are reassessed in relation to expenditure. The
quality of the experience potlatch inspires for the notion of dépense eludes us

because "that which remains of traditional modes of dépense appears atrophied, and the vital sumptuous tumult has been dissipated in the unleashing of class conflict." The contradiction of bourgeois culture, characterized by the supremacy of the commodity, is that it banishes the essential, that which induces fear and trembling from the world of things. Nonetheless one notes that the bourgeoisie has not thoroughly eliminated the notion of dépense, but has more effectively subordinated it to its own purposes. Unlike the feudal aristocracy, it consumes only for itself, isolated from the eyes of other classes, thereby depriving them of the spectacle of loss and destruction. A typical reaction to the degraded evolution of medieval festivities and ostentatious displays within the restricted mode of dépense is that of the romantic revolutionary, whose nostalgia Bataille pointedly condemns for not having recognized that "the domination of the *thing* is never total: it abuses its power only halfway, while in the propitious obscurity, a new truth is being hatched" (VII, 127).

Yet the preceding readings of Mauss demonstrate that anthropology's categories—including don and potlatch—are inadequate to serve as a maieutic for the birth of dépense, a category that defies the economist's restriction of need to "the petty preservation of life," and erupts as "a continual release of vital forces" (II,156). Moreover, the perspective opened by the general economy is blocked by Mauss's presentation of gift-exchange in two directions. First, Mauss wishes to translate the archaic gift into a suitable modern equivalent and must, therefore, purge it of extraneous, irrational trappings. This gift will provide "joy and pleasure" precisely because it is devoid of archaic ambivalence. Reduced to a social form, its economic function as a redistributive device is subordinated to its primarily ethical motivation. Isolated from the archaic structures in which it is tied to virtually every dimension of social activity, the modern gift remains protected from the invasion of the economism prevalent in other domains. The second consequence of the gift thus reconstituted is that it cannot provide the necessary link among the divided parts of modern society. Yet, if there exists an almost universal appeal in the gift essay, surely it is to be found in the revival of the category of totality called for by Mauss. The holistic portrait is grounded in the play of social forces that incessantly cross and intermingle, in marked contrast with a culture of discrete, relatively independent subsystems which produces the splintered subject whose cause Bataille placed at the heart of his anthropological venture: "To ask before another, by what means does he satisfy his desire to be whole: sacrifice, cheating, poetry, morality, snobbishness, heroism, religion, revolt, vanity, money? Several [ways] together, or all at once?" (V, 10).

Mauss is the acknowledged precursor of the anthropological tradition that breaks with the deceptive neutrality of cultural relativism to base its critique of modern industrial nation-states on examples drawn from non-

Western societies. By concentrating his examination on exchange, contract, and prestation in archaic society, Mauss forced a serious polemic with the allegedly ahistorical construct of *homo oeconomicus*. Moreover, the philosophical commentary accompanying these exotic examples shows that "reasons other than those with which we are familiar from our own societies" are responsible for the mode of exchange found among "a part of mankind, wealthy, hard-working, and creating large surpluses" (31). Yet a definitive explanation for the motives behind the elaborate systems of gift-exchange cannot be provided, precisely because of the total nature of the phenomena described. While he asserts that "it is something *other than utility* which makes goods circulate in these multifarious and fairly enlightened societies" (70), Mauss is unable to uncover the secret of groups Bataille admired for equating power with the willingness to lose, superiority with the capacity to destroy.

Bataille's anthropology of giving does not posit a unilateral response, but regards both individuals and social organizations as fundamentally ambivalent, drawn between antithetical solicitations: "One leads to the formation of stable, lasting orders and conquering forces; the other, through the mediation of expended forces and general excess, to death and destruction" (II, 371). The problem is that Western civilization, well served by the handmaidens of high culture, has erected its enduring monuments, convinced it can do so only through the absolute denial of those forces Blackmur called collectively the *moha*, "whose presence in human life disturbs wastes, troubles the noumenal coercion of culture."[18] As part of Bataille's campaign to undermine the "maintaining" material civilization, he introduced the notion of dépense into literature. Only if equal recognition is accorded both solicitations, he contends—the "malediction" weighing on the part maudite lifted and its expenditure once more sanctioned by collective rituals—will totality be restored. Here the gap between the gift as transaction among forces of restricted exchange is widened when contrasted with the destabilizing violence of dépense expanded to the global theory of a general economy.

By dwelling on the distances separating don from dépense, we have perhaps lost sight of the historical destiny of the notion of gift-exchange making them traveling companions. Bataille is considered an important mediator in the current reception of Mauss's ideas, even though the assessments of his role are predictably divergent.[19] In the sections that follow, the Mauss/Bataille readings will be situated in the wake of the debates stimulated by potlatch, following its trajectory through economics, psychology, and anthropology. The purpose of this review of the literature dealing with archaic gift-exchange is to document the parameters of current epistemology, whose influence actively precludes the possibility of conceptualizing alternative theories of "economy," including that of Bataille.

RATIONALITY

The appearance of the "Essai sur le don" in 1923–4 augured for Bataille the demise of economic man, whose mythological genealogy, traced to the earliest stages of human beings, was debunked by evidence "that counters the traditional concept of truck as the original form of exchange. In the case of primitives, at least, the economic interpretation has been difficult to defend . . . . It is only in the modern period that it is justified" (I, 294). Indeed, Mauss's work continues to be the classic reference for current speculations on the nature of social exchange and prescriptions for a revitalization of gift-giving. Yet even Bataille, however wary of economics' tendency to intimidate its potential critics, could foresee neither the expanded role of economic theory in the social sciences nor its development independent of other disciplines.[20]

Nineteenth-century capitalism may have nurtured the growth of economic man, but his portentous conception is attributed to the philosophical test tube of Adam Smith. According to the author of *The Wealth of Nations*, two factors—respectively circumstantial and ahistorical—induced the preternatural birth of *homo oeconomicus*. One was the existence of markets; the other, the alleged propensity to barter, truck, and exchange. Deploring the mixture of prejudice and prophecy in this assertion of economizing traits, Polanyi notes:

> It can be said that no misreading of the past ever proved more prophetic of the future. For while up to Adam Smith's time that propensity had hardly shown up on a considerable scale in the life of any observed community, and had remained, at best, a subordinate feature of economic life, a hundred years later an industrial system was in full swing over the major part of the planet which, practically, and theoretically, implied that the human race was swayed in all its economic activities, if not also in its political, intellectual and social pursuits, by that one particular propensity.[21]

The ascendency of this specious psychology is further underscored by its perseverance well into the twentieth century when

> a host of writers on political economy, social history, political philosophy, and general sociology had followed in Smith's wake and established his paradigm of the bartering savage as an axiom of their respective sciences. In point of fact, the alleged propensity to barter, truck and exchange is almost entirely apocryphal.[22]

Two historical circumstances facilitated the spread of this cultural prejudice. First, the anthropological research that could have provided an

empirical counter to such erroneous notions was abandoned on the
assumption that "primitive" cultures were irrelevant to the issues confronting contemporary societies. Only the propitious meeting between
economic history and social anthropology was able to provide an effective
opposition to the theory of innate characteristics. Second, the progressive
autonomization of the economy "legitimized" the motive of economic gain.
The market economy is thus held responsible for the creation of a new society
in which the economic and productive system is entrusted to self-regulating
devices, with the devastating consequences that "the pursuit of material self-
gain as the institutionally enforced incentive to participate in economic life,
eroded social and community life."[23] Prior to the critical transition to a
market economy, societies—from the most archaic "stone-age" economy
(Sahlins's terminology) through the appearance of eighteenth-century regu-
lationism—were characterized by the incontrovertible fact that economic life
was enmeshed in social relations, and the salient trait of the market economy
is its fostering of social organizations that invert this axiom.

A comparable argument is forwarded in *La Part maudite* where Bataille
cites the example of Tibetan culture, whose economy is totally assimilated to
religious activities. The dubious distinction of capitalism is to have singled
out what it calls "economic" motives as the constant traits of human nature,
thus convincing individuals that interest and profit are in fact the dominant
incentives for their actions. What critics of that theory continue to point out,
however, is the extent to which their efforts are stalemated by the complicity
between theory and practice that has marked economics since its inception as
a formal discipline in the last century. A theory of social action based on
economic motives establishes hunger, gain, or self-interest as the guiding
activities of everyday life. Its societal institutions, therefore, sanction any
means to attain their satisfaction. Any other values manifestly at odds with
those of economism were segregated from these "primary" concerns and
enlisted among the enduring dualities of Western culture.

> Honor and pride, civil obligation and moral duty, even self-respect and
> common decency, were not deemed irrelevant to production, and were
> significantly summed up in the word "ideal." Hence man was believed to
> consist of two components, one more akin to hunger and gain, the other to
> honor and power. The one was "material," the other "ideal"; the one
> "economic," the other "non-economic"; the one "rational," the other
> "non-rational." The Utilitarians went so far as to identify two sets of terms,
> thus endowing the economic side of man's character with the aura of
> rationality. He who would have refused to imagine that he was acting for
> gain alone was thus considered not only immoral, but also mad.[24]

The bitter irony of Polanyi's indictment of economic man and its "delusion of
economic determinism as a general law for all human society,"[25] is that for

market economies such laws hold true. As witness to the market's capacity to confer its particular imprint on all aspects of bourgeois-capitalist culture, he observes:

> State and government, marriage and the rearing of children, the organization of science and education, of religion and the arts, the choice of profession, the form of habitation, the shape of settlements, the very aesthetics of private life—everything had to comply with the utilitarian pattern, or at least not interfere with the working of the market mechanism. But since very few human activities can be carried on in the void . . . the indirect effect of the market system came very near to determining the whole of society. It was almost impossible to avoid the erroneous conclusion that as "economic" man was "real" man, so the economic system was really society.[26]

The portrait of the economizing individual perpetuated by economics may indeed be faithful to the reality of the market and its correlative institutions; but the ideological bias of the discipline surfaces in its tendency to generalize from the specific circumstances surrounding the evolution of the market economy during the eighteenth century to a universal phenomenon. Godelier also notes that while theoreticians of economic behavior may be aware of the interrelation of action and objective circumstance, they nonetheless present their historical analysis in evolutionary terms.[27] Thus the institutional guarantees of economic rationality are depicted as stemming from within the individual actor, thereby confirming the triumph of reason over archaic tradition and custom. "Economic activity (under natural economy) realizes goals established by tradition with the help of means established by tradition, without carrying out a reasoned analysis of either. [Its aims] are established by custom and morality, approved by religion and sometimes also sanctioned by legislation."[28]

Economic theory commanded increasing respect during the last century through its assimilation of the central elements of utilitarianism; atomism, rationality, empiricism, and randomness of ends all systematized deeply entrenched biases of the European cultural heritage. Thus we find that the formal definition of economics as "the science which studies human behavior as a relationship between ends and means which have alternative uses" continues in the utilitarian vein that "economic" behavior emanates from an isolated actor.[29] According to this theory of social action, the choices made by the individual actor are comparable to "those of a scientific investigator" who carries out ordinary, practical activities in accord with reasoned principles.[30]

The formula further assumes scarcity, to which the actor must adjust his unlimited wants, or "presumed hedonism," satisfying these ends through the calculations of a rational choice.[31] This also presupposes a repertoire of values activated at the moment the rational choice is executed; these include the profit motive, or the need to maximize those means available. In Veblen's irony, the famous formula accounts for behavior aimed at getting something for nothing at the cost of whom it may concern.[32]

In the eighteenth century the French physiocrat, François Quesnay, sententiously declared the "perfection" of economic behavior to consist in "la plus grande augmentation possible de jouissance par la plus grande diminution possible de dépense." Bataille pushes back the "humiliating" activities of restricted expenditure characteristic of the bourgeoisie to the seventeenth century, where they parallel the flowering of rationalist conceptions that have "no other meaning than that of a strictly economic representation of the world" (I, 314). Yet Bataille's derisive use of *economic* as a reference to the "vulgar" practice of bourgeois economizing is also connoted by the ostensibly scientific definition. The most far-reaching consequence of the formula, however, results from the means-end relation, which is so generalized as to blur the specificity of economic activity and to impart to it the relevance of a universal principle. Thus, notes Godelier, "if all behavior involving allocation is economic then the relationship of a mother to her baby is just as much an economic one, or rather has just as much of an economic aspect as the relationship of an employer to his hired labourer."[33]

The paradox of modern economics can be summarized as follows: While it defines itself as the study of only one particular form of activity, economics founds its credibility on laws so general as to be nonrestrictive and which, therefore, facilitate its hegemony within the other social sciences. The question of how ultimately to delimit the disciplinary borders of economics is, however, less urgent for us than the questions that have emerged thus far from the discussion: the consequence of the domination of economics and its rationality bias for a theory of gift-giving, and the extent to which this same preeminence corresponds to the economy's real power to determine other cultural systems.

The position taken here has been that a historical investigation into the "social preconditions" surrounding the formation of economics is the most effective tool in undermining its inordinate influence. The model for such a study was proposed by Marx's historical materialism, offering "self-knowledge" within capitalist society by demonstrating that "the totality and the driving forces of capitalism cannot be grasped or conceptualized by the crude, abstract, unhistorical and external categories of the science of the bourgeoisie."[34]

Writing in the early part of this century, Lukács noted that the credibility of historical materialism could be maintained only if it was willing to turn its method on itself. To do so would extend this self-knowledge to include the historical vestiges of precapitalist economic formations. Thus, the "changing function of historical materialism" announced by Lukács means applying its method to archaic cultures.[35] The strength of the method resides in the dialectical understanding of the connections among the presumably "closed" systems of the economy, the law, and the state: "For, as far as *method* is concerned, historical materialism was an epoch-making achievement precisely because it was able to see that these apparently quite independent, hermetic and autonomous systems were really aspects of a comprehensive whole and that their apparent independence could be transcended."[36] The advantage of studying precapitalist formations is to avail readers of a view of culture prior to the reification process Lukács ascribes to capitalism: "Its basis is that a relation between people takes on the character of a thing and thus acquires a 'phantom objectivity,' an autonomy that seems so strictly rational and all-embracing as to conceal every trace of its fundamental nature: the relation between people."[37]

In gauging the scope of historical materialism Lukács was particularly attuned to the ideological issue at stake in the willingness of a method to accomodate a holistic analysis. He also focused, however, on the possible bias regarding how historical materialism determines the specificity of precapitalist societies, which Engels had already warned was of a structural order. The outcome of the analysis was, therefore, predicted on the role ascribed to history and the extent to which the causes underlying the reification of all social relations can be traced to a particular mode of production. Yet the self-knowledge of capitalism provided by historical materialism is itself the result of historical factors. Thus only "now," according to Lukács, can the essential nature of these archaic societies be understood without distortion by the mechanical application of capitalist social categories—whence the caveats regarding a "vulgar Marxism" that would mistake historical categories for "eternally valid ones."[38]

A review of the anthropological studies produced within Lukács's program reveals an unfortunate backsliding from the rigor of his admonitions.[39] The most prevalent critique is directed at the failure to adjust Marxist economic categories to cultures where the "economy" does not present itself as an autonomous system and cannot be identified as such. Structuralism is often proposed as a corrective, resulting in elaborate efforts to juggle a synthesis between the two theoretical constructs.[40]

Bataille viewed Marxism less as wrong than limited, confined to a primarily economic approach unable to account for the emotive turbulence prompting historic upheavals. The materialist dialectic, however, provided an essential tool for Bataille and his peers, who were otherwise ignorant of the major texts of Marx and who acquired their understanding of the dialectic through the Kojève lectures on Hegel.[41] Thus, whereas historical materialism is essential to a critique of Hegelian rationalism, its ability to renew its own categories through the study of archaic cultures must be viewed as considerably more problematic.[42]

If, in fact, Marxism failed to deliver the death blow to utilitarianism, the gift essay fostered alternatives to the latter's prevailing influence.[43] Mauss himself is indeed credited by Lefort with the proposal of a "new rationalism" ("in the tradition of Hegel, Marx and Husserl").[44] Gift-exchange sustained by reason replaced the social sanctions of guilt and shame that guaranteed the transmission of its archaic counterpart. The progressive displacement of collective constraints by reasoned good will provoked this commentary by Sahlins:

> By the end of the essay, Mauss had left far behind the mystic forests of Polynesia. The obscure forces of *hau* were forgotten for a different explanation of reciprocity, consequent on the more general theory, and the opposite of all mystery and particularity: Reason. The gift is Reason. It is the triumph of human rationality over the folly of War.[45]

The concept of reason proposed here is clearly not to be equated with the avatar of economic rationality under discussion; but by not adequately contending with the modern split between the economic and the social, Mauss facilitated the current bias that applies the morality of gift-giving only to exchanges in the social sphere.

Mauss attempted to inscribe the diffuse possibilities of gift-giving within a modern form of exchange in which equivalent values are transferred; yet the essay itself fuels the conviction that the need to give defies such restriction and surfaces within our own time as the desire to offer a thoroughly disinterested "free gift." While Mauss's study documents the variety of functions played by the offering of gifts—to buy peace, to express affection, or to bind generations—it also sensitizes readers to impulses allied with, but not immediately translatable into, the reality of economic transactions. It is, therefore, easy to appreciate how Richard Titmuss was able to spark a heated and protracted polemic among economists and sociologists with a comparative study of blood donorship in Britain and the United States, significantly titled *The Gift Relationship*. By documenting the greater success of the English system, in which no remuneration is provided, he is able to sustain the thesis that "gift-exchange of a non-quantifiable nature has more important functions in large-scale societies than the writings of Lévi-Strauss and others would suggest."[46] Locating himself within the legacy of Mauss, Titmuss also contends that "the application of scientific and technical developments in such societies . . . has *increased* rather than diminished the scientific as well as the social need for relationships." Moreover, "modern societies now require more rather than less freedom of choice for the expression of *altruism* in the daily life of all social groups."[47]

Although Titmuss and others may have succeeded in imposing the issue of gift-giving as a legitimate concern, one must question their impact on the very criteria employed to evaluate their contributions. Thus a typical, and indeed accurate, assessment from within the conventional "rational choice" approach to exchange questions whether the category of a "free gift," prompted by altruism devoid of concern for future benefits, "can be brought within the scope of exchange at all."[48] Ironically, reading Mauss via Bataille leads to a similar conclusion: The particular mode of expenditure connoted by dépense can circumvent the "paradoxes" of potlatch only if removed from the arena of competitive rivalry and practiced exclusively within a form of giving which precludes any acquisition of gain, real or symbolic. The inevitable question, then, is how to situate dépense in relation to the conditions dictated by theories of exchange. For if, as we suspect, dépense falls outside the purview of the categories determined by such theory, or at best is reintroduced under the innocuous guise of the "gift," then an evaluation of the possibility of giving conceived beyond the limits of rationality is in order.

DEPENSE

The hallmark of twentieth-century French anthropology is the central position of exchange as the foundation of culture. Following Mauss's emphasis on the rules and meaning at work in gift-exchange, Lévi-Strauss constructed a communicational model that posits the object circulated as a sign safeguarding communication against the individual's propensity to "keep to oneself."[49] Goods, moreover, mediate the practice of exchange as dictated by the rules of the symbolic order regulating the social obligation to give. The economic assumptions underlying this view of exchange challenge neither the scarcity premise of traditional political economy nor the inevitable conflict between individual desires and social exigencies. Mauss also envisaged exchange as transcending one-to-one encounters. In his social cosmos, however, exchange functions within a cyclical order of restitution returning to individuals benefits in the form of welfare, that they legitimately expect from society but that cannot be guaranteed through the mechanisms of the marketplace. What is eventually returned through exchange is nonetheless understood by Lévi-Strauss as first having been extracted. Myth, he speculates, serves to overcome temporarily the strife incited by the demands of an order to which the subject's wants are subordinate.

Lévi-Strauss laments the demise of the days of pre-exchange and "that atmosphere of feverish excitement and sensitivity which engendered symbolic thought, and social life, which is its collective form," that "can still with its far-off vision kindle our dreams."[50] For him, myth functions as the escape valve through which the antagonisms toward exchange can be vented: "To this very day, mankind has always dreamed of seizing and fixing that fleeting moment when it was permissible to believe that the law of exchange could be evaded, that one could gain without losing, enjoy without sharing . . .

removing to an equally unattainable past or future the joys, eternally denied to social man, of a world in which one might keep to oneself."[51]

Mauss's "social man" extends gifts because he is both reasoned and generous. He experiences joy and pleasure in public expenditure and is psychologically liberated from the onus of constraints that ultimately deprive him of the voluntary nature of his offering. To the extent that the giver of the future must be conditioned to the idea of social gifts, a democratic educational system must execute the socializing process: "There is no need to seek far for goodness and happiness. It is to be found in the imposed peace, in the rhythm of communal and private labour, in wealth amassed and redistributed in the mutual respect and reciprocal generosity that education can impart" (81).

The structuralist paradigm, however, radically "decenters" the Cartesian legacy of a worldless subject by locating its identity and possibilities for thought at the intersection of multiple semiotic systems. The structuralist subject thus inhabits a universe of goods endowed with "value" as meaning, and this *homo significans* exchanges things already inscribed within a symbolic order. Lévi-Strauss, who rejects Mauss's explanation of the "force" of the gift through the indigenous categories of *hau* and *mana,* compares them to the modern French equivalents of *truc* and *machin,* equally "unstable" signifiers of undetermined signifieds.[52] Their ambivalence reflects the economic reality of language—an abundance of signification from which emerges these "floating signifiers," looming on the semiological horizon of culture constituted as "an ensemble of symbolic systems, headed by language, marriage rules, economic relations, art, science, and religion,"[53] incapable of codifying the excess of meaning.

The contribution of the structuralist theory of gift-exchange to economic anthropology expanded the analysis of needs and desires from the purely material to the symbolic. The alleged motives of economic man are now directed toward the acquisition of the signs of power and prestige. The ostensibly irrational expenditures incurred in accumulating cultural capital are reassessed within a cost-benefit analysis calculated with an eye to the entire social ensemble. Perhaps the most subtle move in this direction is found in Baudrillard's "political economy of the sign."[54] It breaks with the specious dichotomy between the material and the symbolic, which maintains that the latter is subsequent and subordinate to a rational mode of production. Drawing on these insights, Sahlins applies them to American culture while making generalizations for all of Western "civilizations." He observes that symbolic differentiation—social distinctions and hierarchies— is encoded at the level of production and provides Western culture with its own panoply of totems and fetishes. The point here is to counter the fiction "that the [Western] economy and society are pragmatically constructed," while for those of archaic cultures "the locus of symbolic differentiation remains social relations, principally kinship relations, and other spheres of activity ordered by the operative distinctions of kinship."[55]

A frequent criticism of the structuralist concentration on rules and meaning is that sentiment becomes subordinate to structure and the behavior of individuals is considered only in light of collective constraints. This antiatomistic position is less pronounced in Mauss, with his desire for a gift-exchange motivated by both individuals and groups. His concern with the psychological basis for the gift is evidenced by the controversy over interest, a response to the utilitarian query, Why give?

In keeping with his assertion that economic man is a recent phenomenon, Mauss complements his examples of the relative disinterestedness of archaic gifts with the philological history of the concept of interest. It is traced to the Latin where it was written in accounting books opposite rents to be collected. For Roman society, however, "interest" meant something other than its modern counterpart, since "in the most epicurean of these philosophies pleasure and the good were pursued and not material utility. The victory of rationalism and mercantilism were required before the notions of profit and the individual were given currency and raised to the level of principles" (77). The cultural differences highlighted by this change in the notion of interest stem from an implicit assimilation of "individual": "It is only by awkward paraphrasing that one can render the phrase 'individual interest' in Latin, Greek, or Arabic" (74).

It is therefore possible to argue that an explanation of the archaic gift resists translation into the discourse of modern psychology because of its collective nature. Mauss's approach to the question follows his adherence to Comte's precept that the psychological attains full significance through the social; and, according to Lévi-Strauss, his anthropological project benefits from a "nonintellectualist" psychology that probes for "unconscious" categories where "incomparable and uncommunicable subjectivities" meet to generate the categories of "collective thought."[56]

The primacy granted to the social by Mauss is evident in the scheme of exchange where no original giver is posited and individuals are considered already within the cycle of reciprocity. The psychological state or motive of any one person is thus absorbed by the group activity, just as the actual governing mechanism activating prestations is attributed to "nothing less than the division of labor itself" (1).

Norman O. Brown tests the viability of the traditional psychological approach to the gift. He contends that the inquiry is skewed by Mauss's formulation of the opening question: "In primitive or archaic types of society what is the principle whereby the gift received has to be repaid? What force is there in the thing given which compels the recipient to make a return?" (1). Here Brown reveals Mauss's unwitting compromise with the assumption "that the original giver needs the assurance that he will not lose in the transaction. But the inadequacies of the psychology of egoism are glaring in their inability to explain the principle of reciprocity of archaic exchange in which there exists no gain."[57] Brown inverts the question to provide an origin for an investigation into gift-giving directed away from the "not-further-analyzable" principle of social solidarity.

> Archaic gift-giving [the famous potlatch is only an extreme example] is one vast refutation of the notion that the psychological motive of economic life is utilitarian egoism. Archaic man gives because he wants to lose; the psychology is not egoist but self-sacrificial. Hence the intrinsic connection with the sacred. The gods exist to receive gifts, that is to say sacrifices; the gods exist in order to structure the human need for self-sacrifice.[58]

Brown then points his psychology of economics toward that "other mental apparatus" posited by Freud as independent of, and possibly more primitive than, the pleasure principle. This is the sector where anxiety, the repetition compulsion, sadism and masochism, guilt, and the death instinct intersect. Brown deviates furthest from the tradition of French sociology in his insistence that archaic gift-giving, like the modern psychology of possession, is finally explained through the psychology of guilt: "The magic quality of objects is derived from their symbolic relation to the unconscious sense of guilt, and the first demand of the unconscious guilt is to be shared."[59]

Bataille and Brown ostensibly agree that the psychology of archaic guilt is indeed self-sacrificial. But whereas Brown asserts that guilt motivates the need to give, Bataille simply states that the need for dépense stems from within; it exists "for no reason other than the desire one may have for it" (VII, 16.) Bataille's anxiety to illuminate dépense itself— repressed by social taboos and repeatedly displaced among the marginal categories of madness, irrationality, poetry, and the sacred—partially explains the vagueness of this observation. The opening pages of the essay "La Notion de dépense" acknowledge the contribution of psychoanalysis to the question: the equation of gift and feces as insight into extraordinary expenditures. He further connects the latter, such as jewels, to his category of the part maudite by their symbolic emanation from the taboo "wounds" of the self-sacrificing individual. Despite their specious flirtation with death, however, contemporary modes of dépense such as gambling or horseracing cannot be considered a form of pure dépense since they designate status within a hierarchy of symbolic distinctions.

In our own culture, adolescence manifests a dépense susceptible to psychoanalytic interpretation. Its "juvenile" prodigality, however, barely intuits the implications of the ecstasy of giving in "a certain orgiastic state." Restrained by a paternal authority consecrated by the light of reason, the adolescent's expenditure reinforces rather than subverts the social hierarchy mirrored in familial relations. Thus, while the paternal censor may not prove effective in imposing total closure on the expression of dépense, he is able to reduce the adolescent to a subservient position. The forces of dépense are neutralized within the sanctioned grace period of adolescence, conceived as a rite of passage between childhood and adulthood when sexual energies are sufficiently squandered such that the adult, equated with the worker, will be more willing to assume the necessity of entering a work force dedicated to production and accumulation. To the extent dépense compromises with utility, Bataille can consider it only a minor or subordinate mode of expenditure.

Bataille's argument based on the evidence of potlatch demonstrates what the adolescent could not understand: that entire societies can find it in their "interest" to spend, not save. The position adopted here was announced earlier with Queneau in a critique of Marxist theory: the "sclerotic" materialist dialectic must be revitalized through the best of "bourgeois" thought: psychoanalysis (Freud) and French sociology (Durkheim and Mauss). Searching for the "foundation" of the Hegelian dialectic, Bataille and Queneau conclude that it arises from "the human condition within a lived experience" such as the tension between father and son, master and slave, and the privileged grounds on which to explore these notions are the "sciences of man, and they alone."[60] The renewed attempts to match the categories of the general economy with those of other disciplines will be documented throughout this study. Yet it is evident that the major emphasis is placed on the social mechanisms that deny the "necessity" for a form of giving that tries "to project oneself, and something of oneself, *beyond the self* . . . which in certain instances can have no other result than death" (I, 265). Because it is a force rather than an idea or sentiment, and because it finds satisfaction in those collective encounters arising from the excess energy of the isolated monad aware of its insufficiency without the other, dépense cannot be exhausted within the categories of individual psychology. Dépense and the part maudite each comprehend the history of such hybrid notions as the archaic gift and potlatch before their split into specialized abstractions. But they also reflect the malaise arising within a culture where the denial of collective means for self-sacrifice "leads a man in isolation to incomprehensible and sometimes even stupid behavior" (II, 13). Brown may posit a domain of experience "beyond the pleasure principle" where impersonal forces sway individual behavior. Yet while he prescribes a "resurrection of the body" exempt from the alleged guilt stalking all economic activity, this erotic exuberance leaves unresolved the nature of the relation to an other.[61]

Another, philosophical reading of Mauss demonstrates how collective categories emerge from the experience of gift-giving. In a conscious attempt to counter the structuralist focus on the rules of exchange, Lefort's interpretation emphasizes the phenomenological reality of the behavior involved. Gift-exchange is lived as a confrontation between the subject and the other, between individuals and groups, such as clans or tribes. Although Mauss indicates that subgroups may, in theory, dissociate themselves from the cycle, they are never cited as doing so. Yet the contract can be breached, explains Lefort, and the cycle of reciprocity perceived as "open" rather than as a duty that transcends persons. Thus the "war of wealth," as Mauss describes potlatch, is not to be condemned as purely divisive, but precipitates a face-to-face encounter Lefort terms a "war of men." More than a call to ostentatious display, potlatch challenges the representation individuals may have of themselves. The gift must be understood as an *act* by means of which subjectivity is conquered through the negation of *things*. Although identity may indeed be tied to property, in this case it does so through the negativity of destruction. Within the gesture of gift-giving can be observed a simultaneous affirmation of *difference* and the discovery of *similarity,* since the idea that the gift will be returned implies that "the other [*autrui*] is another self which ought to behave as I do; the return gesture confirms the truth of my own gesture, that is to say, my *subjectivity.*"[62] Brown reproached Mauss for dwelling on the *return* gift as acquiescing to the psychology of egoism; Lefort reads into the experience its implied reciprocity: "One does not give in order to receive, but so the other will give."[63]

The concrete result of the *lutte des hommes* for mutual recognition is the emergence of "a collectivity trying to behave as a collective 'I' . . . the 'we' of the group exists only insofar as each person affirms his subjectivity through the gift. Moreover, a transcendental consciousness is constituted through the collective experience, rather than the empirical behavior of the subject being deduced from it."[64]

Fundamental to this reading of the gift essay is its demonstration that things structure the formation of social relations. In this precommodity universe even individuals in relative isolation identify with the objects mediating their contact with nature. Giving, however, sunders the ties to things and inaugurates social bonds and human attachments—provided that this negation be both recognized and replicated by the other: "In this way, the emergence of the human universe is coeval with a disaffection from reality; men, in an identical operation, that of the gift, confirm to each other that they are not things. The covenant with the other and the break with nature testify to a collective *cogito*. It is this which allows us to appreciate the sacred nature of the gift without having to appeal to a mystical interpretation."[65]

By exploring the ramifications of gift-giving, Lefort imagines an exchange in which the subject's identity ultimately relies on the collective exercise of individual will. The atmosphere so created, charged with the forces of persons engaged in giving, imparts to the entire act the aura of the sacred without necessitating recourse to an external agent whose authority guarantees its value or meaning. Any violence thus generated is directed toward the destruction of things, thereby opening Bataille's communication as *consumation*. The anthropological model for this eminently positive view of collective life is derived from Durkheim, with whom Bataille agrees on two fundamental principles: that the social whole is greater than the sum of its parts, and that religion is the primary force of social solidarity. Within the immediate context of the individual/group duality, Durkheim's contribution is as follows.

By considering social constraints as the *unconscious* rules that define how a person may realize his/her potential, "we speak a language that we did not make; we use instruments that we did not invent; we invoke rights that we did not found; a treasury of information is transmitted to each generation that it did not gather itself, etc."[66] This area of Durkheim's thought has earned him recognition as a prestructuralist. The label is further justified by the similarity of this "treasure" to the Saussurean *trésor* of *langue* that renders the utterances of individual *parole* possible. It is important to note that the "varied benefits of civilization" that Durkheim wishes to restore to society, Lévi-Strauss and Brown view as having been subtracted from the individual. According to Durkheim, "if we do not ordinarily see the source from which we get [these benefits], we at least know that they are not our own work."[67]

Durkheim's concept of society is further distinguished by his insistence on the *sui generis* reality created through collective encounters. Thus, in Lévi-Strauss's nostalgia for the ambiance of "feverish excitement" recognized as unique to social life in its collective form, he joins Durkheim's harkening for "those hours of creative effervescence" formerly responsible for the emergence of new ideas, including scientific ones: "Perhaps," speculates Durkheim, "a day will come when our societies will know again the contagious frenzy of group life where vital energies are over-excited, passions more active and sensations stronger."[68] In these states of heightened awareness, otherwise "closed" consciousnesses commune and discover sentiments made possible only in such rich moments. These are not rare, disparate revelations, but the gathering of forces that stimulate the awakening of religious thought and, by extension, produce the most comprehensive system of symbolic representations of a culture: "Thus religion, far from ignoring the real society and making abstraction of it, is in its image; it reflects all its aspects, even the most vulgar and the most repulsive. All is to be found there."[69]

Yet the excess arising from such religious ecstasy—even when constrained by ceremonies and rituals—cannot be exhausted. In an outstanding passage, Durkheim sketches his understanding of the particular economy responsible for relaying the surplus of energy among alternative modes of representation.

A surplus generally remains available which seeks to employ itself in supplementary and superfluous works of luxury, that is to say, in works of art. There are practices as well as beliefs of this sort. The state of effervescence in which the assembled worshippers find themselves must be translated outwardly by exuberant movements which are not easily subjected to too carefully defined ends. In part, they escape aimlessly, they spread themselves for the mere pleasure of doing so, and they take delight in all sorts of games. Besides, insofar as the beings to whom the cult is addressed are imaginary, they are not able to contain and regulate this exuberance; the presence of tangible and resisting realities is required to confine the activities to exact and economical forms. Therefore one exposes oneself to grave misunderstandings if, in explaining rites, he believes that each gesture has a precise object and a definite reason for its existence. There are some which serve nothing; they merely answer the need felt by worshippers for action, motion, gesticulation. They are to be seen jumping, whirling, dancing, crying and singing, though it may not always be possible to give a meaning to all this agitation.[70]

Having asserted the primarily cognitive function of religion, Durkheim relegates art to the superfluous, a tributary of the religious overflow. Rites become modes of "dramatic representation," equivalent to games and art forms. Still, some notions, gestures, and sentiments stubbornly resist insertion within any "form" or "precise and economical ends." The recognition of this "meaning"-less agitation, albeit in a religious guise, allows Durkheim to penetrate the uncharted domain of rites and activities serving "nothing." Similarly, when pushed to look for a motive for dépense, Bataille responds that "the human being is responsible for expending in a glorious gesture what the earth accumulates, what the sun proffers. Essentially, man dances, laughs, and gives festivals" (VII, 16).

The tension between the force of dépense and the propensity to ascribe to it form or meaning is undeniable. To what extent this conflict indicates an inevitable dynamic of culture remains subject to debate. The elusive reality of dépense—whether manifested as potlatch, history, or poetry—indicates, however, that few individuals are content to accept the "instant" of unconditional giving as their sole access to the truth. They therefore condemn themselves to an obsessive search for meaning through some form or representation. The struggle to integrate that instant within consciousness is articulated as follows:

In fact, accumulation must be situated in relation to the *instant* at which it will be resolved as pure dépense. But herein lies the difficult moment. Consciousness is opposed to it to the extent that it seeks to obtain some object of acquisition, some *thing*, rather than the *nothing* of pure dépense. It is a matter of attaining the moment when consciousness ceases to be the consciousness of *some thing*. In other words, to become aware that the

decisive meaning of an instant where acquisition will resolve itself in pure
dépense, is precisely the consciousness-of-self, which is to say, consciousness which no longer has a *thing as its object*. [VII, 272]

From these readings on exchange, two distinct issues emerge corresponding to those raised by the part maudite and dépense. The first
question touches on the very existence of a surplus that eludes the
homogeneity of the restricted economy. Its corollary articulates the notion of
a "free gift," or pure dépense, that challenges the codes that could ascribe it
value or meaning. Thus Mauss speaks of the "force" of the gift itself—
circulating among individuals tangled in the confusion between persons and
things; Lévi-Strauss regrets the "feverish excitement" permeating language
and sexual relations; and both borrow from Durkheim's enthusiastic account
of the "effervescence" and "exuberance" of archaic religious cults and
ceremonies. Irrespective of the occasion, Durkheim notes, the expression of
the surplus is the same: "cries, songs, music, violent movements, dances."[71]

The part maudite and dépense are phenomena of excess whose
archaeological strata bear the imprint of all the preceding notions, but
emerge within a culture at the "point" where collective emotions and
discursive categories meet. Laughter, eroticism, ecstasy, heroism, and
sacrifice: all govern the law of communication among individuals, whom the
degradation of collective life would condemn to isolated agony. Concepts
derived exclusively from discursive understanding must be complemented
by those approximating "an emotive yet rigorous mode of understanding,"
until the two (modes of knowledge) dissolve "in the laughter of the
unanimous crowd" (V, 11).

The trajectory between don and dépense does not move in a straight
line from one-dimensional economic man to the Maussian exhortation to
consider "minds as wholes, and not minds divided into faculties." In both its
theory and practice, Western culture is distinguished by its extreme social
fragmentation, as well as an intellectual division of labor into specialized
disciplines with complementary discourses. This increasing tension parallels
that between values promoted by the work ethic and values contrary to them
in the cultural sphere. If the general economy is defined by the forces of
expenditure rather than those of production, then its constitutive categories,
such as dépense and the part maudite, must be considered within the context
of that whole. Similarly, we must examine the extent to which they reveal
subterranean connections obfuscated by the modes of thought and systems
of representation limited by exchanges—material and symbolic—consonant
with the restricted economy of specialized systems.

Within the archaic forms of gift-giving, exchange is understood as a
"total social fact" bearing social, religious, aesthetic, and juridical signif-

icance. In addition, however, it entails ceremonial expenditures that are uneconomic, dangerous, and ultimately "irrational." Subsequent trans-formations of this model expunge the "sacred-superfluous" aspect (Brown) exemplified in potlatch to stabilize contracts within gift-exchange. Mauss advises his readers to revitalize and expand this model, reversing the decline in social bonding brought on by the practice of exclusively economic transactions. The consequences of such gift-exchange are primarily social, performing only a secondary function within the economy itself. The "reversibility" inherent in the gift/counter-gift cycle effectively precludes profit or accumulation since it annuls any intervention of meaning or value within the process.[72] "Symbolic exchange" of this order, however, does not allow for the loss implied in dépense as an active, continual movement. There, "value" is attained only in the instant of total surrender to a force ready to sacrifice things, meaning, and self. While its only truth ultimately defies the containment of an exchange model, the laws guiding unlimited expenditure must be situated in relation to those of the restricted economy. Thus dépense is located within the space of the don. Yet it also obeys the logic of the general economy which dictates that each contributing element derives significance from its place in a whole that exceeds the sum of its parts. With this caveat in mind, the remaining categories pertaining to the general economy will be considered.

CHAPTER

2

HETEROGENEITY

One certainty emerges from the history of the notion of dépense: to liberate a form of expenditure from the criterion of utility demands a radical break with conventional modes of exchange. Only the transgressive violence of sacrifice, disdainful of immediate ends and destined for loss, guarantees access to a domain so alien to the restricted economy that it can relinquish to the part maudite the sovereign force it commands. Moreover, a category must be devised that would be capable of safeguarding dépense from the censure of irrationality. Unlike the alternatives found in philosophy, science, or so-called common sense, heterogeneity perceives excess as the substrate uniting specialized systems. Thus, the study of heterogeneity encompasses three orders in an effort to bridge the discontinuities maintained by other approaches: the social, the personal, and the discursive. Furthermore, it considers how, within contemporary culture, the heterogeneous can be acknowledged and even mobilized to counter the deleterious effects of homogeneity.

The analysis of heterogeneity begins with a broad characterization of social homogeneity as it develops through rationalism and its correlatives—abstraction, specialization, and fragmentation. As a form of social organization the homogeneous sector tolerates only that which is useful, productive, profitable, and concerned with the preservation of self and things. Above all, homogeneity is identified as *commensurability* among elements and a *consciousness* of the process whereby "human relations can be maintained by a reduction to fixed rules based on the identity of person and well-defined situations: in principle, violence is excluded from the course of an existence so defined" (I, 340).

The exclusion of ritualized violence from social relations is one symptom of homogeneity's more general operation. Given its inability to generate an internal unifying force as the basis for its own identity, it must derive its definition from an expelled object. This process accounts for the transition from archaic gift-exchange to Western market economies; a universal currency imposes a common denominator for all objects by removing one—gold—from circulation. The market's subsequent encroachment on the original structures of social exchange precipitates the demise of the hierarchy dictating the categories of exchange within the archaic economy. The flattening process of capitalism is, therefore, coeval with the progressive homogeneity of social life.[1] By extension, to appreciate the consequences of the primary process of homogenization, one must question the identity of the heterogeneous object it spawns: Can it be imputed to a special class within the general order of things, or is it to be found in the subjective reactions elicited by the nature of the objects themselves?

Social homogeneity, for instance, is consolidated through the values it projects onto the proletariat. Although integrated at the level of production, workers remain only marginally related to the benefits of profit since they never appropriate the means of production. The owners may guarantee homogeneity, but the middle sector, caught between owners and workers, is most affected by "the reduction of human character to an abstract and interchangeable entity" (I, 341). Homogeneity thus devolves to the proletariat an ambiguous position resulting from its simultaneous appropriation of the surplus labor of workers and the investment into them of the heterogeneous, irreducible forces it believes to have segregated beyond its own confines. Thus, workers appear to the bourgeoisie "as ugly and as dirty as the hairy parts, and equally base" (I, 85–86). Predictably, observes Bataille, "sooner or later this will lead to a scandalous eruption during which the asexual and noble heads of the bourgeois will be cut" (I, 85–86).

This psychoanalytic overdetermination of the social basis for the capitalist/worker distinction is the paradigm for the hierarchical dualities whose appearance parallels the autonomization of the economy from the archaic state of "original undifferentiation." We recall that one of the signs of imminent change was the split of hybrid notions into specialized terms mirroring the intensified division of labor. Bourdieu thus explains why, in the lexicon of the archaic economy, one finds "double-edged notions which the history of the economy destines to be dissociated because, by reason of their duality, the social relations they designate reflect unstable structures, condemned to separate as soon as the social mechanisms buttressing them begin to weaken."[2] Bourdieu seconds Mauss's praise for the "venerable revolution" among Greeks and Romans which led to the development of clear-cut economic structures. The latter slough off the obligations of ceremonial expenditures, which he views as costly maneuvers to disguise the fundamental economic reality of gift-exchange. Bourdieu rejects, however, Lévi-Strauss's "objectivist" reduction of gift-giving to the mechanical execution of the obligations of reciprocity (formulated as a counter to Mauss's phenomenological approach) on the grounds that within one operation, it obliterates the conditions of the possibility of the *institutionally organized and guaranteed disavowal* which is at the basis of gift-exchange and, perhaps, all symbolic work aimed at transforming, through communication and cooperation, the inevitable relations imposed by kinship, the neighborhood, or work, into elective relations of reciprocity: in *the work of reproducing established relations,* festivals, ceremonies, exchanges of gifts—visits, compliments, and especially marriages—which is no less indispensable to the group than the reproduction of the economic foundations of its existence, the work necessary to dissimulate the function of exchanges becomes no less important than the work demanded to fulfill the function itself.[3]

Bourdieu's "praxeological" model is relevant to the discussion of heterogeneity to the extent it does not reduce the symbolic to the economic, but insists that their inextricability within archaic cultures constitutes a fundamental difference from Western civilization. This ontological unity can be appreciated only if one tries to "hold together" the "double truth of practices which are intrinsically *equivocal* and *ambiguous*" given that they encompass "economic" calculations within a symbolic sphere.[4] Moreover, because he reinscribes the symbolic and the economic within a comprehensive materialism titled "a general science of the economy of practice" touching on the social energies so produced, Bourdieu allows us to examine how the practice of heterogeneity, as manifested through "elective relations of reciprocity," is limited by the conditions of possibility within capitalism.

Bourdieu's goal is to break with the ethnocentrism of economism's "naive dualities," as they insist on differentiating technical from symbolic activity, and productive from nonproductive work. Rather, he claims that those acts touted as most disinterested actually participate in an "economic cosmos," where symbolic and material capital are mutually convertible.[5] In a similar vein, I will argue the importance of heterogeneity as a means for challenging the alleged stability of antinomies grounded in the clear-cut structures of purely economic acts. The purpose of this reversal is not to detect "spiritual" traces within monetary transactions, but to see how the heterogeneous disrupts the oppositions by englobing them within the material, i.e., social, religious, and erotic forces of the general economy. In this way, Bataille's proposal of a heterology, best appreciated as a synthesis of anthropology and psychoanalysis, will allow us to gauge the price paid to maintain the illusion of homogeneity through the repression of its heterogeneous foundation.

The dynamic governing the homogeneous/heterogeneous distinction, as well as that of the capitalist/worker opposition, is explained by the increased rationalism which accompanies the inception of capitalism. While rationalism is a mainstay of classical Western philosophy, its role within particular moments is, as Lukács maintains, qualitative, and must be evaluated in relation to its place within the comprehensive system of human knowledge and objectives: "What is novel about modern rationalism is its increasingly insistent claim that it has discovered the *principle* which connects up all phenomena which in nature and society are found to confront mankind. Compared with this, every previous type of rationalism is no more than a *partial system*".[6] The contemporary form of rationalism in question here is that which evolved from economic theory as a form that equates rationality with economizing.[7] The definition of economics is so general as to blur the outlines of the science and impart to the economizing principle the prestige of a universal law. Yet, despite its ubiquity, economics cannot produce the desired synthesis, and economic man remains a truncated creature severed from any sense of wholeness. Thus, regardless of the claims made for the rationality of economics, it too abuts against a barrier of irrationality. As Lukács crystallized the situation, "In such systems [of rationalism] the 'ultimate' problems of human existence persist in an irrationality incommensurable with human understanding. The closer the system comes to these 'ultimate' questions the more strikingly its partial, auxiliary nature and its inability to grasp the 'essentials' are revealed."[8]

Because it is located within the framework of the general economy, heterogeneity questions the status of the philosophical "thing-in-itself" as the material obstacle to the imperialism of rationality. The inability of conventional economic theory to respond to consumption of goods or the acquisition of "symbolic capital" except through irrational sentiment has already been underscored.[9] The notion of dépense, however, challenges the opposition of rationality and irrationality and reopens to modern experience the equivalent of a sacred space of archaic expenditure. How the special nature of the sacred is determined is the underlying issue for an appreciation of heterogeneity.

THE SACRED

In a review of Jules Monnerot's *Les Faits sociaux ne sont pas des choses*,[10] Bataille identifies himself with the generation that attained maturity between the two world wars and that distinguished itself by its consciousness that "society" was not fixed, but a product of historical change. As heirs to a humanist culture in which the individual remains the measure of all things, these artists, poets, and intellectuals viewed society as, at best, a necessary evil, whose justification was periodically subject to doubt. Added to this essentially cerebral pessimism was the view that society's inability to reproduce itself except by the exploitative status quo generated the "revolutionary impulse" that intensified the intellectual's conflict between thought and action.

Whether they looked to the revolutionary left, the fascistic right, or the politically ambiguous surrealist compromise of a cultural revolution, Bataille and his peers witnessed a surge of activity in which men and women banded together for motives not exclusively political, cultural, nor sentimental. For Bataille, who remained on the margins of these dominant movements, the lure of revolutionary solidarity nonetheless elicited hope for community. The result was a series of experimental *collèges*, secret societies, and short-lived journals. Yet he was equally cognizant of deep-seated fears of individual subordination to an impersonal cause—the drama of men torn between individualism and the need for collective action.

Bataille traces the title of the Monnerot work under consideration—social facts are not things—to the popularity of Mauss's lectures and an inclination for community other than that offered by French society during the 1920s and 1930s. He parallels the fascination with sacred bonds in the primitive cultures studied by Mauss with modern cultural pursuits: "These young writers understood that society has lost the secret of its former cohesiveness, and this is precisely what they were searching for by means of the obscure, awkward, and sterile efforts of their poetic fervor."[11] Bataille also credits his contemporaries—Leiris, Caillois, and Monnerot—with another motive: the preoccupation with a scientific basis of judgment. The main contradiction, however, besetting intellectuals who renounced affiliation with both surrealism and communism was their inability to translate the knowledge acquired from sociological analysis into practice: "Neither the concern for a society capable of creating uncommon values, nor the interest in sociological studies ever led to real action."[12] Moreover, any justification of the revived interest in the avant-garde activities of that earlier period, Bataille suggests, is not to be found in the debatable scientific success of social theory. Rather, the social historian should be attuned to the vague sense of lack and nostalgia which pervades society and which forms the legacy of his generation to its successors.

Bataille's own sociological reading of Monnerot's book stresses the resemblance between the categories that Monnerot applied in his social critique and those used by intellectuals to express their general malaise. The historical significance of Monnerot's work derives from a morality reflecting the conditions of early twentieth-century French society. The primary focus is, therefore, on the set of contrasting organizational structures discovered in the study of precapitalist formations: the dualism of the sacred and the profane, subsumed under the more encompassing opposition between homogeneity and heterogeneity and paralleled by the dichotomies of appurtenance versus contract, *Bund* versus secret societies. Bataille conjectures that because Monnerot revealed to an essentially profane world the sacred ties active in other cultures, he successfully countered Durkheim by demonstrating that social facts cannot be considered only as things.

Monnerot's sociological treatise expresses the sentiments of a generation seeking social adhesion of a different order, and united by a common perception of isolation unaccounted for under existing systems of social or philosophical analysis. On the survival of this sense of urgency in postwar France, Bataille is unequivocal: "The possibility of intentional communities is, for each of us, the decisive question."[13] Although Monnerot demonstrated courage in his willingness to tackle the foundations of Durkheim's sociology, he did not pursue his investigation to the point where the potential meaning of social facts meets with historical reality: "Thus it is regrettable that as a sociologist, Monnerot never elucidated the significance of the categories he set forth within their historical context."[14]

To do so would effectively provide a psychological complement to Durkheim's postulate that the sacred is the primary unifying force of society: "The difference between the *whole* and the sum of its parts does not mean, as Durkheim insisted, that the determinism of society is psychological. Similarly, to concede the influence of a psychological or economic factor does not imply that the whole is merely the sum of its parts."[15] Because he equated psychology with individual predispositions, Durkheim insisted that social facts could be understood only by other social facts. In this way he believed he had divested his work of the conceptual errors of his predecessors. The methodological advance, however, led to an overstatement of the individual/psychological distinction.

Thus a recurrent problem for Bataille was the various connotations assumed by "individual" and "society" in Durkheim's lexicon. Moreover, he never successfully divorced their bifurcation from the influence of Durkheim in a manner consonant with his own demand for a theory evolved from experience. For heterogeneity, the issue parallels similar debates raised by Durkheim's concept of the sacred or Lévi-Strauss's approach to incest. Bataille, however, formulates the problem within the dichotomies of the social/psychological or collective/individual rather than in the culture/nature pair. Since the "subjective" reactions provoked by excrement or menstrual blood, for instance, are subject to universal taboos, it is difficult not to attribute them a basis in nature. As a further complication, these things attain objective status within a theoretical discourse only when affiliated with homogeneous scientific abstractions. To break the impasse, Bataille resolves to treat the heterogeneous as it is located within a total order of things, and by making privileged "the subjective heterogeneity of particular elements [which] alone is concrete" (III, 63).

As a result, the theory of heterogeneity is consistently subordinated to its constitutive facts. Although Bataille agrees that the understanding of social facts must necessarily consider their meaning, the model for exploring such phenomena was provided by Durkheim, who stipulated the criteria for their recognition. Social facts are independent of both the observer and the individual will; they may be ascertained by empirical observation; and they are susceptible to study through external observation (e.g., indicators, legal codes, statistics). Moreover, some social facts are not crystallized in a precise form but are nonetheless subject to objective study and exert ascendency over the individual. Durkheim refers to the "free currents of social life" that the individual discerns as sacred but whose source or origin cannot be readily identified. He therefore ascribes to the sacred a status absolutely distinct from the profane: "The two form distinct and separate mental states in our consciousness, just as do the two forms of life to which they correspond. Consequently, we get the impression that we are in relation with two distinct sorts of reality and that a sharply drawn line of demarcation separates them from each other; on the one hand is the world of profane things, on the other, that of sacred things."[16]

The impetus for the establishment of the duality of homo- and heterogeneity nonetheless remains an enigma, and Durkheim amplifies the mystery.

> When we believed that sacred beings could be distinguished from others merely by the greater intensity of the powers attributed to them, the question of how men came to imagine them was sufficiently simple: it was enough to demand which forces had, because of their exceptional energy, been able to strike the human imagination forcefully enough to inspire religious sentiments. But if, as we have sought to establish, sacred things differ in nature from profane things, if they have a wholly different essence, then the problem is more complex. For we must first of all ask what has been able to lead men to see in the world two heterogeneous and incompatible worlds, though nothing in sensible experience seems able to suggest the idea of so radical a duality to them.[17]

Despite Durkheim's zealous praise for the specific reality produced by collective encounters, Bataille dismisses the descriptions as inadequate scientific basis for the sacred/profane distinction: "[Durkheim] was content to characterize the sacred world negatively, as absolutely heterogeneous in relation to the profane" (I, 355). Yet Bataille initially appears content to follow Durkheim, restricting heterogeneity to a negative function of homogeneity. He presents the former as the passive consequence of nonproductive dépense, that is,

> all that homogeneous society rejects, either as detritus or superior transcendent value. These include the excremental products of the human body and certain analogous materials; those parts of the body, persona, words or acts possessing an erotic charge; the diverse unconscious processes such as dreams and neuroses, the numerous elements or

social forms which the homogeneous sector is incapable of assimilating: crowds, warrior classes, aristocrats and *misérables,* all different sorts of violent individuals, or certainly those rejecting the law. [I, 346]

Bataille's attempt to communicate the fluid dynamism of the heterogeneous closely parallels Durkheim's descriptions of the sacred. Both place strong emphasis on the violence and excess of heterogeneous objects whose power, in individual or collective actions, breaks the laws of social homogeneity. By contrast, heterogeneous objects are clearly apprehended. Their reality is that of solid materials: abstract, neutral, precise—the appropriate and appropriable companions of economic man. Predictably, the heterogeneous is energized by force or shock value, manifesting itself like "a charge, passing from one object to another" (I, 347). Heterogeneity appears in the mystical thought of the primitive and obtrudes into the dream world of modern consciousness because its reality is "identical to the structure of the unconscious" (I, 347). Finally, in its irreducible opposition to the homogeneity of daily life, "charging these terms with the positive value they carry in affective experience" (I, 348), heterogeneity is understood as *tout autre,* incommensurable.

A comparison between Durkheim's concept of the sacred and Bataille's category of heterogeneity provides overwhelming similarities between their styles, systems of classification, or mapping of a general problematic. Yet the "positive" value of the heterogeneous is not necessarily that with which Durkheim endows the sacred. The sacred/profane duality is itself overdetermined by a series of inherited dichotomies capable of fixing its boundaries, and only recently has the imposition of a static hierarchy upon them affiliated the sacred with all that is good, high, and abstract.

Durkheim's legacy provided Bataille with the notion of the ambivalent sacred, found not only among the unstable categories of the archaic world but in the Middle Ages as well; there, *sacer*, designating both sacred and syphilitic, embodied the polarity. Bataille credits the twentieth century's ability to encompass in one category the pure and the impure to the accomplishments of French sociology. Yet recent commentaries on Durkheim trace his stubborn adherence to the sacred/profane dichotomy to "a general love of dualism" and point to the contradictions entailed by the impure sacred: "How is the impurely sacred to be distinguished from the profane, a sacred profanation from a profane profanation?"[18]

Durkheim reserves his strongest praise, however, for the exuberance released by the religious forces of attraction. His enthusiasm for the exceptional social solidarity thus generated indeed appears as boundless as the energy and forces described.

> For our definition of the sacred is that it is something added to and above the real. . . . In fact, we have seen that if collective life awakens religious

thought on reaching a certain degree of intensity, it is because it brings about a state of effervescence which changes the conditions of psychic activity. Vital energies are over-excited, passions more active, sensations stronger; there are even some which are produced only at this moment. A man does not recognize himself; he feels transformed and consequently he transforms the environment which surrounds him.[19]

It is therefore not surprising to find Durkheim offering an entirely sanguine portrait of the morally regenerative currents continually passing among individuals: "Thus the environment in which we live seems to us to be peopled with forces that are at once imperious and helpful, august and gracious, and with which we have relations."[20] Missing, however, is the profound ambivalence of the sacred—its forces of repulsion and attraction—as they appear under heterogeneity. An evaluation of the latter would thus be incomplete without some explanation for Bataille's revival of the impure sacred abandoned by Christianity.

Intending to discover a meaning for the sacred beyond the array of social facts, Bataille attributes the sacredness of certain things or places to dépense. He speculates that the founding moments of such expenditures were stimulated by the revulsion and fear provoked by the presence of a dead body, which menaced the continuity of the group. Thus the feelings of disease elicited by a putrefying corpse must be ritually expelled through the mediation of a sacred person, animal, or object. Bataille revitalizes the truism of humans as social animals by recalling the fears and desires that defy expression or conscious understanding without the assistance of psychoanalysis and sociology. The gathering of individuals into groups, however small or temporary, is inevitably marked by a central dépense "without which I cannot conceive of a human ensemble" (II, 331). The particular intensity of the heterogeneous, however, produces a sacred kernel to mediate the power of ambivalent forces. Without this core of "violent silence" (II, 319) relations would be robbed of their human character.

The heterogeneous is equally present within contemporary religion; the most prosaic church, divorced from its institutional allegiances, represents a *lieu de concentration* of heterogeneous energy. As the resting place for saints adjacent to the burial ground of the community, the church is doubly enshrouded in an aura of death, imparting to it "a certain force of repulsion which generally guarantees an internal silence, keeping noise and voices at bay; at the same time it possesses a force of attraction, being the more or less constant object of affective concentration for the inhabitants, a concentration partially independent of sentiments which can be qualified as specifically Christian" (II, 325). Durkheim's presentation of the sacred identifies the salient traits of heterogeneity: its distinct otherness, supported by its independent laws and economy, first produced by the homogeneous expulsion of certain "foreign bodies" as *ganz anderes*. Bataille points to the usefulness of this notion "to indicate the elementary, subjective identity between excretions (sperm, menstrual blood, urine, fecal matter), and all that has been considered as sacred, divine, or fantastic" (II, 59). Furthermore, heterogeneity is a force that, when not physically constrained, retains its fluidity until "it becomes impossible to speak here of anything more than an ensemble of sacred places, things, persons, beliefs, and practices" (II, 326).

These general characteristics reappear in various contexts pertaining to the "sacred" roles of art, literature, myth, and mysticism in a culture no longer organized by religion. In this way, the assimilation of Bataille to surrealism appears justified.[21] Yet some of Bataille's strongest statements on heterogeneity are formulated in his rejection of the surreal.

THE SURREAL

The twenty years of contact between Bataille and surrealism were punctuated by violent confrontation and surprise reconciliations, both in a series of essays outlining the various periods of Bataille's thought and activity. The earliest of these appeared as a polemic with Breton and contains Bataille's harshest but most sustained critique of surrealism. His particular target is the surrealist pretense of having formulated an alternative to Hegelian idealism: a so-called materialism. The title of the screed, "La Vieille taupe et le préfixe *sur* dans les mots *surhomme* et *surréaliste*" (II, 93–109), contrasts Marx's figure of the burrowing mole with the surrealists' elevated, transcendent prefix. The central issue subtending this opposition—and that between Bataille and Breton—is the role of philosophy in formulating a critique of bourgeois society and the categories it enlists in such a project.

Bataille's theoretical orientation here is more explicitly Marxist than in most of his work; in this essay, philosophy participates in the same ideological formation as the matrix of values, thought, and behavior conditioned by class affiliation, itself determined by the relation of a group to the means of production.

The perceived congruence between infra-/superstructural relations is explicitly stated in his opening assertion of a fundamental agreement between "the present state of affairs, bourgeois moral values, and the intellectual edifice which supports them" (II, 93). The allusion to the "present state" evolves into a critique of the visible disintegration of bourgeois culture, but the Marxist alternatives to that religious and political society are inadequate. For although "in the last instance the infrastructure determines or conditions the superstructure," Marxism has not progressed from that affirmation to a scientific analysis of possible "reactions emanating from the superstructure" (I, 338). Yet, in an addendum, Bataille concedes his own methodological prejudices and argues for the validy of *états élans* over

French sociology, German philosophy (phenomenology), and psycho-analysis. The Marxist influence is manifested in this essay in three distinct areas: the historical perspective on the surreal, the call for a dialectical materialism, and the revolutionary status of the proletariat.

The pattern of cultural estrangement experienced by the Marxist revolutionary is distinguished from those of the surrealists, Nietzsche, and their romantic predecessors by the emphasis on an alliance with the working class. Political engagement, however, must first be translated into terms sensitive to the reactionary tendencies in the discourse of these historical models. The paradigm for the deviations to which even the brilliant Nietzschean etymologies fall prey is in large part determined by a hierarchy so "naturalized" that its ideological component is easily elided. According to Bataille, the first phase of subversion of the dominant ideology relies on categories that claim superiority to those initially rejected. In its early stages, the surrealist revolution was independent of the lower classes and derided by Bataille as "a disturbed mental state, paralleled by a violent phraseology on the necessity for a dictatorship of the spirit" (II, 94). Only later did the surrealists claim the solidarity with workers which is necessary for the bourgeois revolutionary to resist an imposed cultural revolution. Indeed, all revolutionary movements prior to Marx sought validation from a higher authority, from the very idealistic propositions that accompanied a class hierarchy. Moreover, the quest for validation becomes an expiatory rite for the bourgeois son's guilt of having denounced his class, the equivalent of repudiating the father. The product of such a confusion of sentiments is the "idealistic utopianism" of the past, which distorts the revolution into a "redeeming light, rising *above* the world, *above* classes, the epitome of the elevation of the spirit and Lamartian beatitude" (II, 95). The imperative for political action has, in part, eliminated archaic "deviations" in the twentieth century. But if only the moral and psychological turmoil of economic upheavals is considered, one can identify unacceptable developments similar to those of "prematerialist" revolutions.

The model for these moral deviations occurs in the high/low opposi-tion represented by the political symbols of the old mole and the eagle. Bataille reinserts both within the solar cosmology. In appearance and éclat the eagle is most clearly a "virile" icon; in the radiant orbit of the sun he retains a position of "dominant prestige" (II, 196). His absolute virility is evident in the sharp, hooked beak, which "[cuts] down everything that comes into contact with it, devoid of fear and retaliation" (II, 96), and castrates all who challenge its sovereignty (e.g., Icarus, Prometheus, the Mithraic bull). The eagle's ravening sexuality complements his political imperialism: both qualities manifest unbound power that knows no obstacles.

Bataille demonstrates the metaphysics of the eagle's image "identified with the idea, when it is still juvenile and aggressive, and has not yet reached a state of pure abstraction: where the idea is still only the outrageous development of the concrete fact distinguished as divine necessity" (II, 96). Revolutionary idealism is then rebuked for appropriating these symbols for ostensibly subversive purposes: Bataille presents them as "a sur-eagle knocking down imperialistic authority, an idea as radiant as an adolescent eloquently grasping power in the name of utopian illumination" (II, 96).

The inadequacy of a "rupture" with bourgeois culture which leaves its political ideology intact is evidenced in Nietzsche's proposal of a *surhomme* which ignores the working class. Nevertheless, the violence with which he voices his "hatred of the elevation of the bourgeois spirit and its pontifical comportment" (II, 99) exonerates him from conscious complicity with the dominant ideology. Yet Nietzsche seems "condemned to conceiving his rupture as an Icarian adventure" (II, 99), stealing "the fire in the sky," not in the name of a political goal, but "by a simple subversion, for the pleasure of transgressing supposedly intangible laws" (II, 100).

But individuals steal fire only to annihilate themselves. It is precisely the will to autonomy sounded in Nietzsche's cry in the desert that condemns him to a regressive course. This reactionary exaltation is, moreover, linked to the last century's enduring fascination with the sovereignty of the feudal aristocracy. To the socially isolated individual, nostalgia for the values of this group demonstrates an estrangement from contemporary social forms and questions the "derisory" nature of the subject's activity. Archaisms, concludes Bataille, are useful to the conservative but provide for the rebel only an "Icarian illumination" (II, 12).

Such aspiration to the sun also hinders the evolution of a coherent surrealist practice with revolutionary intentions. Bataille is particularly irked by the dualism in which the surrealists vaunt their originality by espousing exalted values manifested in "lower" values of the unconscious: sexuality and scatalogical language. The contradiction is sustained by occulting the socioeconomic reality in which the lower categories participate.

Post-Marxist revolutionaries can look to the old mole as a displacement from the idealist's iconology of utopia. In the *Communist Manifesto*, Marx describes the mole burrowing in the materialist bowels of the proletariat. Bataille rightly foresees uneasiness with his own revival of the high/low opposition "emasculated" of its religious vestiges by secular philosophy. Yet he insists that it is a contrast that informs profane sensibilities despite the castrating effects of philosophers who avoid its diverse, albeit shocking realities.

> The terrifying obscurity of the tombs or caves, and the luminous splendour of the sky, the impurity of the earth where bodies decompose and the purity of airy spaces; within the individual the base parts and the noble parts, in the political domain, the imperial eagle and the revolu-

tionary "vieille taupe," as in the universal order of matter, base and useful reality, and the elevated spirit. This language unknown to the philosophers (at least explicitly) is nonetheless a universal language for the human race. [II, 97]

The historical eclipse of this language results from its mystical overtones, which Bataille subsequently politicizes. The imagery not only discovers physical correlatives for moral imperatives, but explains the sociopolitical base of material correspondence. Although members of all classes are subject to antithetical impulses, the upper classes have become the metaphorical equivalent of the spirit and thus exert a virtual monopoly on ideas: "For even when ideas have a lowly origin, they are nevertheless elaborated from *above*, the higher spheres of the intellect, before taking on a universal value" (II, 98). The disruptive forces of heterogeneity, however, arise from the lower strata of the social geology.

In the *Second Manifesto*, Breton explicates the formerly unquestioned antinomies that inform the surrealist system of representation. There, both analogical thinking and an expansion of the dialectic were viewed as possible alternatives to those oppositions. One oft-cited passage thus deserves reconsideration in light of the surrealist claim to subvert reason and logic in staking the boundaries of the possible.

> It is a matter of experimenting with all possible means, to force at all costs, the recognition of the factitious character of the old antinomies hypocritically destined to prevent all agitation on the part of man, if only by giving him an impoverished opinion of his resources, defying him to escape universal constraints. . . . Everything leads us to believe that there exists a certain point of the spirit where life and death, the real and the imaginary, the past and the future, the communicable and the noncommunicable, the high and the low, cease being perceived contradictorily. In vain would one seek another motive for surrealist activity other than the hope to determine this point.[22]

Because Breton appears to collapse the tension between high and low into a mechanistic dialectic, it is easy to appreciate why Bataille would reject a system where the degenerate contingencies of nature and society are ultimately reintegrated into a traditional Icarian scheme.

Heterogeneity avoids the idealist pitfall by insisting on the very content of the irrational so that it cannot be appropriated as an epistemological or aesthetic problem. The heterogeneous asserts a "base" materialism exhibiting intractible, unsubmissive forces. By extension, it demonstrates that Durkheim's presentation of the sacred as a simple derivative of the profane betrayed his own law that social phenomena assume a life of their own, qualitatively distinct from anything the individual can produce or experience. The heterogeneous, which for Bataille encompasses the sacred, may ultimately be determined by the boundaries of the profane restricted economy, but the homogeneous itself also depends upon that limit for its definition and derives its internal cohesion from an initial ejection. The attraction/repulsion dynamic therefore shifts the frontiers between rationality and irrationality as they are established by the inside/outside limit.[23]

The permutation of these antinomies within the political structure of the moment provides a psychological reference point for a group, class, or nation. It either imposes the subject-object relation as an expulsion of the object-Other beyond its limits, or it segregates the heterogeneous within the existing system's ghettos, reservations, asylums, or prisons.

Bataille contends that the significance of the surreal resides in the spiritual assimilation of that which it originally negated. His critique of the role of Sadism within the movement further substantiates this attitude. Featured in the polemical dossier with Breton of the early 1930s, "The Use Value of D.A.F. de Sade" (II, 55–80) argues that the author of *The One Hundred Days of Sodom* has effectively been emasculated, that his potential impact and shock value have been defused by his very champions against bourgeois censorship. Bataille rejects the surrealist counter-apologia for the scandal of Sadism, especially because of the supposed affinity between the two movements. Since it is claimed that the latter phenomenon antedates the marquis himself, it is possible to raise the value of Sade above historical practice, and the most apt analogy that exclaims the surrealist attitude is found in the process of sacralization common to archaic societies: "The behavior of the admirers of Sade resembles that of primitive subjects regarding their king whom they adore and execrate, showering him with honors and paralyzing his movements. At best, the author of *Justine* is in fact treated like any other *corps étranger,* that is, he is the object of adulation only insofar as this adulation facilitates his expulsion or excretion" (II, 56).

The gesture of exclusion that concerns Bataille is the surrealists' mistaken belief that one can dispose of the heterogeneous by demoting it to the status of excrement. Just as the social ramifications of heterogeneity are complex, Sadism itself possesses a duality unsuspected by the surrealists: "It appears as both a positive eruption of excremental forces (excessive violation of modesty, positive algolagnia, violent excretion . . . vomit . . . defecation) and a corresponding *limitation,* a narrow subjugation of all that is opposed to this eruption" (II, 56). As a global phenomenon, Sadism proposes its own economy, which distributes material in a cycle of appropriation and excretion. These are then subsumed by Bataille under the broader categories of homogeneity and heterogeneity and appreciated through heterology.

The study of the heterogeneous cannot take place within the conventional restrictions imposed by science, confined to a mode of representation that depicts humanity's adaptation to "production, rational consumption, and the conservation of products" (II, 63). This intellectual process is self-limiting and produces as its own waste a scandal to human thought. Heterology is now conceived as "the complete reversal of the philosophical process which, from the instrument of appropriation that it was, enters into the service of excretion and introduces the claims of violent satisfactions implied by social existence" (II, 63).

By underscoring the "use value" of Sade, Bataille restores to Sadism its historical specificity denied by the surrealists. He hopes to prevent the heterogeneous from being reclaimed by the homogeneity at work in the surreal. Thus he must also contend with the dialectical presentation of appropriation and excretion since "it will be too easy to find within objective nature a great number of phenomena that, *grosso modo,* correspond to the appropriation/excretion schema in order to, once again, attain the notion of the unity of being in its dialectical form" (II, 64). This unnatural unity so reconciles the tension between opposing forces as to impose on the cycle an ahistorical, eternal status, rendering it impossible to grasp its practical effects. For this reason, he explains that "excretion is not a median term between two appropriations" (II, 65).

The inability to conceive of rot, detritus, or nonproductive dépense as an end in itself can be traced to an intellectual prejudice. Dreams, for instance, invert the commonsense view; there appropriation is the intermediate stage between two excretions. The social equivalent subverts the popular image of the worker and implies that he/she accumulates in order to spend. Historically, the worker has been identified with the slave destined to produce goods expended by an aristocracy or leisure class. The "abominable appropriative morality" is thus foisted upon a group elected for this purpose; but only when the homogeneous values are abandoned will men and women learn "to link their *raison d'être* to the violence of their excretionary organs and open themselves to the possibility of the excitement of trances, heterogeneous elements, and debauchery" (II, 65).

This last statement captures well the unusual mixture of sensations discerned within both the heterogenous and potlatch. How the figure of the heterogeneous Other—whether Sade or the "primitive" as nostalgic projection—of Western culture is periodically reappropriated by the homogeneous is the question central to the essays on surrealism examined thus far. To them must be added Bataille's postwar reflections, including a 1948 lecture entitled "La Religion surréaliste" (VII, 381–95), which can be taken as an indicator of his later sentiments.

Unlike his early acerbic attacks, this essay evinces Bataille's solidarity with the surrealists. Bataille and Breton share the perception that no system which denies the necessity for collective action can overcome the "old antinomies." Similarly, surrealism questions whether any radical transformation—through art, religion, politics, or philosophy—can succeed within the context of bourgeois culture. The *ganz anderes,* heterogeneous forces within the working class, Sadism, or the primitive—all must preserve their subversive potential from appropriation by the homogenizing power of romantic utopianism, the discourse of anthropology, or Fascism.

Thus, Bataille warns the surrealists against their anachronistic plunder of the archaic world for solutions to twentieth-century discontents. Yet he himself succumbs to a similar impulse, characterizing the surrealists' primitive as a paradoxically "religious" figure who, unhampered by reason, remains susceptible to "savage" instincts and violent outbursts of emotion. The primitive evokes envy by participating in religious ceremonies whose extraordinary "effervescence" permit access to the intimacy of deper- sonalized communication. During sacrificial rites, effusion and destruction meet in the exquisite though anguished instant of revelation. The barriers between individuals and the universe collapse as the community recaptures its sense of life's proximity to death. Destruction negates the utility and "thingness" to which the sacrificed object was reduced, and the liberation experienced flows from the perception of having "consumed without profit . . . a realization of pure dépense" (VII, 63).

Surrealism is a religion to the extent that it approaches the impassioned quality of archaic rituals of destruction. Yet it must also recognize the ability of primitive religion to convince a community bound by material interests of its efficacy. Thus it cannot simply negate the material, nor claim to supercede it, but must reassess its significance within the contexts of capitalism and individualism. The denial of the material can only lead to a "mythologizing of intuitive understanding"[24] or an apotheosis of passion untainted by reason. Ancient religion contains the "impossible" unleashing of passions by the "possibility" of material benefits; one must somehow avoid meeting this antinomy with only contemplation. The alternative, suggests Bataille, is to "plunge into consciousness" and "transgress the difficulties of the present world which requires the subordination of the instant to transcendence. Only by working within the specificity of the modern condition—its ineluctable consciousness—can the ancient forms of the primitive be captured through the alterations imposed by this state of awareness" (VII, 391).

To abandon the "material" value of rites for a purely poetic or aestheticized version of the sacred is to lose a strong unifying force. Art, notes Bataille, does not possess the power of religion to bind individuals any more than it can provide the key to lost totality possessed by the primitive. While it is clear that surrealism cannot effect cohesion through the same order of claims as those of materialism, it fails to recognize that the reality of such an experience can be attained only by "a communal existence" (VII, 390). It is unacceptable to proclaim the foundation of a community or any gathering of individuals, whether elaborated into a formal "religion" or not, without articulating its relation to the "utilitarian, rational, aesthetic, and moral imperatives that the surrealist act necessarily avoids."[25] The refusal to do so produces a category such as the surreal which, couched in a pseudopolitical language, disguises an unregenerate idealism. By not recognizing the "inevitable" world of rational utility, surrealism forces the majority to reject a movement that disseminates "a general malaise, a sense of ineffectiveness" (VII, 390).

In the shift toward communism by Breton and other surrealists, Bataille observes a political reflection of their rage against possessive individualism and private property. The failure of the Russian Revolution is explained through the specific feudal conditions of czarist Russia rather than by any intrinsic weakness of Marxism-Leninism. Yet we cannot know directly what life could be like without personal interest. Whether the surrealists propose the poetic act as privileged communication, or automatic writing as a mode of "rupture," the error is the same. For no one experience can transgress the restricted economy unless it engages more than the private relations of dyadic exchanges. Words themselves partake of the profane— only a willed "depersonalization" can lead to the sacred subversion of dépense.

Breton equated surrealism with the creation of a collective myth.[26] Bataille paradoxically regards the contemporary "absence of myth" as the point of departure for the myth-making of the modern individual who is incapable of surmounting his/her scepticism. A mythology grounded in the "absence of myth" avoids the divisiveness intrinsic to its archaic progenitors. At the inception of every religion, identity is asserted through opposition, yet religion unleashes emotions capable of suppressing differences among individuals. Thus the surrealists could convert nostalgia for the past into enthusiasm for the present by simulating the fusion common in ancient religious festivals; they created "a new individual whom we could call a collective individual" (VII, 394).

Bataille views the surrealist quest for sacred activity relevant to the contemporary, markedly profane world as symptomatic of a pervasive nostalgia derived from romanticism, and Nietzsche in particular. This general longing attempts a "reconstruction of the foundations of humanity before human nature was enslaved by the necessity for technical work . . . or tied to ends dictated by exclusively material considerations" (VII, 386). Although *homo faber* may have broken with his former identity, work itself is not the cause. The discontinuity stems from capitalism and society's inability to divorce it from the future and rediscover the immediate, communal emotions of the primitive sacred—its horror and ecstasy, its fear and desire, its sense of the possible and impossible.

The history of Western civilization offers little evidence of cultural forms willing to value the "instant" of dépense. According to Bataille, surrealism ought to be regarded as one such effort. His closing statements in the lecture on "religion" exhort resistance to the humiliation of modern life "dominated by a God that is nothing more than hypostasized work" (VII, 395). And one must admire the general exuberance of surrealism—an expenditure whose éclat illuminates the lesser value of art conceived as isolated works.

The investment of nonproductive dépense nonetheless remains a gesture restricted to the privileged few who have access to the vehicles of art. By shifting the significance of surrealism away from art works toward a concept of life, the movement satisfied the criteria of totality and collective action called for in Bataille's revitalization of "religion." The tension between theory and practice also constituted the basis for earlier invectives against the literary—imaginary—limits of the vision of Sade, whose negativity was truncated by surrealism. The condemnation of surrealism's phraseology as "simple verbal prestidigitation" enhanced Bataille's own revolutionary aspirations to implement the teachings of Sade. The critique falters, however, when political ambitions are not grounded in objective social conditions but are propelled by "a will that remains obsessed with a need for agitation and activity" (II, 57). The abrasive theses on heterology are intended to disorient the intellect stupefied by science and thereby justify the fact that "I put off for later the arduous and interminable exposés analogous to those of any other developed theory" (II, 57).

In the postwar lecture, Bataille's appraisal of surrealist propositions on the art/life, contemplation/action, high/low antinomies underscores how the "impossible" surplus is calculated into the "possible" archaic economy of debt and retribution. The purpose is not to demystify the material base of the old antinomies, but to investigate the surrealists' declared materialism within its hierarchial structure. Heterogeneity also asks how to reconsider objects from one system of values (in this case, one that demeans them as vulgar, base, or lewd) within another, contradictory or subversive, value-system. Further, what is the status of effervescence embodied in material objects, beings, words, signs, symbols, songs, or dances when it denies any temporal reality beyond the "instant" of dépense? The failure of surrealism to confront these questions head-on provoked Bataille's disdain: "If one determined under the name of *materialism* an offensive emanation of human life poisoned by its own moral system, a recourse to all that is shocking, impossible to destroy and even abject—all that debases and ridicules the human spirit—it would be possible to determine at the same time *surrealism* as an infantile disease of this base materialism" (II, 93).

Heterogeneous "facts" are sacred. They are also foils to the homogeneity of the restricted economy. Although not fixed by any simple criterion, the element common to sacred objects is their ambivalence to the proximity of death. Associated with those primal elements of excrement and sperm, which are subject to near universal taboos, the sacred must also be identified within those "rare, fugitive and violent" (II, 446) moments of inner life that eventually translate into the social compositions of the church, the army, or secret societies. This explains the impetus motivating the creation of a "collège de sociologie" among "equal peers united by elective affinities"[27] and dedicated to the revival of the sacred as it is manifested in "the points of convergence between the fundamental obsessive tendencies of individual psychology and the guiding structures that preside over social organization and command its revolutions" (II, 446).

The collège was in existence between 1937 and 1939. It represents the last in a series of prewar endeavors initiated by Bataille and it enlisted the participation of Roger Caillois, Michel Leiris, Jean Paulhan, Pierre Klossowski, and Jean Wahl. Despite several joint declarations of principles, sharp divisions rapidly surfaced among members gathered to study *la sociologie sacrée*. Ironically, the definition of the sacred proved amenable to consensus, whereas that of sociology did not. As a formal discipline, sociology is subject to the same criticism incurred by philosophy or any other partial system. Moreover, sociology evinces a historical paradox when it emerges from the "supreme stage of the division of labor" at the same moment "the total social fact" is discovered: "It is thus incapable of drawing the lessons of its own discovery."[28] Only a marginal, self-designated institution such as a collège could accomplish the task, announced by Mauss, to "graft onto the total fact a 'totalizing' goal."[29] Despite the proclamation of this project, Bataille's obsession with "mysticism, madness, drama, and death" was subsequently condemned by Caillois as irreconcilable with "our founding principles" (II, 336). Aware that his increasingly subjective attitude could be interpreted as inconsistent with Durkheim's "rules," Bataille offered statements regarding his methods. Unfortunately, most of them serve only to justify his repudiation of any one school of thought. Along these lines, the rejection of Hegelian phenomenology is instructive.

> The negativity of which I speak is of a different nature. I first represented it by projecting its interference in laughter or sexual activity. I will now represent it in its concentrated form. And without a doubt I will continue to give these facts what I describe as an interpretation that is in part personal, but this time I will keep close to classical descriptions and interpretations. [II, 324]

The issue in question overflows disciplinary borders by touching on Bataille's concept of an "active" sociology equated with the sacred. Since the latter is distinguished by its contagious force, then the collège ought to foster collective activities leading to its own version of "a virulent and devastating *sacré*, a rite that would end in an epidemic contagion, converting and exalting the person who had sown its first seed."[30] In his memoirs of the collège,

Caillois recalls a growing impatience with the secretive nature of Bataille's activities. Although consistent with exhortations to bridge the gap separating theory from practice, Bataille's desire to spark "an irresistible expansion of the sacred," intended as "an irrevocable ritual gesture—the enactment of a voluntary human sacrifice," would be condoned neither by Caillois nor by the collège.[31]

The naiveté of Bataille's gesture, a capitulation to his need for violent action that could "lead to the worst" (VII, 461), trivializes the legitimate demand for a holistic approach to the study of social phenomena. To do so would encompass an understanding "of violence and the will to transgression to the extent they form the basis of all power," as well as necessitating taking on "perversion and crime, not as exclusive human values, but ones that must be integrated into the totality of human experience" (II, 274). The shift from intellectual recognition to active assent of these values is never justified. Moreover, the stress on spectacular activity underestimates the power of heterogeneity in writing and as an innovative category.[32]

By illuminating the heterogeneous with the dépense of the general economy, Bataille revitalized the notion of the sacred by inserting economics into Durkheim's argument for religion against science: "Science is fragmentary and incomplete; it advances but slowly and is never finished; but life cannot wait. . . . Religion exists; it is a system of given facts; in a word, it is a reality. . . . Also, in so far as religion is action, and in so far as it is a means of making men live, science could not take its place."[33] Because he insisted on the profoundly social nature of religion, Durkheim was able to extricate its value from the simplifying consequences of opposing the rational to the irrational. Moreover, the philosophical dualities codifying the two-sidedness of human nature into the mind/body, spirit/matter antinomies are reinscribed within their social origins. The study of the elementary forms of religious life, claims Durkheim, demonstrated that "we have even found the basis for conjecturing that the fundamental and lofty concepts that we call categories are formed on the model of social phenomena."[34]

While the strong point of Durkheim's argument demonstrates the need for "religion" as fundamental to collective life, its weakness leaves ill-defined the nature of the "social." Thus the unanswered question lacing the documents of the collège concerns the status of subgroups, such as itself, in relation to dominant political structures. Durkheim pointed out that "there are periods in history when, under the influence of some great collective shock, social interactions have become much more frequent and active . . . men become different. Under the influence of the general exaltation, we see the most mediocre and inoffensive bourgeois become either a hero or a butcher."[35] How a movement is "to win the energies of intoxication for the revolution," however, is never clear.[36] Durkheim's sanguine outlook does not account for the "independent" movement of "the whole world of sentiments, ideas, and images" emergent from the collective experience being manipulated by the homogeneity of political forces.[37] Bataille's reflections on this issue appear in the essay "La Structure psychologique du fascisme" (I, 339–71). The specter of Fascism haunts discussions by the collège of violence, action, cults, and myth without focusing on its immediate historical incarnation. How the force of heterogeneity is appropriated by an individual, class, or locus of power cannot be avoided in a study of the category of sovereignty.

CHAPTER

3

SOVEREIGNTY

M more than any other category, sovereignty challenges the limits of modern consciousness in its ability to conceptualize the general economy as an affirmation of *loss*. Dépense, because of its proximity to the don, is ambiguous. It can, but does not necessarily, connote a reciprocal form of giving which enlists the other and in which there is neither loss nor gain. Heterogeneity encompasses the social, ritualized expression of energy generated by collective encounters but which often finds expression in political goals. In its radical otherness the heterogeneous may be extreme, but it never implies privilege. Sovereignty, however, is associated with a hierarchical order imposing high and low, dominance and subordination, freedom and slavery. Like the nostalgia surrounding gift-exchange, sovereignty evokes naive aspirations for feudal values antithetical to utilitarian bourgeois-capitalism. Yet Mauss insisted that, "especially" in potlatch societies, the social hierarchy is established by means of gifts: "To give is to show one's sovereignty, to show that one is something more and higher, that one is *magister*. To accept without returning or repaying more is to face subordination, to become a client and subservient, to become *minister*" (92). Similarly, the feudal aristocracy grounded its sovereignty in conspicuous consumption, an obligatory mode of nonproductive dépense. The master's apparent autonomy masks the reality of his double dependence upon the slave for the production of the goods he consumes and for the recognition of the superiority he seeks.

Bataille initiates the project to extricate sovereignty from these ideological associations in the 1933 essay on dépense. Published in *La Critique sociale,*[1] a review founded by disaffected surrealists and former Communist party adherents, the article's main thesis locates potlatch at the origins of class division and conflict.

> In potlatch, the rich man distributes the products furnished to him by other men. He seeks to elevate himself above an equally rich rival, but the

ultimate goal is to raise himself above these miserable creatures. Thus dépense, though it may serve a social function, ends up as an antagonistic act of separation, in appearance antisocial. The rich man consumes the waste of the poor man by creating for him a category of abjection which opens the way to slavery. [I, 314]

Mauss introduced this perspective on potlatch by showing that economic wealth signifies both prestige and power. He also questioned whether "our own position is different and that wealth with us is not first and foremost a means of controlling others?" (73).

Bataille points out that the degraded imitation of feudal spending among the bourgeoisie is characterized by the disappearance of its former generosity and nobility. The bourgeoisie conceals its dépense, using it not for public festivals, but to consolidate a private, symbolic code of distinctions between itself and the worker:

> As a class possessing riches, having received with this wealth the obligation of functional dépense, the modern bourgeoisie is charac- terized by its refusal to comply with this obligation. It has distinguished itself by insisting on a dépense only for itself, within itself, which is to say, hiding its dépense as much as possible from other classes. [I, 313]

While the bourgeoisie retains the surface signs of prestige evidenced in archaic and feudal cultures, it relinquishes access to the sovereign domain of nonproductive dépense. Lost is the aesthetic, magical aura imparted to objects destined for destruction. The lesson of potlatch lies not in the disparity between the appearance of generosity and the reality of "gain," but in the fundamentally ambivalent nature of the things exchanged. It is critical to recall that even the famous Kwakiutl copper "has its own value, in the full magical and economic sense of the word, which is regulated by the vicissitudes of the potlatch through which it passes and even by its partial or complete destruction" (43). Similarly, archaic money incorporates contra- dictory attributes: "The Trobriand *vaygu'a,* armshells, and necklaces, like the Northwest American coppers and Iroquois's *wampum,* are at once wealth, tokens of wealth, means of exchange and payment, and things to be given away or destroyed" (71–72).

To restore to sovereignty the ambivalent forces of the sacred through contemporary modes of communication demands a rethinking of funda- mental categories and the laws governing their determination. The preceding chapters therefore traced the fragmentation of "original undifferentiation" and its resolution within the specialized roles of the division of labor. Money, determined by the gold standard, reflects a one-dimensional value system. And when introduced into archaic exchange, it precipitates the breakdown of distinct categories. Women, for instance, though controlled by the laws regulating their transfer among men, are never directly exchanged for other objects.[2] Rather, they belong to the category of gifts, services, honors, duties, and artifacts constituting the "symbolic" wealth that individuals and groups are compelled to relinquish, reciprocate, and on occasion destroy.

This behavior follows the norms of an "economic cosmos" in which the material and the symbolic are mutually "convertible."[3] The laws of this universe dictate that their "systematic accent on the symbolic aspects of acts and relations of production tend to impede the formation of the economy *as such,* which is to say, as a system governed by the laws of interested calculations, competition, or exploitation."[4] Bourdieu's proposed inter- pretation of the symbolic dissimulates the "economic" ends of the acquisi- tion of wealth—albeit of a nonquantifiable nature. But he makes this claim in order to demonstrate that the pursuit of the symbolic is no less real, rational, or potent than the desire for the material. Nor does there exist any intrinsic means to distinguish the worth of objects located in either category which would justify their respective labels. As stated by Polanyi:

> No protest of mine, I realize, will save me from being taken for an "idealist." For he who decries the importance of "material" motives must, it seems, be relying on the strength of "ideal" ones. Yet no worse misunderstanding is possible. Hunger and gain have nothing specifically "material" about them. Pride, honor, and power, on the other hand, are not necessarily "higher" motives than hunger and gain.[5]

Only economism, Bourdieu argues, with its "restricted definition of eco- nomic interest which is the historical product of capitalism," demotes the symbolic to irrational sentiment or passion.[6] By measuring all activity against the "unambiguous standard of monetary profit, the most sacred activities are also constituted negatively as *symbolic,* that is, with the connotations often carried by this word as devoid of concrete material effect, in a word, *gratuitous,* in the sense of *disinterested* but also *useless.*"[7]

From the vantage point of archaic cultures, the classical notion of utility is metaphysical; "material" motives are no more powerful than the striving for nonmaterial ends; even in modern Western economies goods acquire their symbolic, social intent in production, and not as a secondary result of their circulation. This melding of the material and the symbolic, according to Bourdieu, must be restored to the study of culture viewed as the collective energy generated within social practices.[8] Bataille also called for the expansion of economics to a theory of a general economy that regards "human sacrifice, the construction of a church, or the gift of a jewel, as bearing no less significance than the sale of wheat" (VII, 19). And the first law of this general economy declares that "the sum of energy produced is always superior to that necessary for production" (V, 385). But Bourdieu's position represents symbolic activity as a game whose destructive energies never culminate in an irrevocable definitive act.

Sovereignty, however, is "a dissipation without reserve of riches; if this dissipation were restricted, it would create a *reserve* in view of other moments, which would limit—annul—the sovereignty of the immediate moment" (V, 215). Moreover, the "science" responsible for relating the objects of thought to sovereign moments is the general economy, "envisaging the meaning of these objects in relation to each other, and finally, in relation to the *loss of meaning*" (V, 215, emphasis added). Sovereignty is this useless, meaningless loss.

Divested of the historical meanings indicated above, sovereignty must remain a subjective experience that incessantly undermines the objective order bent on appropriating its force. Just as the potlatch ceremony captures the effervescence of dépense within an object encoded within a hierarchical order, so the surrealists consecrate sovereignty through images that transmit the values they purport to subvert.

Thus, one common question prompts the discussions of the surreal, the heterogeneous, and the sovereign: How is each determined within the existing order of classification and categories? More precisely, how is the general economy situated by its reference to the restricted economy?

Before turning to the various responses explored by Bataille, it is important to consider the archaic model of recognition and containment of the sovereign, as he summarizes it in this exceptional passage:

> At all times and in all places, a principle of divinity fascinated men and overwhelmed them: under the names of the *divine* and the *sacred,* they recognized a sort of internal animation, an essential frenzy, a violence seizing an object, consuming it like fire, and which, without hesitation, carries it to its ruin. This animation was believed to be contagious, and, passing from one object to another, it brought to whatever touched it a miasma of death. . . . *Religion certainly seeks to glorify the sacred object and to impose a principle of loss as the essence of power and all value, but it also seeks to reduce its effect to a delimited circle, which an insuperable limit separates from the world of normal life or profane existence.* [*L'Erotisme,* 200, emphasis added]

Bataille seems to yield to the religious model of a taboo/transgression cycle when he anticipates the sovereign moment as the violation of an interdict. He also follows Durkheim's qualification of the heterogeneous/sacred as "tout autre" by designating it as incommensurable with the profane. But unlike the society that alternates law and license, that of modern men and women fosters only "humiliation," whether "in offices, in the street, in the countryside, not to mention in religion, dominated by a God that is nothing more than hypostasized work" (VII, 395). When the sovereign spark does galvanize individuals into mass action, too often the force concentrates into the figure of a "sovereign" leader. In the prewar period, Bataille's creation of the controversial *Contre-Attaque*[9] group wanted to counter Fascism with a parallel mobilization that would liberate rather than subjugate the masses, and highlight the "anachronistic character of classical proletarian movements" (I, 419). The role of intellectuals is "to contribute to the awareness of the force of the popular masses; we are certain that *force* results less from strategy than from collective exaltation, and exaltation arises from works that touch not the reason but the passion of the masses" (I, 411).

The surrealists, also under the influence of Durkheim, compared their efforts to "the collective creations of exotic peoples."[10] Yet they did not adequately free their materialism from metaphysical criteria; the bodily energy and the excretionary forces suggested by heterogeneity must remain unassimilable to spiritualized goals. If the artist/poet is to make contact with the proletarian masses, it will be on the common ground of a sphere of action organized by images, not metaphor.[11] Those energies of intoxication that Benjamin understood must be marshalled for the revolutionary cause are fundamental to the materialism of the general economy of dépense: "In their accentuated form, the states of excitement which are comparable to toxic states can be defined as illogical and irresistible impulses rejecting material or moral goods which it would otherwise have been possible to utilize rationally (in keeping with the principle of balancing an account)" (I, 319). Matter, moreover, "represents in relation to the economy of the universe that which crime represents in relation to the law" (I, 319).

Sovereignty is use-less, meaning-less negativity; matter is the motor-force of transgression; bodily energy can be revolutionary. These fundamental axioms announced the critical rupture with the metaphysical materialism of the nineteenth century and inaugurated the anthropological materialism of the general economy.

POETIC SOVEREIGNTY

In *L'Expérience intérieure,* Bataille qualifies the master/slave dialectic as "the decisive moment in the history of the consciousness-of-self, and, one must say, to the extent we must distinguish each thing that touches us one from another—no one knows anything of himself, if he has not grasped this movement that limits and determines the successive possibilities of mankind" (V, 28). Bataille's own encounters with Hegel were initiated by the Kojève lectures, whose Marxist interpretations underlined both the dialectic and the idea of Absolute Knowledge.[12] The dialectic so presented, as it pertains to Bataille, can be summed up as follows: The master's status is established by risking his life. He has defied death, subjected himself to the anguish of confrontation, and survived the ordeal. The slave, however, has not exhibited the requisite courage and founds his existence on the desire for self-preservation. Instead of engaging in battle, he works. But the truth of the master's experience can be verified only if he keeps his life long enough to profit from the fact of having risked it. His truth is therefore dependent upon the "conscience servile" of the slave for recognition. When the latter becomes master, he will have retained a trace of his repressed origins, but will be able to transform himself in an act of complete independence. This inequality constitutes the kernel of Bataille's impasse—the superiority of the slave over the master. The latter has risked his life and survived in order to be recognized by another, who is the slave. The master is presented with two possibilities: either to ruin himself in pleasure or to die on the battlefield, but he cannot live "consciously knowing he is satisfied with what he is."[13] Ultimately, the slave presents the superiority of the project of work, transforming Nature through creative action in contrast with the ideal, unmediated goals and nonactivities of the master. The latter is dedicated to the existence of pure consumption of the material objects fashioned by the slave, whose work is synonymous with the creation of discourse, science, and history. For Kojève, work gains significance by inaugurating social relations in the form of exchange:

> The manufactured object incarnates the idea (of a project) that is independent of the material *hic et nunc;* this is why these objects are "exchanged." From this follows the development of the "economic" world, specifically human, where there appears money, capital, interest, salary, etc. . . . Perhaps it would be more accurate to say: the world changes essentially (and becomes human) through "exchange," which is possible only as a function of Work and the realization of a "project."[14]

The philosophical basis of the theory of a general economy can now be clarified. Hegel insisted upon the preservation of the life of the master, since without this "economy of life" the supreme proof of self would be eliminated. A simple defiance of death, without any consideration for its meaning within some system, becomes a hollow gesture. Hegel termed it "abstract negativity" and opposed it to the principle of *Aufhebung:* "The negation of consciousness which sublates in such a way that it preserves and retains that which is sublated."[15] The Hegelian subject remains ultimately attached to that which he/she tries to preserve: the self and the meaning derived from a consciousness-of-self.

Bataille wrote *L'Expérience intérieure* with Hegel glaring over his shoulder, and in the ensuing struggle to evolve an experience formulated in terms of dépense rather than the economy of life, one of sovereignty rather than mastery, it is evident that the Hegelian influence is not easily overcome. Bataille emphasizes most the differences in the respective attitudes of the two theorists toward death. His anthropology considers the taboo imposed on the dead body as the sign of human consciousness, marking a limit between nature and culture and the transition from animal to human. Death projects violence into the profane world of work and homogeneity, and contact with it is mediated by the observances reserved for the sacred. Surrounding the taboo are those rituals constituting the symbolic order of representations that evoke the same terror and anguish as the body itself. Fear of death subordinates the slave to the master. Unable to persist in the anachronistic ideal of testing his courage in battle, the modern putative master must confront death through a simulacrum: "This difficulty announces the necessity of the spectacle, or generally, of representation, without the repetition of which we would remain ignorant of death as are animals. Nothing is less bestial, in fact, than fiction, more or less at a distance from reality, from death."[16]

Humans do not live by bread alone; we indulge in cults and spectacles. We also read: "Literature, when authentic and sovereign, prolongs in man the obsessive magic of spectacles, whether comic or tragic."[17] In the ongoing confrontation with Hegel, however, literature as an experience of limits is temporarily displaced by laughter and ecstasy as they challenge the Hegelian system: "To convene all the tendencies of man in one point, all the possibilities he represents, to pull together the harmonious agreements and violent discords, to no longer leave out the laughter that rends the texture of which man is made; . . . in this sense, my efforts repeat and undo the *Phenomenology of Hegel*" (V, 96). "Le rire déchirant"—Bataille's laughter is an explosion in the master's philosophy of work, of the project. From the unknown to the knowable, its movement is toward a science subordinated to the goal of Absolute Knowledge. Bataille laughs. The goal is sovereignty, liberated from the inert words of rational discourse and immersed in the night of "non-savoir." For Bataille, "to the extent that [knowledge] takes itself for an end, it founders on the blind spot. But poetry, laughter, ecstasy are nothing, and Hegel hastily disposes of them; the only goal he knows is knowledge. His immense fatigue, in my view, is linked to his horror of the blind spot" (V, 130).

Hegel's clarity about death obscures the significance of sacrifice as a will to experience death's horrors through a social form of representation; the sensation of sadness he admits to remains secondary and subordinate to consciousness. To the individual for whom sacrifice rather than philosophy mediates the experience of death, the emotive impact of ritual is primary.

Sovereignty is located within the moment of sacrifice and sacred horror as they constitute the "entire" movement of death. This refusal of a higher synthesis through discourse is comparable to the state experienced by the *conscience servile* known as *négativité-négatrice*.[18] Because it did not focus its fear on any one object, nor seek to dispel its anguish over time, the servile consciousness withstands the horror of death in all its intensity. Thus, "it trembled within itself, and all that is fixed and stable trembled in it. This pure universal dialectical movement, this absolute dissolution of fixed stability, is the essential reality simple or indivisible of the Consciousness-of-self, the absolute negative-negativity."[19] Sovereignty simulates this "déchirement absolu" if discourse is disrupted and the movement of the dialectic suspended.

Bataille further compares the rite of sacrifice to a festival and its extreme of human sensations: "It announced a deleterious and blind joy, as well as its dangers: it exceeds and menaces with death whomever is drawn into its movement."[20] More predictable is the one-dimensional sadness described by Hegel, whose acknowledgment of death's ubiquity nonetheless precludes the ambivalence of an "anguished joy."

In its ambivalence, the expérience intérieure is best compared to the "conscious mysticism" Bataille counters to the classical version. Qualified as atheistic, it is aware that it "makes of Nothingness a Being, and defines this impasse as a Negativity without a field of action [at the end of history]."[21] Bataille's "mystic" would live within the "déchirement absolu" of conscious mortality, and contemplate the negative as did Hegel. While for Hegel this phase was temporary, for Bataille it is the essence of the experience: "Ultimately unable to transpose the Negative into a being, and refusing to do so, the conscious mystic sustains this ambiguity."[22]

Sovereignty thus suggests the possibility of an "operation" other than those offered by the master or the slave. It rejects negativity as action, leading to a taking possession of things—the intellectual, political, and economic activity Bataille equates with work. To them he opposes sacrifice, laughter, poetry, and ecstasy: disruptive "breaks" with the closed systems resulting in appropriation. While defined as a putting into action, negativity also activates a putting into question. Within this dual movement, alternately responding to the solicitations of concrete production and of death and destruction, humanity is defined. Because Hegel confused the meaning of life with work, he could not break with the project—the philosophy of work—in order to see those "irreducibles" that lead to "a more accessible philosophy of communication" (V, 223).

As the favored experience of sovereignty, laughter communicates intimacy that avoids appropriation and induces fusion. In poetry, Bataille seeks this mode of communication—a dépense of the self in union with the other, since we are whole only outside ourselves.

Sovereignty is the instant when meaning, presence, knowledge, and the reserve of mastery are annulled, thus reaching the limits of existing systems of representation. Yet it effects a profound unity, comparable to that of "theopathic states": "a point where laughter no longer laughs, and tears no longer cry, where the divine and the horrible, the poetic and the repugnant, the erotic and the funereal, coincide. *It is not a point of the spirit.* . . . Sovereignty is the reign of a miraculous *non-savoir*" (V, 251).

This point, which itself resists definition, "has given an optical form to experience. At the moment that it posits the point, *the mind is an eye*" (V, 138). Since conventional scientific discourse avoids its blinding glare, the sovereign sun has become the privileged symbol of literature: "The need to dazzle and to blind can be expressed in the affirmation that in the final analysis, the sun is the sole object of literary description" (II, 140). It is equally emblematic of Bataille's own demons. In *L'Expérience intérieure* he recounts the tribulations of the writer/poet burdened to reveal what he alone has seen.

Hegel was able to elevate philosophy to the seriousness of death. In wanting poetry to simulate sovereignty, Bataille contemplates the limits of words. Like the objects sacrificed in potlatch, they help the reader to undergo the sensation of dissolving into the unknown, while remaining tied to the familiar things represented by them. The dilemma was explored by Hegel and paraphrased by Kojève in his account of the initial stages of the awakening of the consciousness of self. The "subject of knowledge" loses itself in the object of contemplation. Awareness of self is stimulated by desire, defined by Hegel as a negativity that actively creates the separations it must then synthesize. Sovereignty demands from poetry not a dialectical overcoming, but an original fusion.

To do so, poetic sovereignty helps divest the individual of impediments to communication determined through expenditure. The first stage of this process questions the superiority of rational, philosophical discourse in which each word is subordinate to the next within a linear progression: "For the most part discursive, the movement of philosophy is reducible to a chain of words, and discourse, those words that help us easily reach objects, cannot gain access to internal states, which remain strangely unknowable" (V, 162). Following these criteria, poetry murders words. Death is teased and imitated in a *mise en jeu*, as evidenced in the recurrent imagery of *L'Expérience intérieure*.

Yet Bataille insists that he uses language in a "classical" fashion, implying that the experience of sovereignty cannot be transmitted through plays on words. Although at this stage of his work the political implications of sovereignty appear to recede, he does not forfeit the "economic" spirit of dépense. The analogy with potlatch cannot be satisfactory since it represents the aleatory nature of the universe through a collective, socially sanctioned spectacle. The nexus of its political, social, and economic meanings is inadequately reproduced in a modern counterpart.

Bataille nonetheless underscores the ability of the theory of general economy to make statements regarding all social practices involved with the manipulation of signs—including poetry—as an ordered relationship between words and things.

The question of a general economy is located at the same level as that of political economy, but the science designated by the latter refers only to a *restricted economy* (to market values). The general economy deals with the essential problem of the use of wealth. It underlines the fact that an excess is produced that, by definition, cannot be employed in a utilitarian manner. Excess energy can only be lost, without the least concern for a goal or objective, and, therefore, without any meaning. [V, 215–16]

The subversion of that established order of things is expressed in *L'Expérience intérieure* by "contestation," a more explicitly political term than most employed by Bataille. But because of its dependence on words, poetic contestation is deemed inauthentic and incapable of testing limits. Compared to the treachery of shifting sands, words exhaust the poet, "a man engulfed, whose efforts only sink him in further" (V, 26).

Sovereignty so determined appears locked into a verbal equivalent of the impasse of the idle master in which words are buried and meaning sacrificed. The twofold project of *L'Expérience intérieure* was to reintroduce a sacred aura into writing and to simulate ecstasy. Unlike meditation, expérience, or knowledge, sovereignty "is the power words have to evoke effusion, the unlimited dépense of its own forces; thus, to an already determined effusion (comic or tragic), sovereignty adds not only the rhythm and overflow of the verses, but *the special capacity of the disorder of words to annul the ensemble of signs which constitutes the realm of activity*" (V, 220, emphasis added).

Yet poetry remains subordinate to its thematic content. Only if it renounces the literalism of theme and recognizes the insignificance of rhythm can it begin to approach true sovereignty. The elimination of themes, however, risks anarchy: "a game without rules which, in the impossible condition of no longer possessing a theme, is incapable of controlling its violent effects. In its turn, modern poetry becomes subordinated to that which is possible" (V, 220). To remain a "major" expression of sovereignty (since no discourse, philosophic or poetic, is immune to subordination), poetry must integrate within the text its own affirmation, "providing an indication of its absence of meaning" (V, 220).

Without this declaration of intention, poetry would resemble laughter, sacrifice, eroticism, or drunkenness, and would not be subordinated, but recovered through a median term. These "minor sovereigns" have not avoided all forms of activity and are therefore inserted within the appropriative system.

Major sovereignty is distinguished by its spontaneity and independence of external authority; otherwise, "it would acquire an external referentiality, and thus seek control and duration. But these are denied to sovereignty by its own demand for authenticity, since it can only be powerless, unstable, violently (or gaily) destructive, eternally dissatisfied" (V, 223). Because it pushes meaning and discourse to their limits, placing them in relation to the absence of meaning and the absolute non-discourse, sovereign writing is best compared to a potlatch: a transgressive, defiant sacrifice of words.

Sovereignty leads from a dialectical to a transgressive approach to language. The analogy with potlatch indicates that words exist as a social institution, whose laws organize the economy of meaning into discourse. For sovereignty in writing to be effective, these laws must be violated. Transgression, argues Bataille, is understood as "an operation of a Hegelian sort . . . which corresponds to the dialectical phase described by the untranslatable German *Aufheben:* to transcend without suppressing" (*L'Erotisme,* 41). It differs from a "return to nature" since it lifts the taboo without eliminating it. The relevance of the sublating process in social terms has already been underscored in the master/slave dialectic. Because the subject (thesis) retains a trace of its original identity, the true master remains a repressed slave. Bataille's anthropological presentation stresses that the taboo does not designate the content of an absolute law, but is tantamount to a limit whose inscription within a culture is historically displaced by transgressive acts. The limits that tempt most exist primarily in the consciousness of those individuals who defy them.

The assimilation of grammar as the law of language is for Bataille, in the wake of Nietzsche, equivalent to the internalization of the idea of God. The negative theology exposed in *La Somme athéologique* is said to be shared by Blanchot, who acknowledges the inhibiting face of a supreme being. "It is said of the word God that it exceeds the limits of all thought—how false!—for it in fact concedes to a definition and, therefore, to a limit" (V, 207).

The death of God is therefore coeval with access to the impossible, since God marks the outer limit of thought and experience for a society, the rational limit beyond which meaning and experience dissolve into nothingness. The deity is the object of mystical experience, but also the fountainhead of reason, the father, and the source of the word. The deity is the origin of an order in which all things remain subordinate to the possible. But once it is dead, what will fill the void? "Sacrifice is the remedy to a world devoid of transcendence . . . the impossible is liberated through a crime, its locus now unveiled" (V, 207).

The "acéphale," godless, headless society will come to power in the wake of a bloodless crime. With the restoration of sacrificial practices, albeit of a symbolic nature, the order of transcendence will have been razed. That hierarchy perpetuates the high/low model of antinomies subverted by Bataille's "irreducibles," and its moral correlates, such as good/bad, have been demystified as well. The indictment of the class-based determinations of such values echoes the Nietzsche of the *Genealogy*. The major guarantee against such reduction is to allow the subject to be swept along by the forces of change in a sovereign relinquishment of meaning and self. By sacrificing God, by murdering the deity, the subject is also annihilated.

The sacrifice that we consume is distinguished from others in that he who executes the rite is affected by the sacrifice himself; he succumbs to it and loses himself along with his victim. Once more, I insist that while the atheist is satisfied by a world complete without God, this sacrificer, on the contrary, is anguished by having to confront an eternally incomplete, incomprehensible universe, which moreover destroys him (just as this universe destroys itself). [V, 176]

In philosophical terms, Foucault views the collapse of philosophical subjectivity not as the end of philosophy, but rather as the "end of the philosopher as the primary and sovereign form of philosophical language."[23] The sacrifice of the deity, the effacement of the outer limit, leads modern experience to be an expérience intérieure or personal meditation. As yet another consequence of the death of God, literature is thus compelled to replace the effect of physical communion elicited by sacrificial rituals: "Literature is situated in the wake of religion, to which it is heir. Sacrifice is a novel, a story, illustrated in a bloody fashion. Or rather, in its most rudimentary state, it is a theatrical representation, a drama reduced to a final episode, where the victim—animal or human—plays alone, but plays unto death" (L'Erotisme, 96).

Words remain inadequate to the demands of the sovereign experience, for to understand is to reject the philosophical discourse of knowing and to attempt to seize meaning from within. Hegel recognized the role of desire in extricating the subject from the object, but for Bataille the recognition and experience of oneself proceeds from an exploration of ecstasy and the jouissance of sovereign dépense.[24] Thus, the "dissolution of discursive reality" (V, 231) gives way to a new locus of communication, where the fusion of the subject and object explores the unknown, the impossible, the "non-savoir" through a dramatization of their effects. The revival of sacrifice, with its violent mixture of anguish and ecstasy, is an effort to externalize what would otherwise remain a purely internal experience: "If we did not know how to dramatize, we could never move beyond our immediate selves. We would live isolated yet suffering lives. But a sort of rapture, caused by anguish, leaves us at the frontier of tears; thus we lose ourselves, we forget who we are and communicate with an unreachable beyond" (V, 23).

To attain communication through the written medium and liberate the individual from an isolated existence is an arduous task, especially when accompanied by a firm resolve to spurn notions of good and evil, reason and madness, "independently of any moral end or at the service of a God"(VI, 12). Despite frequent comparisons with Nietzsche, Bataille views his "parole" as a failure.

By suppressing the obligation, the *good,* or denouncing the emptiness and treason of morality, [Nietzsche] destroyed the efficacy of language. The moment we cease to insist on a burning intensity as the condition of relation to another . . . the proposed state appears as a futile, empty expenditure. . . . By not committing this *consumation* to some form of enrichment, such as the force and effulgence of the city (or of a God, church, or political party), it remains an unintelligible gesture. [VI, 12–13]

Within the general economy, the alternative to the threat of unintelligibility does not lie in a specific theological or political affiliation. Certainly this would be the most blatant form of subordination. Nietzsche did not confront the paradox of writing, in which "the positive value of loss can, apparently, only be expressed in terms of profit" (VI, 12). Tragedy, as a compromise between words and their dramatization, is an excellent case in point. It introduces the sovereignty of silence in verbal communication, thereby heightening the spectator's awareness of the inadequacies of all language. Yet the disparities between its moments of silence (which do not, however, completely suspend the production of meaning within the play), the sovereignty of its experience, and the inevitable meanings attached to its spoken message must be dealt with: *"Explanations cannot be suppressed by simply avoiding them:* tragedy that does not explain itself is nonetheless subject to interpretation. The tragic author does not explain himself, yet is vulnerable to the explanations of others."[25]

Thus, the only resource available that presents writing in a major vein is that which, through a series of signs within the text, provides a declaration of its absence of meaning. It is all the more necessary for the text to provide these guideposts to its ideological stance, since the poet is usually cut off from direct interaction with the audience.

"'La poésie doit être faite par tous, non pas un'" (V, 172). The surrealists appropriated Lautréamont's challenge to accepted notions of individual genius and inspiration as their collective slogan. Intended to reflect their own communal orientation to the production of literature, it served to reinforce revolutionary intentions in literature, not politics. By renouncing the surrealist shibboleth, Bataille asserts his belief that "genius remains stubbornly personal" (V, 172). The claim by followers of Breton to change the world through words and enlist poetry in the service of the revolution is a confusion of realms. Power is the basis of the established order, and the subversion of that order can never be effected exclusively through words: "At this point, it is clear that poetry must confront the inevitable question of power. Ultimately, poetry can only be an evocation that challenges the order of words *but not of the world*" (V, 220–21).

This is a *mise au point* on the subject of literature. It does not imply a disavowal of previous revolutionary declarations and earlier sympathies toward the proletariat. It simply clarifies Bataille's attitude on the relationship between the individual and the group and his criticism of the surrealists' unquestioning acceptance of the ideology implicit in their writing. While Bataille acknowledges the necessary and inevitable claims of the group on the artist, he insists on the isolation of the *act* of writing. Not the production, but the product itself, poetry, will induce communication at its most significant level. Perhaps the final word on the matter can be found in the "avertissement" of the *Méthode de méditation;* at the risk of having presented a privileged experience, the author introduces the concept of a "continuum," which allows him to place his expérience in a new perspective: "The continuum that I propose is a continuous milieu of the human ensemble, opposed to rudimentary representation of indivisible or decidedly separate *individuals. . . .* Of the criticisms leveled at *L'Expérience intérieure* which impute a purely individual meaning to 'supplice,' they are only indicative of the limits of those who make them in relation to this *continuum*" [V, 195]. Bataille subverts philosophical discourse and escapes fixed polarities by introducing laughter, the spirit of chance, and renewing old debates that confront the artist/poet's social role.

Constellations of short, separate paragraphs form the basic unit of Bataille's philosophical writings. Rather than act as building blocks to construct a solid argument, one cluster of thoughts appears to cancel the next; the poet is playing dice, and at every page he has thrown a new game: "Each one of my sentences reflects the acceptance of the game, until the one where I finally reject it" (III, 536). Play, in the sense of risk, is an obsessive theme throughout this work, and its primacy is explained by the fact that "all is *jeu,* that being is *jeu,* that the idea of God is both intolerable and a failure in that God, which initially can only be conceived outside of time, is in fact harnessed by human thought to an idea of creation, which is the antithesis of *jeu.*"[26] Once again the concept of a transcendent deity has been immolated, but not on the bloody altar of sacrifice. From the circumscribed world of knowledge, reason, morality, and servitude, Bataille has released human thought and its potential for free play with a vigorous outburst in the face of death. God is dead, and in pity for Him does humanity laugh.

The liberation of the individual does not necessarily prove to be the deliverance it promised. The fundamental movement is toward freedom, not as an absolute state of being, but contingent upon the transgression of social prohibitions. Liberty is crime that seeks excess, including the violation of the integrity of the other. From this rending transgression of limits arises communication since "it cannot take place between two intact entities: it demands beings who have faced risks, placed themselves at the limit of death and extinction; the moral summit consists of putting oneself into question— the suspension of being beyond oneself at the limit of nothingness" (VI, 43). Evil in this context has shed its theological associations and can no longer be equated with a solitary, self-indulgent act harmful to the community. "Le crime du mal" refuses a folding in on oneself and responds to an awareness of the "principe d'insuffisance," which describes existence at its most painful. In recognition of the presence of the *néant* at the core of being communication occurs. The continuum of human interaction leading to communication usually finds fullest expression in sexuality.

The last consequence of the "death of God" is manifested in its effect on modern sexuality. By removing the absolute limit—contemporary experience—the expérience intérieure, or sovereignty, becomes the experience of the impossible. Only the impossible is truly sovereign, the possible being reducible to an obvious goal or morality. Almost immediately, however, one discovers that the exploration of the impossible becomes the realization of limits, and the anguish of the experience is the attempt to transgress those renewed limits. Only the *mise en jeu* of life and erotic excess, the "assenting to life to the point of death" (*L'Erotisme,* 15)—complete dépense—could risk to push the hallucinatory repetitiveness of the taboo/transgression cycle to its extremes.

God is dead, the reality created through discursive language is dissolved, and the philosophical subject has been sacrificed. The experience of limits would be meaningless without its corollary, the *mise en question* of the limits of language itself. The field of language and writing must now be extended to encompass a discourse that can answer the needs of transgression; yet transgression, despite the absence of the notion of the sacred, is ultimately expressed in acts of religious profanation and most often in terms of the loss of God. Foucault analyzes transgression within a historical perspective: "the speech given to sexuality is contemporaneous, both in time and structure, with that through which we announce to ourselves that God is dead."[27]

The loss of God is linked to changing attitudes toward language. Most pertinent to Bataille is the problem of language as it relates to a preoccupation with sexuality: "our sexuality has been absorbed by the universe of language, denaturalized by it, and placed in a void where it establishes its sovereignty and ceaselessly imposes itself as the law of limits that it transgresses."[28]

These broad generalizations and rather daring claims compel us to extend our discussion to the domain of sexuality or, more accurately, eroticism as Bataille envisions it. At the outcome of this struggle to understand the role of literature in terms of a sovereign experience, we find Bataille, both in his theoretical work *L'Erotisme* and the so-called pornographic novels, again forwarding a defiance to the limit of thought as reason and the human experience as grounded in exchange. Eroticism is the ultimate dépense, the sacrifice of self in the most complete gesture of communication.

EROTIC SOVEREIGNTY I

The aphoristic fragments of *La Somme athéologique,* unburdened of any pretense at narrative coherence or temporal continuity, are acclaimed by their author as the record of the expérience intérieure of "total man." Bataille makes the case that to intuit the self as a whole is to provide for "la part du feu, de la folie, de la part maudite," which in the restricted economy are ceded by reason grudgingly and from without, parsimoniously doled according to "liberal norms" (VII, 23). For this experience there exists no definitive formula.

> I must be content with empirics. I mean by *expérience intérieure* that which is usually designated by the term "mystical experience," the fact of living states of ecstasy, rapture, etc. But I envisage less "confessional experiences"—those that are conventionally invoked—than the experience itself, free of attachments, be they vague, to any confession whatsoever. Hence the relinquishment of the term "mystical," which I could not have retained without leading to confusion. [V, 427]

The course of the expérience leads through myriad experiments and tentative commitments—one ultimately cancelling the other—until Bataille begins to play with the notion of sovereignty. Composed of a variety of moments rather than a sustained revelation or state of being, these epiphanies cannot be organized or appropriated into a discursive system of understanding. Yet by their very disparity and disconnectedness, the sovereign instants—lightning flashes that escape the conscious mind— aggravate the individual's sense of internal discord. This tension between the contradictory impulses of dépense and accumulation cannot be accommodated by any available experience or mode of thought without distorting the relative significance of either force. Past representations of sovereignty as a simulated surrender to death tend to negate its ambivalence—precisely that which renders it at once dangerous, menacing, and elusive, as well as the object of reverence and defilement—by consecrating it within "aristocratic" values such as glory. This containment of dépense is most evident in the sun imagery discussed earlier and in the nineteenth-century images of power revived by the surrealists. Nor is the sun of *La Part maudite* exempt from the contamination of a utilitarian morality. Thus, when the bourgeois tries to deny his secret aspiration to be sun-king, "one can say that the sky is closed to him: he ignores poetry and glory, and in his eyes the sun is only a source of calories" (VII, 191). The sovereign vision of Bataille promotes the image of a light, "pure, radiant and glorious, above a night charged with horrors and nightmares as well as above the flat expanses of homogeneity. It [sovereignty] is the analog of a sun and, like the sun, shines with a light so cruel that it is necessary to turn one's eyes" (VII, 225).

The reworking of the sun imagery followed "the revolutionary negation of royalty" (*L'Erotisme*, 184) exemplified by Sade. This transfer of
sovereignty to literature explains why the agonistic terminology of master/
slave relations pervades the modern discourse pertaining to words, writing,
and literature: "Neither able nor willing to have recourse to ascesis, I must
link contestation to the liberation of the power of words, which constitutes
mastery" (V, 28).

Moreover, the anguish of the "dual solicitation" highlights the tensions
between the economies of language and poetry found in *L'Expérience
intérieure*: "In the debate that opposes the will to lose and the will to gain—
the desire to appropriate and the desire to communicate—poetry is at the same
level as the states of consolation, as visions, as the words of mystics" (V, 165).

One finds that even poetic images (those of Proust, for instance)
manifest an internal economy indicating "a proprietary sentiment, the
persistence of a 'je' reflecting everything back onto itself" (V, 165). Heterogeneity demonstrates the need for a sacred silence to mediate the antitheses
of excretion and appropriation, attraction and repulsion. Although the
movement toward sovereignty leads to anguish, one must recognize it as the
inevitable condition of ecstasy: "Anguish is the fear of loss, the expression of
the desire to possess. Recalcitrance in the face of communication stimulates
desire as well as fear. Acknowledge the desire to possess and suddenly
anguish turns to ecstasy" (V, 169).

The next phase of the *expérience* seeks the *continuum* through which
sovereign moments produce a sense of mutuality. True satisfaction defeats
by reciprocity the inequality of the master/slave relation. Without this,
Kojève insisted, pleasure would never exist. Bataille stipulates as the
condition for communication a shared *dépense* or *déchirement* emanating
from the desire for totality within the conscious mind as it leads to a
transcendence of meaning: "a total existence is located beyond any one
meaning, it is the conscious presence of man in the world to the extent he is
non-meaning, having nothing to do other than to be what he is, no longer to
be able to go beyond himself, nor to give himself meaning through action"
(V, 20).

The writing of *L'Expérience intérieure* objectifies Bataille's doubt that
anyone but an individual can achieve the sovereign experience which,
however, carries its own social effect since it demands a revision of the social
covenant through transgressive acts. And yet the sovereignty of this gesture
must be preserved against degradation by the individual who profits
from his crime. One must then formulate precise criteria for communication, in order to impede individual indulgence from preventing total
immersion within the community.

Access to the *vue d'ensemble* is elusive. Consequently, Bataille engages in
a dialogic project comprising all the discourses incorporated into his text.

The determining influence of anthropological notions in this work has already been underlined, and is complemented by a clear antipathy to philosophy. The rejection is justified by philosophy's perceived reductionism, when it attempts to impose "intelligibility" by abstracting general laws or principles from an immediately perceptible reality intractable to ready-made categories such as "absurdity" or "horror" (IV, 397).

More serious is philosophy's resemblance to science in the primacy placed by both on the study of objects. The subjects of modern philosophical investigations are "sujets connaissants," knowledge of which need not be rigidly controlled by the dictates of reason and logic. Bataille calls for a "science du sujet" while immediately acknowledging its impossibility. In the expérience intérieure of sacrifice, the place of the subject is constantly related to its destruction as a *mise en jeu,* the willingness to risk the self by annihilating the ego. The subject/object dichotomy is only temporarily retained since the goal of the desiring subject is the fusion of individual identities.

From the traditional portrait of an individual incited by hedonistic demands, Bataille's anthropology hypothesizes a state in which minimal needs are met. Liberated from daily material concerns, one then explores the possibilities of a being for whom the excesses of *jouissance* have displaced the demands of desire in a universe whose first law of economics posits a surplus at the very basis of life. Nature not only guarantees the reproduction of the species, but the paradox of eroticism—the *conscious* activity of the sexual animal—reveals death within this very excess. The abundance of sperm beyond what is biologically mandated for survival of the species does not obviate the fact that within procreation—the instant when the zygote is fused—the "economy of life" requires that the two donor cells "die." From this evidence of the presence of death in life, Bataille spins off a series of observations regarding the nature of eroticism as it arises when the forces of sexuality are channeled into social structures.

Despite the rejection of the "definitely puerile" feudal models of sovereignty (VIII, 273), traces of the traditional association between the aristocrat and sexual prowess linger in this work. Their foil is the "castrated" bourgeois, whose respect for law and order, including its repressive apparatus, is emasculating. The alternative view of eroticism Bataille proposes, however, ultimately depends on a more enduring, allegedly universal archetype for male consciousness, that of the *giving* female.[29] Within the economy of energy, gender is a central category dividing the labors of male production from those of female donation: "To give [of oneself] is the fundamental feminine attitude" (*L'Erotisme,* 127), and the culmination of giving is in the erotic act. Thus, while Bataille aims to expand the limited visions of science and philosophy, it is also evident that the study of the subject from the vantage point of the general economy cannot remain blind to sexual differentiation. He then proposes a circuitous trajectory via anthropology, religion, and sociology as a way to the *vue d'ensemble.*

The point of departure for reflections on erotic sovereignty within the context of exchange was provided by Lévi-Strauss's *Les Structures élémentaires de la parenté*, which appeared in 1949. Despite a "closed" title, Bataille insists that its subject—incest—dovetails with his own. Until the structuralist approach provided an explanation, the taboo on incest constituted the central enigma of anthropology. Lévi-Strauss was the first to relate its presence to the social structure of kinship relations and not, as was commonly held, to the nuclear family. At the social level, the taboo emerges as an isolated manisfestation of the more generalized principle of exchange. Thus his main conclusion inverts the traditional view of the prohibition and demonstrates it to be an *obligation* imposed on men to relinquish their sisters and daughters by making a gift of them to men outside the family. The injunction on sexual contact with women of one's group or clan was established in order to avoid the hoarding of women and to maximize their distribution. Essential to biological reproduction, women have to be carefully circulated among men willing to deny themselves the unrestricted sexual satisfaction that would jeopardize the future of the social order.

This interpretation, insisting as it does on the social function of female sexuality, reveals women to be but one more link in the symbolic chain men have forged among themselves. Along with goods and words, they complete the three levels of communication that, according to Lévi-Strauss, constitute the symbolic order of primitive social organization. Even with the evolution of society, however, the original value of woman has not been degraded. She was never relegated to the status of a sign, which became the fate of words,

> since even in a man's world she is still a person, and since insofar as she is defined as a sign she must be recognized as a generator of signs. In the matrimonial dialogue of men, woman is never purely what is spoken about; for if women in general represent a certain category of signs, destined to a certain kind of communication, each woman preserves a particular value arising from her talent, before and after marriage, for taking her part in a duet. *In contrast to words, which have wholly become signs, woman has remained at once a sign and a value.*[30]

The hasty attempt to conclude on a positive note nonetheless fails to specify the quality of the signs women can possibly produce within a male-devised symbolic order. Such an analysis would complete while modifying the structuralist one, by looking at behavior as more than the execution of the laws governing exchange. These rules qualify as markers on the horizon of that which can be said, thought, or done within the norms they set. Furthermore, the performance engendered by the rules will be regarded as dialectical, with special emphasis on the inducement, and not the restriction, of certain acts and sentiments through the prohibition. One must further question the impact of individual manifestations of the need for dépense in altering the structures themselves. One appreciation of Bataille's sense of the "impossible" has stressed that dimension of behavior inaccessible except through collective experiences. With the study of eroticism, however, he aspires to a province of sensations in such proximity to the law that it demands a reevaluation of the categories of individual and society.

Bataille first contests the structuralist emphasis on the "economic" strategy involved in the distribution of women; this scheme, he argues, downplays a total, systemic appreciation of all taboos and their transgression. The injunction men agree to constitutes "the origin of the potlatch of women, of exogamy; the paradox of giving away the coveted object" (*L'Erotisme,* 234). Such exchanges must be understood within the context of a culture where the overriding function of the gift is to prohibit isolation and to consolidate communication. The result promotes generosity among those participating in the ceremonial extravagance of the festival, unlike the cold calculations necessitated by exclusively economic transactions.

> Thus women seem primarily important as a means of *communication* in the strongest sense, the sense of effusion. Consequently they have to be objects of generosity on the part of their parents whose gift they are. The parents must give them away, but this happens in a world where each act of generosity contributes to the cycle of generosity in general. The sexual relationship is itself communication and a movement, it is like a celebration by nature, and because it is essentially a communication it provides an outward movement in the first place. [*L'Erotisme,* 229]

Bataille claims that the significant moment in the creation of a social order does not occur specifically in the incest taboo as a curb on sexuality, but in the general process of establishing limits. The moment of critical transition from nature to culture, from animal to human, discovers an order of sexuality qualitatively different from the biological impulse. Eroticism is a social phenomenon arising from the vacillation between attraction and repulsion or affirmation and negation. Its violence is menacing and has been forced out of the marital situation as it now exists, but it cannot be banished beyond society's limits. Archaic society foresaw the need for a balance between the impossibility of taboos and moments of transgression. Paradoxically, marriage was at one point that transgressive experience. Its evolution, however, has led to a rejection of erotic extremes, paralleling the more general effacement of sanctioned transgressions. The survival of society demanded the creation of an impenetrable space willing to deny and censor the disruptions of eroticism: the household became this sanctum.

The center of the domestic scene is the woman, just as she is the focal point of kinship rules and incest taboo. Whether the prohibition weighs upon a woman from another clan, a sister, a cousin, or eventually a mother, she alone is its object. Bataille rejects this as an outsider's point of view, because the female cannot be reduced to a pawn in an elaborate give and take.

Generosity flows not just from the father who makes a gift of his daughter to the community; the real don is the gift a woman makes of herself. By turning to eroticism as the form of dépense most accessible in contemporary society, Bataille focuses on what appears as the greater potential for erotic exuberance among women. The possible relation of their transgressive sexuality to the position ascribed them in the exchange system of patriarchal society is never explicitly considered. A final evaluation of this general thesis will be reached after we consider the portrayal of women in Bataille's novels.

Bataille's work is distinguished by its explicit juxtaposition of death and eroticism. The latter is characterized as a disruptive force, antagonistic to homogeneity. It involves a total giving of oneself in an effort to restore a semblance of continuity through communication with the other. As part of the destructuring process of the rational, Cartesian subject, it can lead to a fusion that defies physical boundaries. The subject transcends itself not to rejoin a lost union of oneness with the universe, but to participate in an experience that pushes Being to the limit during orgasm, the "petite mort" simulating death.

When social theories advocate total abandonment of taboos (and their ritualized transgressions), they tend to have in mind a relatively domesticated form of sexual practice.[31] What Bataille refers to—and here he can have recourse only to comparisons—are sensations analogous to those evoked by sacrificial rituals. Sacrifice (and the entire realm of the sacred) cannot be reduced to a symbolic gesture. Society does more than reaffirm the supremacy of the prohibition in a formalized exercise rendered anachronistic by the rationalizations of Christianity. The divine disorder of the festival inaugurated by sacrifice is a transcendent experience uniting the community through the contagion of its violence. It projects individuals beyond themselves, and the presence of death (via the ritualized murder) exposes them to an experience of almost limitless possibilities. A continuum is restored among those whom the profane world of work reduced to atomized, isolated entities: "Violence alone, blind violence, can burst the barriers of the rational world and lead us into continuity" (*L'Erotisme*, 54). While neutralizing the extremity of erotic desire, the consumer society has been able to profit from its inherent mystery, the force of its attraction, by associating it with objects of prestige and status. In this way, the potential force of dépense, rejected by religion (and philosophy), has been channeled into an acquisitive ethic under the guise of sexual freedom. Thus Bataille's understanding of eroticism deviates from the prevalent condemnation of taboos as irritating anachronisms that can, and must, be legislated out of existence: "In this instance, in spite of appearances, I am opposed to the tendency that seems to prevail today. I am not among those who see in the rejection of sexual taboos a solution. I actually think that human potential

82 READING GEORGES BATAILLE

depends on them" (III, 510–11). Because sexuality is violent, because it is fundamentally ambivalent (the genitals causing moments of "mutual repulsion" [II, 318]), it participates in that region of sacred experiences which cannot be articulated through rational discourse. But it must be mediated. By imposing a silent space between a man and a woman, the interdict will not hamper erotic passion, but render sexual relations more "human" (II, 318). Yet the problem of how to transmit these subtleties in the fictional works is a serious one. Not only does Bataille deal with an experience that is verbally transgressed with great difficulty, but the language of sexuality often carries the negative associations of pornography. A brief analysis of the incomplete posthumous novella, *Divinus Deus* (IV, 169–311), examines how these challenges are met.

Bataille's novels avoid the conventional trappings of classical hard-core pornography—the isolated chateau, the sado-masochistic scenes with a panoply of chains, whips, and leather boots. Rather, they share more the techniques of the contemporary novel where social and political settings are reduced to a minimum, characters have no surnames, and psychological motivations are rarely elaborated. At the outset it is understood that only the desire for an erotic experience introduces disorder, divine hysteria, effusion, and ultimately borders on annihilation of the conscious subject.

The basic Bataillian pattern presents an anguished young male narrator surrounded by (usually two) disturbingly aggressive females. He is a twentieth-century Robinson embarked on a re-creation of self in terms of desire, often with a great deal more trepidation than assurance. For he quickly realizes that the movement toward ecstasy entails a painful relinquishment of all the social and historical "points de repère" that help to solidify the sense of identity of a social being. This erosion of the "sujet unaire," the subject subordinated to the repressive forces of the family, state, group, or clan, constitutes the transgressive power of eroticism.[32] Superficially, this tendency is not unlike the isolation found in Sade. The fortress-castle, the assassination of mothers, the aristocratic status of libertines are all part of the evasion of social responsibility and work and permit the liberation of energy for exclusively erotic purposes. The individual becomes a thing or machine, geared for fulfillment and gratification of the most elaborate fantasies. Tension is not elicited by the conflict between a specific law and the desire to defy it. Rather, it arises within the individual out of the horror of an attraction toward what is repugnant and, more disturbing, from the force of the desire which propels his obsessions to a sacrifice of self.

The section "Ma Mère" is a rambling, loosely strung series of episodes involving the transformation of the narrator from a pious adolescent to a fervent erotomane. The sentimental education of Bataille's hero would not differ greatly from the sexual diversions of any adept young narrator of erotic novels, but the transgressive element is introduced when we realize that it is Pierre's mother who organizes her son's initiations. Although mother and son never exchange more than one passionate embrace (after which she kills herself), their relationship is all the more deeply solidified by her collusion in his affairs with other women, since the latter are usually her former lovers. Here is the first step in a process that aims at breaking down the notion of erotic exchange as found only in one-to-one relationships. The alternative is not simply a quantitative increase in lovers, but a reevaluation of the notion of identity in a form of experience that disturbs conventional concepts of personal love. The women in Bataille's novels are profoundly aware of their transgressive role and actively pursue experiences that will satisfy their most arcane desires. They view themselves as a luxury, not as a sign to enhance the social standing of lovers or husbands. Their sexuality is an abundant source of energy offered at will: "I received underneath the table the offering Hansi made of herself" (IV, 267).

The appearance of this new type of female character in pornographic novels has already been noted, and Sontag contrasts the heroine of *The Story of O* with her Sadian counterpart: "Justine is the stereotype sex-object figure (invariably female, since most pornography is written by men from the stereotyped point of view): a bewildered victim, whose consciousness remains unaltered by her experiences. But O is an adept; whatever the cost in pain and fear, she is grateful for the opportunity to be initiated into a mystery. *That mystery is the loss of self*" (emphasis added).[33] In much the same process, Pierre's mother consciously explores all possible routes that will provide her with the most extreme instance of self-negation. This intensely violent desire and her insistence on transgressing all limits is also reflected in the relationship with her son. From the very moment his mother chose to recount adventures of her sexual past, Pierre was aware of the particular complicity that she was instigating. Yet the presence of a limit, an undefinable obstacle, persists between mother and son, and no conventional explanation in terms of the incest taboo resolves the enigma of the situation. In this most transgressive, libertine of atmospheres, Bataille attempts to instill in his reader a sense of the "impossible" nature of a relationship that cannot be consummated because of the excessive quality of the emotions at play. Pierre and his mother encounter eroticism in its most disruptive and anonymous form—not the inhibiting effect of a social injunction. The characters themselves are aware of this, prompting Pierre to reflect that he has become indifferent to the particular identity of his partner.

The conflict dramatized here focuses on the relative types of experience "love" and "eroticism" propose. The latter has been described as impersonal, dominated by the will to release the powerful and anguishing forces of dépense, and the ability to face risk. The contours of what Bataille refers to as love are less clearly delineated. Moreover, how does one justify the

conscious movement toward disorder and confusion, the continual ques-
tioning of a relationship that is often considered the only source of pleasure
and stability in a hostile environment? Bataille answers that the so-called
stability of love is spurious, that it is *necessarily* disturbing.

> The most significant manifestation of the necessity for this alternation of
> balance and lack of balance is the violent and tender love of one being for
> another. The violence of love leads to tenderness, the lasting form of love,
> but it brings into the striving of one heart toward another the same quality
> of disorder, the same thirst for losing consciousness and the same
> aftertaste that is found in the mutual desire for each other's body.
> [*L'Erotisme,* 64]

While love shares these qualities with eroticism, it also implies the
intense emotional attachment to one individual accompanied by a haunting
fear of loss. To refuse this "risk" debases love: "The ridiculous thing about
the urge toward transcendence in which concern for the preservation of life is
scorned is the almost immediate transition to the wish to organize it in a
lasting way, or at least a way intended to be lasting, with the disequilibrium
[caused by] love protected—if possible—from disequilibrium" (*L'Erotisme,*
64).

The underlying tension in "Ma Mère" arises from the elaboration of
these contrasting experiences. For his mother, Pierre identifies sensations
analogous to those of his earlier religious attachments, a violent impersonal
force clearly related to the notion of dépense: "There existed a love between
us similar to that which, according to the mystics, God reserves for man, a
love calling forth violence, never leaving room for peace" (IV, 236). With a
young, intelligent woman and former protegée of his mother, Pierre
discovers a more personalized attachment: "I trembled at the thought of
losing Hansi, I sought her out like the thirsty man a source of fresh water.
Hansi was the only one; in her absence, no one could console me" (IV, 236).
At the thought of losing Hansi, the narrator often experiences anguish. In
fact, the only real threat to the idyll is Pierre's mother, having instilled in
Hansi the fear that she will not be able to satisfy the desires the mother has
aroused in her son.

When evoking the intensity of the erotic experience, Bataille approaches the subtle limit that separates eroticism as the transgressions of
dépense and communication from the more conventional sexual violations
of hard-core pornography. In one parodic scene, Hansi arrives in a flaming
red riding habit brandishing the obligatory whip and belatedly confesses that
she has no predilection for vices. Yet she affirms that she could kill a man with
the intensity of the voluptuousness she offers. And this is precisely what the
narrator sets out to demonstrate as the couple indulge in a protracted orgy
that leaves them at the border of exhaustion and whose culmination becomes
a metaphor of death. They have reached the "plaie profonde"; the open

wound is willfully exposed and reveals the dependence on the other, which allows for the deepest form of interaction to exist. The effort to attain the wound determines the success of communication. Too often, sexual relations in pornography are regulated by rules that lend them a superficial similarity to religious practices or the more familiar codes governing all social relations.[34] Bataille deplores in most so-called erotic literature those characters who appear to have embarked on a "voyage au bout de la nuit" but who have not been compelled to engage their egos beyond their immediate selves.

In "Ma Mère," the problem of communication manifests itself in the comparison between the narrator's relations with Hansi and his mother's with her lovers. Pierre's mother is an incarnation of unbridled eroticism drawing others into the whirlwind of frenzied orgies. She entices, seduces, and at every point is conscious of the extraordinary force of her trangressive desires. She is willing to push herself to the limit, but her pursuit of extremes is ultimately a failure in its isolated search for absolute sovereignty: "The solitary desire for sovereignty is its own betrayal of sovereignty" (IX, 316). In this desire resides the significance of the character of "mère." Consistent with Bataille's profoundly altered notion of communication as exchange, she has bypassed words and immersed herself in an endless profusion of erotic encounters. Yet her lovers, male and female, seem reduced to mere objects of her pleasure. She is a disconcerting figure, indicative of the difficulty Bataille and Lévi-Strauss both encountered in accommodating female sexuality to their social schemes.

If the attraction between the sexes is an outgrowth of the need to give and to violate the barriers of the individual ego, then the opposition between Pierre's mother and Hansi is crucial. The former is a product of a patriarchal society, and her erotic desire is menacing and violent because it exists only as a reaction to the laws that try to maintain it within their order. (It is important to recall that Pierre's father rapes her in the woods and then compels her to marry him.) This explains why Bataille must then present the relationship with Hansi as an alternative to Pierre's mother's glorious, self-consuming eroticism, which is destructive in a conventional way. The mother does not move toward others from a sense of insufficiency, seeking with them the same gratification that she pursues in a chaotic, isolated surge of desire. Only the inner sense of limits leads to communication because it returns the individual to the community in a search for recognition.[35]

The contrast between these two female figures demonstrates the relation of economics to eroticism. Bataille already pointed out the connection with his characterization of potlatch as "the simultaneous transcendence and epitome of calculation" (*L'Erotisme,* 233). In women, the imperatives of the two economies meet. Men agree to delay gratification for the higher good of the social order, yet their deprivation is enmeshed with the sensations of giving and collective communication. Moreover, the taboo on women enhances the value of the forbidden female: first, because she accrues symbolic wealth as she circulates within the system; second, because the act of denial increases her appeal.

Thus, the distinction of eroticism from sexuality lies within the complementary cycle of taboo and transgression, the paradox of potlatch, and the ambivalence of the *Aufhebung*, which "supercedes while maintaining." Their common denominator is the calculation whereby men consciously deny what they desire for the reward of increased pleasure.

Bataille repudiated a purely economic explanation, which would demean the mysteries of eroticism to the logic of a transaction. Yet he ultimately demonstrates that the erotic is a product of a profoundly economic notion, not unlike the maximization principle of economic rationality on which the restricted economy relies. In the materialism of the general economy, however, the only apparent gain is measured in terms of loss. The deprivation entailed is not understood within a psychology of guilt, debt, and retribution. A restricted economy of meaningful signs carrying power and prestige do not reinscribe the limits transgressed. Rather, the ritual of dépense is played out within an "empty" form of the *Aufhebung* and never exhausts the need for renewed expenditure.[36] Thus, the moment at which eroticism surpasses sexuality and accedes to sovereignty is a consequence of transgression, rendered possible by a social institution that simultaneously enforces the law of restriction and administers its violation: "The law does not modify the violence of sexual activity, but it does open the door of transgression that animal sexuality could never enter" (*L'Erotisme,* 241).

Bataille intended *L'Erotisme* and his novels to be a polemical challenge to a culture where the prevailing consumerism has wedded desire to appropriation. His erudite, often opaque, inquiry into the nature of eroticism shows that it is irreducible to empancipatory slogans whose neat oppositions between sex/work, freedom/repression, immediate/delayed gratification appear inadequate. Most impressive is the capacity of his idiom to penetrate the taboo domains where death and sensuality converge. The transgressions into the inviolate recesses of fantasy and horror, violence and passion, mysticism and degradation, once regarded as impossible to assimilate within literary discourse, indicate Bataille's modernity. Moreover, by relating dépense and communication to Lévi-Strauss's structuralist analysis of social exchange, Bataille anticipates the arguments of later critics of structuralism, providing them with the requisite alternatives to the model of culture and behavior it imposes.

EROTIC SOVEREIGNTY II

The irony of erotic sovereignty is that it projects an anthropology modeled on the behavior of women. Thus it confirms our earlier conclusion that the possibility of a thoroughly disinterested gift could not be posited within the exchange mechanisms as described by Mauss and Lévi-Strauss. Because women are excluded from the rules governing exchange they are less likely to have a stake in the maintenance of the system, and therefore are more prone to give without restraint. Yet the energy they emit is primarily identified with the life forces of biological reproduction and nurturance, unlike the death and destruction associated with dépense. Bataille's presentation of ideas is often not amenable to systematization; but the nexus of women, sexuality, and death is such a volatile issue that it merits further scrutiny. It is also important that the special quality of the expérience intérieure be divested of the morbidity surrounding most discussions of death.

By concentrating his tableau of eroticism on its female figures, Bataille could be accused of adhering to the conventions of gender identity by viewing the propensity to give as sexually determined. According to this traditional scheme, women are located along a natural life-giving, emotive, self-sacrificial axis, while men represent culture, death, reason, and appropriation. Recent French feminist theory reinforces the contrast by celebrating the positive, vital expenditures of women as often portrayed in the literature of men.[37] Men give, but only when motivated by gain. The neurotic reflexes conditioned by the awareness of mortality are responsible for the humiliating subordination to work, production, and the self-imposed deprivations such activity presupposes. By suppressing the rituals of sacrifice, Western civilization has displaced the anguish of death onto the anxiety of work: capitalism profits from the fear of instability—the *chavirement* and dissolution encountered by the *conscience servile*—by incorporating the vagaries of the market into the daily life of the worker. Bataille deviates from Hegel most by eliminating the accession of the slave to master through work. Instead of seeking to escape death through the dialectic of overcoming, sovereignty avoids the anguish it provokes by living in the instant. History demonstrates that the condition of enslavement may be necessary, but not sufficient, to foment revolution. For this reason Bataille studied society so that, once its economic determinants were established, he could then analyze those "emotions" capable of sundering the masses from their bonds.

Bataille explains his affinity with Hegel's philosophy of death by the seriousness it grants to a topic often subject to facile dismissals. His sentiment toward death, however, is not Hegel's "sadness"; rather, it approaches the *joie angoissée* of Irish wakes or the anguished ecstasy of eroticism. Death must be located within the sovereign operation that simulates the unsettling effects of laughter, intoxication, poetry, or sacrifice: "Effusion is obtained through a modification, willed or not, of *the order of objects:* poetry disposes of changes on the plane of images; sacrifice, in general, destroys beings; laughter results from diverse changes. . . . Intoxication, on the other hand, leads to a voluntary change in the subject . . . the same can be said of meditation" (V,

219, emphasis added). Science, reason, and discourse are not absent from the *vue d'ensemble,* but integrated through a "dialectics of intoxication" (to use Benjamin's terminology). Such expenditure without reserve entails two phases: first, the demotion of the status of idealism's logos by the materialism of heterogeneity. Sovereignty then transgresses the opposing systems of the material and the ideal by *exceeding* them, but it also highlights the inability of most discourse to "see" beyond its own blind spots.

Although attracted to the *représentations distinctes* of science, Bataille stresses their inability to dazzle: "that is, to capitulate to that which a troubled vision brings to me: that which is blinding. More precisely, the disturbance of which I speak is that of poetry. I can admit to it: poetry troubles me, it enchants me, it provokes another truth than that of science. It is the truth of death, of disappearance" (III, 521). The section to follow, an anthropological reading of *Histoire de l'oeil* (I, 14–78), will demonstrate how the repertoire of poetic images generated by the sun constitutes the subterranean connections within Bataille's canon, giving insights into a new order of totality.

The *Story of the Eye* is a difficult work to describe.[38] It defies the standards of fictional form and content because its ostensible subject matter—a sequence of sexual encounters—is narrated by means of metaphors syntagmatically connected by objects relayed from one episode to the next, and which eventually displace humans as the main figures. The reader's attention is riveted not only to the object, but to the particular form of erotic activity in which it engages. According to Barthes's admittedly formalist analysis, the structure of the *Eye* is comparable to a poem, if one accepts Jakobson's distinction that the novel is organized syntagmatically and the poem metaphorically.[39] The main "object," the eye, is declined following its possible metaphorical avatars, thus constituting an erotic paradigm of linguistic and sexual associations: *oeil, oeuf, soleil, couille.* The second series of metaphors evolves from sensations of fluidity which modify the nouns of the first. These include tears, milk, the yolk of an egg, the fluid of sperm, and urine. As Barthe rightly points out, so long as an object is attached to the verb or function most clearly dictated by common sense or pragmatic experience, the images remain acceptable: a crying eye compared with liquid flowing from an egg and light pouring from the sun are readily assimilated into the most conventional discourse. When Bataille upsets this scheme, however, to produce images of a broken egg, a pierced eye, or a urinating sun, the transgressive mechanism becomes evident. Moreover, each metaphor is associated with the violence of an erotic game, but these transgressive gestures cannot be divorced from the linguistic play that parallels them.

In the opening cat's "eye" episode, for instance, the concrete referent is a saucer (assumed to be of white porcelain) that contains the milk in which

Simone cools her bared posterior. The male narrator witnessing the scene is overcome by the sight of her genitals and the two simultaneously reach orgasm. Neither has spoken to or touched the other. The unifying paroxysms of their transgressive play is contagious: soon Simone is cracking eggs with her *derrière*. The climax of the association occurs at a bullfight under the "liquefying" Spanish sun. The matador's eye is torn from its socket, and Simone requests to be served the testicles of the freshly killed bull which, not surprisingly, she inserts between her legs. The final episode shifts to a Spanish church: a young priest is murdered and we witness Simone tearing his eyes from their sockets to play with them as one would . . . an egg.

Thus the *Eye* violently condenses all the objects of the metaphor within its compulsive span: eye, egg, sun, and testicle. As in Bataille's provocative assertion that "eroticism is assenting to life to the point of death" (*L'Erotisme*, 29), the metonymic chain is exhausted, that is, the narrative suspended, only when a murder is executed. Yet it is obvious that the transformations of these signifying objects are not infinite, nor are their peregrinations without end. But the source of their limitations, the "signified" of the story, remains unclear. In the "Coincidences," Bataille's afterthoughts on the *Eye,* he recounts a traumatic event in which the author witnesses his blind, paralyzed, syphilitic father trying to void while seated. At that moment, his blanket slipped, exposing the genitals, while his eyes revolved in their orbits exposing only the whites. The genital association egg/eye is later confirmed by a doctor who informs the author that animal testicles are indeed called *oeufs,* adding that human testicles are in the ovoid shape of eyes. These sexual determinants thus limit the metaphorical associations. Ultimately, the "Coincidences" frustrate any illusion that an exclusively psychological key will decode Bataille's semiological puzzle.

Barthes suggests that the transgressive impact of the *Eye* is explained by its linguistic deviations.

> Thus, the transgression of values, which is the explicit principle of eroticism, parallels—if it does not found it—the technical transgression of the forms of language, for metonymy is nothing else than a forced syntagm, the violation of a limit of the signifying space; at the level of discourse, metonymy allows for a contradivision of objects, usages, meanings, spaces and properties, which is the very essence of eroticism: thus, that which the play of metaphor and metonymy in the *Story of the Eye* ultimately transgresses is *le sexe:* which is not, of course, a matter of sublimation, quite the contrary.[40]

The transgression of sexuality points to the violence of eroticism, which is not simply communicated or shared by the actors of the *Eye,* but a force contagiously suffusing the objects among which the human figures must circulate. Barthes concludes that the *Eye* "signifies," in the manner of a "vibration," the nonverbal sensory communication of sovereignty which always renders the same sound.[41]

This vibrating quality also permeates potlatch and other ritualized gift exchanges, where the objects exchanged bear the supernatural force of *hau* and *mana*. Yet the unsolved riddle of these ceremonies lies precisely in the value hierarchy governing the patterns of exchange. Is there a central figure supplying the objects, a chief or deity to whom they are offered? How are the objects themselves designated; do they possess an intrinsic value or acquire a special significance by dint of their participation? Similarly, is there an underlying principle by which to explicate the objects chosen by Bataille?

The initial stage of my response assumes a parallel between the version of gift-giving revised through the notion of dépense presented in *La Part maudite* and the circulation of objects in the *Story of the Eye*. Their common denominator is a challenge to the rationality that has dictated commodity exchanges since the advent of market economies. One finds in this work an explicit correlation between the value of objects in exchange and the sexuality destined primarily for reproduction. For Bataille, the only acknowledged value is *intensity,* a concentration of energy antithetical to the husbanding of scarce resources advocated in social planning or to the maximizing behavior of economic man. And the surplus part maudite is the recognized metaphor for dépense as transgression, ready to accuse the distorted conjugation of economics and sexual morality in the modern world: "the moment of ecstasy is very different from the experience of sexual pleasure: it is closer to a pleasure that is *given"* (VI, 301, emphasis added).

Eroticism is to sexuality as the nondiscursive is to language. Bataille laments the inadequacies of discourse, unable to penetrate the violence inherent in eroticism. By extension, he warns against a "puerile, rhetorical concept of freedom" (II, 131).

> I do not distinguish between freedom and sexual freedom because depraved sexuality is the only kind produced independently of conscious ideological determinations, the only one that results from a free play of bodies and images, impossible to justify rationally. . . . *Because rational thought can conceive of neither disorder nor freedom, and only symbolic thought can, it is necessary to pass from a general concept that intellectual mechanisms empty of meaning to a single, irrational symbol.* [II, 131–32, emphasis added]

Bataille's analysis of potlatch introduces symbolic objects as mediators between states of order and disorder. There it is recognized that the dilapidation of energy could be apprehended only within an order of things. Similarly, Durkheim does not view the use of objects as indicative of linguistic or symbolic deficiency within an indigenous system of communication. He actually stresses a thing's ability to facilitate access to superior modes of consciousness: "In a general way, a collective sentiment can become conscious of itself only by being fixed upon some natural object."[42]

The general economy encompasses the total energy of the planet, with the sun as its privileged, radiant center. Simultaneously concrete and in a state of constant flux, it emanates boundless energy producing light and life, yet can blind and destroy. Within Bataille's essays and novels, the sun is a recurrent figure associated with sacrifice. The disturbing connection between dépense and immolation becomes more evident when their common source is revealed: "the *necessity* to project oneself, or something of oneself, *beyond the self* . . . which is the principle of a psychological or physiological mechanism that in certain instances can have no other result than death" (I, 265). Within a cosmos envisioned in sexual terms, the sun is the "scandal" of the universe, where animal and human life are overcome by their desire to meet solar energy in an incandescent encounter. In passages of his early writings, Bataille juxtaposes the heliotropism of the plant world with human sexual erections, but humans inevitably and necessarily avert their eyes from the sun's intolerable glare. Human eyes can sustain the view of "neither the sun, nor a cadaver, nor darkness, but with varied reactions" (I, 85). At other moments reference is made to "castrated eyes," a metaphor for the inability or unwillingness of humans to recognize the repressed reality of being, given that the collective forms of sacrifice serving such a function in primitive societies have practically disappeared.

Starting with the *Story of the Eye* and culminating in *La Part maudite,* the sun, dominating all other images, is subject to many possible interpretations. As the evident representative of dépense, however, it offers some of the difficulties encountered by Mauss in trying to ascribe meaning to the phenomenon of the gift. The latter is a hybrid notion whose present limited range of connotations is the result of historical erosion. Yet it was equally evident that the convergence of economic and moral meanings could be achieved only at the price of a serious contradiction within Mauss's own work. He examines the gift within the context of a whole society where the gift indeed appears as but one strand of an intricate social fabric. Then from these archaic structures he must prove its applicability in a modern society lacking this affective (and only tangentially economic) form of human social relation. From this it is unclear whether Bataille's formulation of dépense can exist except in the extreme, distorted version of the exchanges described by Mauss. The latter discovered that the polysemic gift lent itself to a variety of interpretations, depending on which dimension—economic, social, psychological—is arbitrarily isolated from its total context. Bataille explores that which by definition has no meaning, a notion that exhausts the significance of the very signs by which it is to be transmitted. Yet the sun is also the paradoxical natural object Durkheim praised, expressing in a solitary symbol the ineffable dépense.

The analysis of sun imagery thus requires a dramatic shift from Mauss's philology to contemporary semiology. Assuming the arbitrary, conventional relationship between the signifier and the signified, a semiotic analysis makes it possible to estimate the value of an object within a theoretically unlimited quantity of systems. Thus, the object under consideration is momentarily liberated from the weight of its historical past and insertable within any relevant system. Bataille's own work provides examples of the sun which evoke the Platonic sun of reason and truth, the Aztec deity of sacrifice, and the sun of Van Gogh's self-mutilation. Each of them can be correlated with a particular discourse, such as philosophy, anthropology, or psychoanalysis. It is against the one-dimensionality of contemporary discourse, bound to hierarchical differentiation and therefore suitable for a successful semio-logical evaluation, that Bataille argues.[43] Bataille's sun is symbolic in the Saussurean sense that there appears to exist a "natural" (motivated) relationship between its signifying elements. The assessment of the sun is further complicated by Bataille's endowment of it with exceptional symbolic power by concentrating a sequence of childhood traumas within this one emblem. Yet the sun of a personal mythology also appears at the head of a system of general economy which transcends literary rhetoric to meet with social and political systems of representation.

Rather than dismiss Bataille's efforts as rife with insurmountable contradictions devoid of scientific value, or resolve them at the level of "a mythological, scriptural potlatch,"[44] it is possible to consider how this imagery forges an anthropology of human behavior.

The trajectory of Bataille's sun can be traced to the "Dossier de l'oeil pinéal" (II, 13–47), a short, posthumously published text contemporaneous with the *Eye*. Bataille details in it a dream version of the incidents related in "Coincidences," thus providing the raw material from which the egg/eye association was to evolve. The dream evokes a disturbing confusion of sentiments, "a sort of ambivalence between the most horrible and the most magnificent. A blinding souvenir like the sun seen through closed eyes, all in red . . . a bloody genital like the sun. My father slaps me and I see the sun" (II, 10). The young Bataille returns to the scene where the original incident impressed upon him the egg/eye rapprochement. He has repressed the traumatic event and, unable to confront it, he is "blinded" as one is blinded by the sun when one tries to gaze at it too long. What he sees is his father urinating: the genitals are red and bloody like the sun, which from that moment on will be described in adjectives of fluidity or liquidness, such as urinating or sweating. Suddenly his father slaps him and he "sees" the sun, marking the moment at which it becomes the metaphor for both the blind father and the son's new understanding of the father/sun association.

The information gleaned from the *Eye* and "Coincidences" alone would validate a psychoanalytic evaluation: the dominant central figure of the father in both dreams has been virtually expunged from the *Eye* as well as other fictional narratives, and his absence frees the protagonists. The only sexual limitations are internalized and stem from the "horror" elicited by extreme desires. But to explain the repression of the father as part of the personal history of Bataille's psyche is to avoid the question to which he himself incessantly returns: Why is it that no one can bear to look at the sun? The *Eye* provides an obscene Bataillian cosmology that contrasts with the mutilated perception of the universe of "decent people."

> I stretched out on the grass, my skull on a large flat rock and my eyes staring straight up at the Milky Way, that strange breach of astral sperm and heavenly urine across the cranial vault formed by the ring of constellations: that open crack at the summit of the sky, apparently made of ammoniacal vapors shining in the immensity (in empty space, where they burst forth absurdly like a rooster's crow in total silence), a broken egg, a broken eye, or my own dazzled skull weighing down the rock, bounding symmetrical images back to infinity . . . . To others, the universe seems decent because decent people have gelded eyes. That is why they fear lewdness . . . . In general, people savor the "pleasures of the flesh" only on condition that they be insipid. [*Eye*, 56–57]

This sexually defined sun represents a possibility encountered as people witness a radiant energy and intensity that is not, however, immune from a disturbing tension between sacrifice and death. As the metaphor for dépense it progressively encompasses the association of death and eroticism in the anal image of the sun. This is dépense as waste or excrement, and the figure of the pineal eye is presented in all its ridiculous, grotesque, even comic (not to say cosmic) contradictions. The dossier of the pineal eye recapitulates the production of this particular image, locating it physically at the summit of the skull, comparable in its absurdity to a "horrible volcano in eruption" (II, 19). Bataille then confirms the association in his mind between the eye and the sun. That the figure (of the pineal eye) should appear absurd is not surprising, but for Bataille it indicates a fantasy fulfilled. After so many years of servility to the higher demands of reason and logic, the possibility of an alternative expression of energy not exclusively concentrated in the head and possessing some of the "violence and disturbing effects of the anal area" (II, 19) thereby vindicates his extravagant imaginings. Yet even these exorbitant claims are tinged with irony and a confused sense of awareness seeking its own elucidation.

Bataille's "necessity to break, in one way or another, with the limits of our human experience (II, 15) implies a cosmology that opposes the erect position of *homo sapiens* to the horizontal position of animals. The verticality of humans has diverted them from the lower forms of existence, understood as all that is by convention inferior, material, and subject to the controlling powers of the mind. As a good example of Bataille's subversive talent at play, the pineal eye is an obvious pun on *pine,* a slang word for "penis," allegedly used by his father in "Coincidences."

A simple description, however, of the grotesque dimension of the pineal eye and anal sun trivializes their intended impact by imposing a gratuitous shock value. For Bataille is equally sensitive to the historical dimension of horror and evolves an extended argument for its recognition throughout *Documents* (I, 159-274), a collection of early essays whose common denominator is their anti-Hegelianism. The argument of *soleil pourri* (literally, "rotten sun") serves as the prototype for all the others. It reveals Bataille's criticism of the dialectic that limits the radical attempt of negativity to transgress language and the conventional imagery of loss and destruction.

The *soleil pourri* is the image of dépense with the added dimension of waste, or *déchet,* a rotten sun that tells us we can no longer afford to ignore the material reality of existence. The sun of "high noon," the elevated, abstract, and emasculated sun of philosophy, is dethroned for a rotten sun symbolizing all that has been rejected by reason as irrational and censored from consciousness as lewd, obscene, vulgar, and repulsive. The second can be explained only in light (or more accurately, shadow) of the first, the "beautiful" one that has "poetically the significance of mathematical serenity and of an elevated spirit/mind" (I, 231). This sun, however, is never observed. And if, contrary to all good reason, one should fix it with a determined stare, then *production* of light and energy will no longer appear, "but the waste, excrescence, that is, combustion, well expressed psychologically by the horror emitted from an incandescent lamp. Practically, the fixed sun is identified with a mental ejaculation, with the foam of lips and an epileptic fit" (I, 231).

Neither can the first, "philosophic" sun be seen, however, for when rational understanding yields to the qualitatively different order than that of idealism or dialectical philosophy, to the urge for dépense, this same sun appears ugly. Mythologically, the scrutinized sun is identified with a man slitting the throat of a bull (Mithra), with a vulture devouring the liver of Prometheus, and the person who looks is identified with the slaughtered bull or the devoured liver. The ritual association of the Mithraic cult of the sun engaged in a spectacle of sacrifice corroborates Bataille's own associations. Naked humans were placed in a pit covered with wooden slats on top of which a priest sacrificed a bull, spraying those below with a shower of blood "accompanied by a bellicose roaring from the bull: a simple means for appropriating the moral benefits of a blinding sun" (I, 232). Thus, all that is most elevated "is practically confounded with a sudden fall of inconceivable violence" (I, 232). Similarly, in the myth of Icarus the first sun illuminates his ascension; the other melts his wax, "thus determining his defection and clamorous fall" (I, 232).

The ideological trap of the Hegelian dialectic is convincingly demonstrated in another *Documents* essay, "La Figure humaine" (I, 181–85). Bataille places himself in the position of an ethnographer contemplating a curious group photograph lifted from a provincial marriage album dating from a chronologically recent, but psychologically remote, past. The ludicrous distortions imposed on the human body, the comic seriousness painted on the subjects' faces, comprise the starting point for his reflections on the eternal constants and historical variants of "human nature." For amateur anthropologists who would be prone to reject their ancestors as historical aberrations, some implicit model of humans must permit them to pass such judgment. They must invoke a "natural" human form recognizable only when liberated from Victorian corsets and plastroned-front shirts. They are the children convinced that their ancestors have been totally superseded, banished to the wooden trunk in the attic. They argue for an eternal, higher order of nature which has nothing in common with this absurd deviation that evokes only a derisory grimace. But the other anthropologists admit that the bizarre figures have not ceased to haunt them entirely, that the excesses of the past continue to inform the sensibility of the present. The negation of human nature as a fixed set of characteristics implies two "absent forms of relationships" (I, 182). The first is the absence of a "common measure" among diverse human entities, which in part reflects a more general lack of proportion between humans and nature. Such a disproportion can be understood only within *concrete* terms. Bataille offers as his example the Dadaist paradox that the "absence of relation constitutes a relation" (I, 183). Were this true, Bataille argues, "each apparent contradiction [would become] logically deducible, in such a way that reason would no longer have anything shocking to conceive. Disproportions would only be the expression of a logical being who, in his becoming, proceeds through contradiction" (I, 183). The alternative to Hegel's dialectic is the scientific concept of *improbability*. Hegel slights such apparitions as "imperfections of nature" (I, 184), whereas the contrary operation in the universe of the improbable would reduce the apparition of the self to that of the fly on an orator's nose. But why pursue the search into an improbable past? Because the same madness and exaggeration could unpredictably surface within our own contemporary scene as the phantoms of our psychic "prehistory." Nor is it inconceivable that we can still be moved and shocked by the ghosts that pursued our grandfathers. With its elaborate series of pineal, anal, and ocular associations, the sun imagery that first appears as the personal repertoire of phantasmatic obsessions is indeed a metaphorical cluster serving as a barometer of modern sensibility.

In the documents of the pineal eye Bataille rails against the inadequacies of so-called scientific anthropology. By definition, it is a discipline bound to the "degrading logic" (II, 22) and ethnocentric categories of a society dedicated to *productive* expenditure. Mythological anthropology, on the other hand, investigates alternative domains of experience and understanding, such as those metaphorically described by the pineal eye. The latter is not "a product of understanding, but of immediate existence: it opens and shuts like a consumation or fever that devours the being or more precisely, the head" (II, 25). Bataille's "other" anthropology would conjure modern equivalents of ancient myths or phantasms which, like the Icarus parable, encompass not only binary oppositions but the paradoxical elements of dépense as well.

At the very moment Bataille's project appears most self-defeating, when it tries to accommodate the unrepresentable violence of his phantasms to the partial illuminations of science, the sun of *La Part maudite* emerges. There Bataille has consciously stripped from his exposition the outrageous fantasies of earlier works, allowing him to leap from the relatively stable terrain of archaic organizations to the unsettled surface of modern "hot" societies. The central argument still hinges, however, on sacrifice. Considerable weight rests on evidence of Aztec rituals, where sacrifice was represented through the sun symbol. Yet he concedes that even the sun as a source of unlimited light and energy can be subordinated to the restricted notion of a deity: "For the popular consciousness, the sun is the image of glory. Light for the naive man is the symbol of divine existence. It possesses splendor and brilliance that are of no utility, but imparts a sense of deliverance" (VII, 189). Thus, it is not surprising that the superb sacrifices documented among the Aztecs are tainted with anthropomorphism: the sun was believed to be a human deity who immolated himself by jumping into flames. Bataille is aware that this is the traditional interpretation of the sun-god imparted to students of Incan culture: sacrifice to the gods is extracted by the deities in exchange for a benevolent disposition toward their subjects. The caloric sun can be traced to a philosophical tradition as well as to the social reality of the bourgeoisie. It is affiliated with reason, logos and economic rationality. As a conventionalized image it is ensconced in the rhetoric of Western culture, which asserts its identity by denying the "other," rotten sun whose heterogeneous rays continue to flicker in its shadow. The Aztec sun is not completely dead, nor has the universe burnt its brightest star. Merely eclipsed by the so-called intelligible light of reason and understanding, the sun of Bataille, Van Gogh, and Nietzsche flashes its sensuous brightness for those who dare to look. And among those who do there persists a "nostalgia for a life that ceases to be separated from that which is behind the world" (VII, 395).

The nostalgia so described is not the aspiration of a privileged few. Bataille's description is notable for its absence of any ultimate presence beyond the immediate perception of the universe. The conventional interplay of light and darkness, surface and depth, implying such a final being is significantly abandoned for the disturbing ambivalence of the sun of the general economy. Nontranscendent, nondominating, the light of Bataille's sun is not aimed above those who attempt to perceive it, but within, illuminating sensations robbed of alternative means of expression.

If one were to ascribe me a place within the history of thought, it would be, I believe, for having discerned the effects, within our lives, of the moments at which discursive reality disappears, and for having drawn from the description of these effects a disappearing light: this light may be blinding, but it also announces the opacity of the night; it announces only the night. [V, 231]

The sequence of episodes in the *Story of the Eye* recapitulates the movement from one flashing epiphany to another, progressively shrouded by the night of *non-savoir*. The sun connotes dépense with its classical complement, the eye. Both figure as representatives of reason, knowledge, consciousness, and conscience, but this Platonic cluster is completed, or more accurately transgressed, by the appearance of a third term—the egg. At the origin of life, and therefore a female as well as male symbol, the egg acquires an obscene force through the "games" of the protagonists.

From the first erotic episode, the absence of verbal communication is striking. Yet the narrator is not immune to the temptation to ascribe meaning to the play with eggs initiated by Simone, and questions her by means of free association.

Upon my asking what the word *urinate* reminded her of, she replied: *terminate,* the eyes, with a razor, something red, and the sun. And egg? A calf's eye, because of the color of the calf's head and also because the white of the egg was the white of the eye, and the yolk the eyeball. The eye, she said, was egg-shaped. She asked me to promise that when we could go out doors, I would fling eggs into the sunny air and break them with shots from my gun, and when I replied that it was out of the question, she talked on and on, trying to reason me into it. She played gaily with words, speaking about broken eggs, and then broken eyes. [*Eye,* 45]

Shortly thereafter, the narrator firmly states that he and Simone abstained from further attempts to impose on their erotic diversions any particular significance, although the inevitable question they posed formed a secret, unstated link.

At any rate, it will be shown by the end of this tale, that this interrogation was not to remain without an answer indefinitely, and above all, that this unexpected answer is necessary for measuring the immensity of the void that yawned before us, without our knowledge, during our singular entertainments with the eggs. [*Eye,* 47]

The narrative of the *Eye* never achieves closure and can be more accurately described as suspended, once the inner compulsion directing it has been exhausted. It is therefore erroneous to equate the murder of a young priest in the last episode with the ultimate meaning of the text. Even this clichéd version of Bataille's rapprochement between eroticism and death, however, is redeemed by its connection with the subterranean interplay between eggs and eyes: "Thus death, in the midst of the coherent order of things, is an effort that upsets this order, and that through a sort of negative miracle, escapes this coherence. Death destroys, it reduces the individual to NOTHING . . . he who thought himself inserted within the order of things discovers that order within himself" (VIII, 264).

The distinction between order and disorder clarifies the juxtaposition of *two* suns. One, the elevated representative of philosophy, reason and logic, symbolizes the good, true, and beautiful. It is the ideal sun of the father and source of the spoken word. The other is the material, base, sexual, sweating, urinating, anal, pineal sun of dépense and disorder. It provides understanding of a qualitatively different order opposed to the castrated knowledge of those who fear to laugh in the face of the first. The two suns meet, collide with and rebound off each other, playing in one another's shadow. Their mutual presence and uncomfortable cohabitation is necessary within the transgressive universe in which they orbit. And the moral of the story is that neither sun will permanently displace the other.

If it is possible to read the "meaning" of the *Story of the Eye* primarily through the syntactic interplay of its signifiers, it is nonetheless pertinent to question why Bataille refused to ascribe to each an identifiable signified, rejecting all other discursive forms of language as inadequate to transgression. In the presence of the sacred, a zone of silence is created by the tension between a taboo and its transgression. Unlike Sade, who chose to demonstrate this phenomenon through an alternating pattern of sex and philosophical disquisitions, Bataille reveals a somewhat more complex process at work in the *Eye*. When the play with eggs begins, signaling the transgression of sexuality, language breaks down at the edge of the void opened to the protagonists. In the place of discourse arises communication produced by the mutual awareness of having attained the fearful limit separating life from death.

As Foucault stresses, the war on language waged in Bataille's text cannot be equated with a more pervasive musing on the "difficulty with words," since this position is determined by the anthropological limits of language itself.[45] Language cannot be divorced from the play of taboo and transgression. Thus philosophy, to redeem its position among those disciplines that study humanity, must abandon the limitations of language and the realm of discursive reality. Philosophy, as the staid speaker of the possible, must now study human problems from an explicitly historical point of view. It must question the origin of negation and interdictions and, most notably, the taboo that defines humanity in terms of work. The error of the modern world, with its progressive diminution of the sacred (though not institutional religion), has been to dismiss transgressions and taboos as anachronistic and imposed from without, a manifestation of the "neurotic" negation that ties us to death and destruction.[46] On the side of transgression, Bataille explains:

> To give to philosophy transgression as its foundation (this is the intention of my thought) is to substitute for language a contemplative silence. This is contemplation at the height of being. Language has not disappeared: Would the summit have been accessible if language had not revealed the way to it? But the language that described it no longer has meaning at the decisive instant when transgression substitutes itself for the discursive exposé of transgression, but a supreme moment is added to this successive apparition: in this moment of profound silence—in this moment of death—is revealed the unity of being, in the intensity of experiences where truth is divorced from life and its objects. [*L'Erotisme,* 303]

Having exhausted his linguistic analysis, Barthes wondered if what was needed to understand the *Story of the Eye* was not in fact a *"psychologie profonde."* [47] Similarly, at the conclusion of a critique of *L'Expérience intérieure* Sartre submits that a radically altered psychoanalysis is overdue if critics are to contend with Bataille's imponderable text. The reading offered here is psychoanalytic only in a broad anthropological sense, by proposing that Bataille's text serves to probe symptomatically the obsessions of a society through an individual's confrontation with the "impossible." In this anguished struggle to slip from the profane to the sacred, from tranquility to violence, from respect to horror—in this willed determination to sovereignty—Bataille reveals in our most private disorders the force of order.

CHAPTER

4

TRANSGRESSION

After locating sovereignty—the supreme instant of dépense—within transgression, Bataille had to justify using an anthropological notion tied to the conservative power of law. Although obedience to the incest taboo creates the structure for the gift-exchange of women, this deprivation is compensated by the privileges of transgression reserved for men.[1] Moreover, violation of the taboo is often equated with regression, a temporary atavism to the animal state. Certainly the most alien dimension of transgression is its religious affiliation. In the universe organized by the antithesis of sacred and profane, work, prohibitions, kinship rules, and marriage bonds are set against war, ritual sacrifice, sexual license, and religious prostitution. Parallel to this social structure is the economic division, alternating work with festivals of expenditure. The latter include the transgressive celebrations sanctioned by religion: "For if dilapidation is the basis for the festival, the festival is the culminating point of religious activity" (*L'Erotisme,* 76).

But Bataille does not see the slash separating taboo and transgression as a formal boundary, nor as a mechanical mediator harmonizing the antithetical demands placed on culture within cyclical alternations. Nor is it to be compared to all the other dividing lines between the dualities that structure Western logic and experience. Rather, it signals a challenge: to awaken individuals to a conscious appreciation of being through their accession to a sacred domain.

Sovereignty is a category animated by the laws of a general economy, asserting a transgression, not a simple inversion of the restricted economy. This implies a moral imperative dedicated to understanding the distinctions between good and evil and their eventual transcendence. The insistence of the sacred/profane opposition in modern culture questions their correlative economic value judgments: dépense is bad and work is good. To restore to the general economy its own force, therefore, requires an examination of the history of all dualisms.

Bataille's review-essay of Simone Pètrement's study of dualisms in history repeats her central thesis: beyond the varieties of religious and philosophical dualisms, one discerns the decisive moment when reflection posits "divine transcendence." Dualism "at its highest level" marks this point and inspires descriptions of "total transformations, sudden insights, and evasions so profound that one must call them ecstasies." The quality of this description is primarily derived from Platonism, founded on the separation between the sensible ("objective matter and subjective ignorance") and the intelligible spheres. The division in and of itself does not necessarily correspond to the opposition between good and evil. Nor does evil emanate from the sensible passions except when they "chain" reason and subordinate it to their own ends. Bataille quotes Pètrement: " 'Evil is when reason thinks according to passions, and not itself; good is the deliverance of reason, of light, and the reestablishment of an order where knowledge dominates ignorance.' "[2]

From this "external" dualism, in which one of the two principles exists beyond this world, evolves an "interior" version in which both orders are found within the realm of the sensible. The stages leading to the equation of light with good and darkness with evil are summed up by Pètrement.

> The dualism of the visible and the invisible, of the real and the sensible, of the divine and the human, of the eternal and the temporal, of the nether world and this one, leads to those of the soul and the body; spirit and matter; and this last opposition imposes a principle of understanding and one of ignorance, which can be named Light and Darkness. It is easy to appreciate how, after having explained evil by the confusion and disorder of these two principles, and good by order, little by little one slips from this theory to a much simpler one, which makes good the product of light alone, and evil that of darkness.[3]

The origin of the movement that initiated dualisms is traced to the quest for transcendence. A radical alterity between two orders is first posited, and the distance separating them is described as " 'an absolute rupture; a total absence of connection; an impossible, incomprehensible passage.' "[4] In Bataille's estimation, the search for the other domain is provoked by a "disturbance." The derived dualism (interior to the world of principles) facilitates the movement that dulls the awakening and slides toward Aristotelian monism: "Spinoza and Leibniz, after Descartes, Fichte, Shelling, and Hegel after Kant, like Aristotle after Plato, establish a correlation between opposing principles, renounce the scandal of absolute separation, and of the skeptical, subjective position concerned with total conversion, reversal, salvation of the dualist philosophy."[5] Because Bataille sees the sacred as equivalent to the divine, he argues that Pètrement's history is inadequate unless completed by the sacred/profane dualism that subtends all religions. He grants that indeed it may be difficult to relate the idea of the sacred in archaic cults to that of transcendence since it does not fall within the intelligible.

The "paradox" of the sacred surfaces in the attempt to understand the doctrine of the "attention éveillée" historically. Independent of intellectual forms, the divine is sensible, and therefore *immanent;* transcendence (the intelligible sphere) is found within the *profane.* In this way, the classical form of the religious dualism is the inversion of its primitive form.

To stress the nature of the reversal, Bataille characterizes the archaic sacred as follows: "Primarily, it is *tout autre,* but essentially, it is communion and communication of unleashed, dangerous, contagious forces, from which it is necessary to protect the realm of the useful, reasonable operations of life." Because the modern routine is guided by precisely these utilitarian criteria, "life" itself appears as a sacred force, irreducible to the "things" of the profane: "Not life reduced to practical activity, but life as play *[jeu],* when it has no other meaning than itself, or no meaning at all at the apex of the awakening."[6]

The categories of the sacred and the profane are clear and trenchant; only the reversal, which substitutes the divine for the transcendent and the profane for the immanent, has led to confusion. A further complication arises with the polarization of the sacred itself into a "transcendent, celestial, and pure sacred opposed to a diabolical, terrestrial and impure one."[7] The equivalent division within the profane separates the idea (reason) from matter and aligns the rational idea to the transcendence of the sacred, and diabolical impurity to matter. The motive force of the "instant of awakening," insofar as it remains possible within Platonic dualism, is stilled in Aristotelian monism. Durkheim formulated this internal duality well, without drawing out its consequences. It remained for Bataille to investigate its impact on contemporary moral categories.

Yet Bataille envisions an "instant" beyond the transcendence of Platonism, in which the awakening is determined by the will to open the eyes, and truth is apprehended within a "luminosity without enlightenment." Such a moment would be guided by divine passion, not reason, and in this sense would recapitulate the founding moment of awakening where "nascent reason" was indistinguishable from "the unreachable horror of the sacred."[8] This truth, Bataille realizes, demands no less than the sort of reversal effected by Platonism. In the final analysis, it entails the development of a moral position that could effectively counter the dominant economic rationale hostile to any sovereign principle: "a *sacred* value escapes moral justification, and allows itself the pure, unfettered freedom and ruinous innocence of poetry."[9]

Thus the transgressions carried out in the name of the general economy engage the sovereign forces of heterogeneous dépense irreducible to utilitarian ends. Yet sovereignty does not merely invert the priorities of the existing order: that was the error of the surrealists. The sun of *La Part maudite* and *Histoire de l'oeil* glorifies expenditure as the paramount happiness, though the joy of consuming without return is undoubtedly fused with the anguish of loss. This profound ambivalence was once celebrated in the festivities of ancient religions without their respective principles being confused and must be revitalized in modern symbolism.

The "impossible" that haunts Bataille is a conscious representation of sovereign needs: ceremonial infractions of taboos have virtually disappeared, and the sacred is discredited by the ideologies that minimize its difference from the profane. A neutralizing discourse can thus promote the "good," "natural," "healthy," "animallike" pleasures of sexuality purged of sacred violence. Pornography fantasizes the perversion of sovereign disinterest through dominance and subjugation. In this sense, the "normal" person must condemn Sade, whose unleashing of the sovereign forces of destruction is modeled on the privileges of the class he claims to repudiate. By sundering the bonds of loyalty toward those subjects who grant him recognition, Sade annuls the dialectic and becomes the victim of his own sovereignty through self-negation. The systematic denial of the other is the outcome of a pathological attitude that has lost a sense of its own violence. Admiration for Sade must be qualified: to do otherwise, as Bataille reproaches the surrealists, is to underestimate the seriousness of his rage. The didactic value of Sade's writings lies not in their disquisitions, but in the compensations it offers for the improverishment of sovereignty in scientific studies. It also serves as a corrective to the belief that violence can be thoroughly eliminated. Finally, the reader understands that the potential for Sadism resides, and must be recognized, in everyone. Only then can the sovereign need for the expression of excess be satisfied within appropriate limits.

Sovereignty contests the primacy placed on a life defined by reason, utility, and order. Special attention is therefore given to those religious practices and philosophical systems that acknowledge death as a force of life rather than its tragic demise. A recurrent theme in the study of eroticism is the universal taboo surrounding death, with considerable emphasis placed on the horror elicited by the putrefying body. The characteristic reaction to the decaying corpse is violence, held in check by interdiction; this maintains a permeable barrier between homogeneity and the transgressive menace of heterogeneous forces. Since the parameters of society's taboos are congruent with boundaries imposed on the human body, religion and philosophy inevitably make some reference to bodily pollutions; thus the most comprehensive and coherent systems are those that manage to affirm what is generally denied. Bataille, for instance, rejects Hegel's monism, which declares that "everything actual is rational, that evil as an element dialectically required must be pinned in, and kept and consecrated and have a function awarded to it in the final system of truth."[10] Hegel, and Kant before him, recognized the classical antinomies and their hierarchical structure, but treated them in a static, mechanical fashion (see I, 97). At best, Hegel sought to incorporate the lower elements into this realization—a dialectic aimed not at unity but at the *identité des contraires*.[11] The materialism of the general economy tries to avoid this implied conciliation by transgressing the binary oppositions.

The assertion of a materialist doctrine marks Bataille's strongest challenge to the Hegelian element lingering in his work. Hegel is the ubiquitous presence, the straw man at whom the vitriolic attacks on an abstract God or nondialectical materialism are directed. He replaced them with a heterology/materialism possessing its own laws antithetical to those of classical philosophy or modern science. The caveat reiterated in the early writings on materialism is to avoid subordination to authority. Greater consideration must be shifted to that which is *bas* ("low") and to the recognition of its profound attractions, as evidenced in the Gnostic doctrine:[12] "It was a question of confounding the human spirit and idealism with something *base*, to the extent that one recognized that the superior principles were irrelevant" (I, 225).

Heterology reveals the disruptive consequences for a society that persists in the delusion that it has irrevocably disposed of heterogeneous detritus and waste. Their resurgence at the heart of a social order is most evident at the moment of death. To the shame and silence that enshrouds the dead body in contemporary society Bataille opposes the attitudes of primitive religions where, as Mary Douglas corroborates, the critical factor in the transgressive experience is that the confrontation with death be willed.

> Punishments, moral pressures, rules about not touching and not eating, a firm ritual framework, all these can do something to bring man into harmony with the rest of being. But so long as free consent is withheld, so long is the fulfillment imperfect. . . . When someone embraces freely the symbol of death, or death itself, then it is consistent with everything that we have seen so far, that a great release of power for good should be expected to follow.[13]

The impulse toward death is dramatized in transgression through sacrifice. Bataille's immediate anthropological reference is the well-known treatise by Hubert and Mauss, who regard ritualized murder as a form of exorcism aimed at eliminating the potential threat of violence.[14] The scapegoat serves as the instrument of the purge; the sacrificial victim mediates between the sacred and the profane, with the rite itself providing the means for all spectators to enter the orbit of the deity. They remain steadfast, however, in their functional evaluation of sacrifice, viewing it as a remuneration to the gods who participate in a global accounting system of exchanges between debtor and debtee. The only gratuitous, disinterested sacrifice is one that brings about the death of a god; otherwise, ritualized murder is justified by its stabilizing benefits to the social community. Similarly, Bataille points out, the Greek tragic hero was pitted against law, social traditions, and elementary religious taboos such as murder and incest: the very underpinnings of the entire moral and social order. The purpose of ritual transgressions was, however, fundamentally conservative, serving to reaffirm the inherent value of laws from which society derives its foundation, structure, and organization. The vagaries of primitive deities can be viewed as so many tests of their subjects, and Greek tragedy as an essential device in perpetrating the cathartic terror evoked by the transgressions of the deviant protagonist. Only with the advent of Christianity was an effort made to lift God out of the sphere of violence and arbitrary provocations. Christ's actions were rationalized into a higher scheme, initiating an uneasy compromise between faith and reason: "In Christianity there exists an equivocation between God and reason which nourishes a malaise, whence the effort of Jansenism in the opposite direction" (IX, 181).

The transgressive connotations of evil for Bataille are now more accurately discernible. In the Christian concept, sin is a passive acquiesence to temptation which distances the faithful follower and his perfect God; here, evil is a willed exploration beyond acceptable limits. If writers are characterized as guilty, it is because they alone, through the vehicle of literature, have sought to confront sovereignty. The irony of Bataille's contribution to literary modernism is that his pornographic narratives took up a controversy long abandoned by philosophy and religion.

The historical demise of socially sanctioned, collective forms of transgression shifted the arena in which such transgressive acts could be played out to literature. The first generation of postrevolutionary romantics recognized the correlation between values fostered by competitive capitalism and the exploitation of the environment. Yet the apotheosis of nature which devolved from this awareness is, for Bataille, symptomatic of a general romantic retreat away from more pointedly political critiques. He rebukes romanticism for having

limited itself to an exaltation of the past naively opposed to the present. It was only a compromise: the values of the past were conjugated from utilitarian principles. The theme of nature is often only a provisional evasion, since the love of nature is also susceptible to an accord with the primacy of utility. It has been the mode of compensation most encouraged by—and the most innocuous—utilitarian societies: obviously there is nothing less subversive and threatening, less savage, than the wildness of rocks. [IX, 206]

Bataille's stated enthusiasm for *Wuthering Heights* as the fulfillment of a certain romantic freedom is not expressed as the triumph of nature over social conventions. Rather, Brontë's rebellion is considered a crime, a transgression against a source—less evident but presumed equally potent—of moral and social cohesion: the law of reason. The error of Christianity (like the misunderstanding of anthropology) was to expel the Dionysian element of primitive religion and break with the traditions of ritualized sacrifice. Contact with the sacrificial animal, the exposure of its mutilated entrails, and the effusion of spilled blood aroused a contagion of emotion in a festive atmosphere which ultimately united the community more effectively than the rationalizations forwarded by Hubert and Mauss. The histrionic dimension of the ritual, its violence and cruelty, contributed to what Henri Lefebvre terms its style—diluted beyond recognition by the homogeneity of contemporary life.[15]

The historical sequence of events just outlined subsequently placed literature in a position of preeminence among other cultural forms, ·providing space from which to perform a role tantamount to transgression without undermining the necessity for the social contract.

> Only literature could expose the game of the transgression of the law, without which the law would have no meaning independent of an order to be created. Literature cannot assume the task of ordering collective necessity. . . . Literature, in fact, like transgression of the moral order, is dangerous. [IX, 182]

The success of the challenge of conventional boundaries and the communication induced by transgression for individuals whose ethical values are most sure enables Bataille to forward his controversial theory of resemblance between mysticism and eroticism. Based on his observation of the shared participation of the mystical and the erotic he posits an "inadmissible" communication and linkage among all passions.

> We cannot deny the fundamental unity of all movements whereby we escape the calculations of interest, in which we experience the intensity of the present moment. Mysticism escapes the spontaneity of childhood . . . but it borrows the expression of trances from the vocabulary of love, and from contemplation liberated from discursive reflection, the simplicity of a child's laughter. [IX, 184]

Between the mystical and the erotic there exist no walls, he continues; they use the same words, exploit similar images, yet continue to ignore each other. Bataille laughs: "How comic" (VI, 50). Death is the obvious common denominator, but to bind both eroticism and mysticism to this single force distorts the significance of their energy which strains beyond limits. The mystic most effectively reveals the temptation to gravitate toward extremes.

These trances, these raptures and these theopathic states described by the mystics . . . all have the same meaning: it is always a search for *detachment* vis-à-vis the maintenance of life; *indifference* to all that tends to reassure; *anguish* experienced in these conditions; *opening* to the immediate moment of life that is generally stifled, which is suddenly liberated in the overflow of infinite joy. [*L'Erotisme*, 269]

Another facet shared by eroticism and mysticism commands Bataille's attention. Both are institutional deviants defying the conventions of acceptability, which condone sexuality in the name of reproduction and access to divinity by way of dogma. Although mysticism must be regarded as the epitome of values fostered by Christianity, it poses a tacit challenge to the authority of traditional theology. At the very least, the lavish poetry of the most renowned saints undoubtedly inspires discomfort among the clergy. But whereas the voice of the mystic ultimately can expect to be heard, arousing esteem, however cautious, the nondiscursive violence of eroticism remains silent.

Yet Bataille's study of eroticism cannot be reduced to a tract espousing the cause of eroticism to a world marketing sexuality but embarrassed by saintly fervor. Nor does he aspire to a strictly anthropological approach as did Caillois, who later apologized for having introduced metaphysical considerations into his own study of taboo and transgression.[16] The historical perspective on the sacred in *L'Erotisme,* serves as an objective constant, structuring reflections from an "internal," but not necessarily personal, point of view. The eclipse of collective transgressions and the gradual internalization of the sacred sensibility contribute to the individual's heightened sense of disconnectedness. The divorce from both nature and others poses the seemingly insurmountable gaps characteristic of a modern condition of discontinuity: "We are discontinuous beings, individuals dying isolated, lost in an unintelligible adventure, but we also have a *nostalgia for lost continuity*. . . . At the same time that we are possessed by the anguished desire for the duration of the perishable self, we are obsessed by a primary continuity, which generally links us to being" (*L'Erotisme*, 20, emphasis added). Solitude, isolation, and despair are momentarily overcome within ecstatic instants of continuity labeled sacred in primitive cultures, divine in our own, and which Bataille himself subsumes under the nonmystical, atheological category of the expérience intérieure. Having searched for a *vue d'ensemble* among disparate intimations of the sacred in a profane world, Bataille first encountered God, the "obsessive" figure of the religious conversion of his youth. Childhood memories and adolescent visions fill the original well of internal experiences from which later nostalgias are drawn. Bataille remains convinced of their unity, an "incomprehensible cohesiveness" that brings together erotic élans and mystical transports.

In the sacred rituals of the primitive, the continuity of being was unveiled to those willing to face the death of their discontinuous selves.

> There exists a domain where death no longer simply means *disappearance,* but the intolerable movement where we disappear *in spite of ourselves;* whereas, at all costs, one should not. It is precisely this *at all costs* which distinguishes the moments of extreme joy and the unnamable but marvelous ecstasy. If there is nothing that transcends us, in spite of ourselves . . . we cannot attain the senseless moment we alternately struggle to reach with all our force and resist with all our might. [III, 11]

Pleasure is despicable without this "terrifying transcendence" (III, 11), not unlike that encountered by Christian mystics.

Bataille's declarations raise several interrelated questions, the first of which is elicited by his insistence on the movement beyond oneself found in the introduction to *Madame Edwarda* (III, 9–14). A footnote by the author to the volume in which it appears, along with other narratives and poetry, tells us that *Edwarda* is contemporaneous with "Le Supplice" (1941), which itself forms the second part of *L'Expérience intérieure.* The two texts are solidary—the first a bravura piece of metaphysical erotica and the appropriately scandalous companion to the philosophical treatise destined to curb its obscene contagion. The author is convinced he would have been unable to write "Le Supplice" without having first provided its "lubric key" (III,491). Much of *L'Expérience intérieure* is indeed divided between aborted attempts to explain the expérience itself and Bataille's outraged refusals at having to do so. With the lucid acknowledgement that "even the search for ecstasy cannot escape a method" (VI, 297), Bataille is convinced of the futility of awaiting spontaneous revelations and manifestly proud of the struggle entailed in his deliberate probes into the unknown: "To go to the end of man, it is necessary, *at a certain point,* to no longer submit, but to force one's destiny" (V,53). Thus the effort to reproduce for readers a method of meditation, to provide prescriptive exercises à la Loyola which would facilitate the way to the expérience, accompanies fulminations against "poetic nonchalance, the passive attitude and literary *déchéance"* (V, 53). The question that surfaces is why transcendence is automatically equated with mysticism or necessarily leads to some variation on the notion of a deity. Buddhism is offered as an alternative to this Western assumption.

The "truth" of the expérience intérieure is paradoxically discovered in the transgression of the ubiquitous taboos that all societies have devised to mediate contact with death and sexuality. Unfortunately, the capriciousness with which the taboos have been imposed has lent them a "superficial insignificance" (*L'Erotisme,* 42). The interaction between taboo and transgression, however, is not a function of absolutes, where the interdiction erects a permanent dividing line between nature and culture. The description of the *Aufhebung* as philosophical approximation of the anthropological phenomenon insists on the relativity of prohibitions: "It is the human world which, within the negation of animality or the negation of nature (formed by work), negates *itself* and, in this *second negation,* goes beyond itself *without ever returning to that which it originally negated"* (*L'Erotisme,* 94, emphasis added).

The variability of the incest law corroborates the historical perspective. And although obscenity is defined as a "relation," since there are no absolutes governing sexuality, utility becomes a significant factor.

> If utility no longer plays a role, men will eventually neglect obstacles whose arbitrariness has become shocking. On the other hand, the general meaning of the taboo reinforced by dint of its stability and its intrinsic worth became more evident. Each time it is convenient, however, the limit can be extended; thus divorce in the Middle Ages, where theoretical incest, devoid of practical consequences, served as a pretext to the legal dissolution of royal marriages. [*L'Erotisme,* 240]

These reflections on incest and taboo were prompted by Lévi-Strauss's *The Elementary Structures of Kinship,* where the latter's nature/culture distinction was faulted for reifying them into abstractions irrespective of their historical contingencies.

What interests Bataille is not the specific content of the denial, but the device that effectively erects and perpetuates boundaries, so that the complement of the original negation—the negation of the negation, or the forces of dépense—can erupt within the uniquely "human" instant of transgression. Negativity is considered action leading to possession, unlike the sovereign expenditures of sacrifice, laughter, poetry, and ecstasy.

The historical relativity of taboos applies in microcosm to Bataille's personal history, documented in *La Somme athéologique,* where the negation focuses on God as the presumed incarnation of the expérience intérieure. In Bataille's speech, God translates as the absolute dépense: "God means for me the fulguration that raises one above concern for self-preservation—or the desire to accumulate—to preserve riches within time" (*L'Erotisme,* 259). Although God may initially be viewed as the limit-form of dépense, mysticism has not provided the path to sovereignty. The ambiguity of mysticism, common to all inferior exercises of dépense, rests with the desire to experience death, but also with the desire to live—or to die without ceasing to live—the hope for an extreme at which, in the words of Saint Theresa, the subject "meurt de ne pas mourir." In contrast, Bataille alludes to "theopathic states" that have apparently abandoned the reservations of the mystic: "What distinguishes them is the greatest indifference to whatever may occur" (*L'Erotisme,* 272). Theopathic states come closest in their ability to efface the distinction between subject and object, to attain the moment at which a sense of linear, measurable time is effaced: "The object of contemplation having become equal to *rien* [Christians say equal to God], [it] appears equal to the contemplating subject . . . and the instant alone is eternalized" (*L'Erotisme,* 272).

Thus eroticism displaced mysticism as the most consistently sovereign form of dépense, for "eroticism can say what mysticism never could (its strength failed when it tried): God is nothing if not the surpassing of God in every sense *[sens]* of vulgar being, in that of horror or impurity; and ultimately in the sense of nothing" (*L'Erotisme,* 294). The play on the multiple dimensions of *sens* is intentional; the expérience intérieure and the dépense that it necessitates lead to an extinction of meaning, to the "non-sens" of nothingness. Entailing a defiance of limits, the spiral of transgression does not automatically lead upward to challenge the limits of the ontotheological presence. Bataille's transgression moves in all directions *(depassement dans tous les sens),* including a conscious vilification of God's sanctity paralleled by a move toward degradation. Yet, even stripped of theological affiliations, the expérience can avoid external validation by a deity only with great difficulty. God looms on the philosophical horizon of any discourse or experiment in communication as the ineluctable point of reference for dispersed individuals bereft of an alternative source of unity. In the words of Denis Hollier:

> The keystone for the profane world is God: it is He who guarantees the identity of self, who guarantees compensations according to merit and justice, and who guarantees stability of meaning in the ordering of words which is language. Linked to the isolation of individuals separated into discrete selves, He is the Supreme Being, the idea of which enables humans, in spite of their separation and limits, to communicate among themselves.[17]

Transgression supersedes, without totally eliminating, the original negated condition or limit. Nor does the forbidden boundary necessarily resume the same position from which it was temporarily lifted. My insistence on this perhaps unduly literal paraphrase of the process of transgression is prompted by its manifestations in Bataille's work. In particular, I refer to the disturbing persistence of a Christian terminology. The philosopher Jean Hyppolite confronted Bataille with the question of this vocabulary following a lecture on sin.[18] Hyppolite concedes that "written in another language, your work would not produce the same effect." Logically, he continues, Christian concepts could easily have been eliminated, but then again, the object of the expérience is not a "logic": "There is a profoundness in your experience that goes beyond all logical systems." Bataille's reply reveals less a dependence on the cultural structure of the Catholic church (as Klossowski claims[19]) than an effort to transcend the limits of the nonreligious, purely poetic experience and erect a somewhat shaky bridge between two otherwise irreconcilable worlds: "Not a bridge on which one can walk—it is not a matter of passing from one side of the abyss to the other—but a bridge that helps us get closer, and perceive the continuity of an experience that has been followed, that is being followed, and that has been so since the pre-Christian era until Christianity, and since then, in other ways" (VI, 342).

With this statement, Bataille offers a historical perspective on the continuity of the expérience, placing it beyond its immediate "God is dead" predecessors. With claims to forebears including Gnostics as well as Kwakiutls, the expérience intérieure acquires a quasi-universal significance, but its actual presence and expression within any linguistic or cultural system poses specific challenges. In the following sections we will trace the historical vicissitudes of the expérience by examining its impact and reception among major French intellectual figures since Bataille began writing in the early part of this century.

CHAPTER

5

COMMUNICATION

SARTRE READING BATAILLE

In 1943 Sartre opened his review of *L'Expérience intérieure* by lamenting the crisis of the essay and the failures of criticism.[1] Bataille's work challenges both issues by highlighting the inadequacy of classical discourse for the experience of modernity, "for if we really try to express our thoughts of today in the language of the past, what metaphors, what circumlocutions, what imprecise imagery."[2] The break with linear narrative and the conventions of objectivity is evidenced in the tortured syntax and discontinuous fragments of *L'Expérience*. Writing is drama; the text, a stage for the *mise en scène* of self. Sartre discredits the expérience as "inutilisable," yet admires the denuding of the man, "his sumptuous and bitter soul, his neurotic pride, his self-hatred, his eroticism, his often magnificent eloquence masking the incoherence of thought, his impassioned bad faith, his vain quest for an impossible escape."[3]

Sartre situates the essay's originality within a hybrid genre also cultivated by the surrealists in which philosophy is crossed with confession and spawns the *essai-martyr*. Breton's comparable exhibitionism fulfills the wish to destroy all literature by exposing the true monsters lurking behind art's façades. Even more potent than the lure of scandal, the desire for direct access establishes "a sort of carnal promiscuity" between author and reader. Finally, by eschewing the tranquil project of writing for the histrionics of the "risk," these writers endowed their enterprise with "the perilous seriousness of a veritable act; *Les Pensées, Les Confessions, Ecce Homo, Les Pas perdus, L'Amour fou, Le Traité du style, L'Age d'homme;* it is within this series of 'impassioned geometries' that *L'Expérience intérieure* takes its place."[4]

Sartre severs form from content to better appreciate the "feverish, bitter, often mistaken" language of the orator who hates words: the Bataillian text seeks silence.[5] Sartre rightly notes that speaking engages the subject in the temporality of the project where totality is parceled among noun, verb, object, and where the subject experiences the rending sensations of deferment; but "M. Bataille wishes to exist entirely, immediately, instantaneously.[6] The result is a juxtaposition within the same text of "the sentence of intuitive delight condensed within the instant" and the exposition of discourse.[7]

These two modes signal the tensions that generate Bataille's work, but Sartre resists their coexistence. At the very outset of his critique he stresses the futility of answering opposing claims. Bataille may expose himself; yet, "no sooner has he shown us his miserable nudity, than he covers himself, and now we go along with his reasonings about Hegel's system or Descartes's *cogito*. And then reason stops short, and the man reappears."[8] Or, it is one thing for poetry to "sacrifice" words, another for "M. Bataille to give us the *reasons* for it."[9]

The quality of the work is equated with the quality of the author's experience. In Bataille's dramatization of its effects, all roles are played by one subject: actor, playwright, director. He even gives the reader cues when to laugh: "To witness the downfall of tragic natures and *to be able to laugh,* in spite of the profound emotion, sympathy, and comprehension one feels, this is divine" (V, 9, Bataille citing Nietzsche).

In the translation of experience into discourse, Bataille vents contempt for his reader, is reluctant to speak, and recoils from his own voice. This meta-commentary, Sartre argues, recalls the disdainful aggressions of the sur-realists but produces a mode of expression adapted to "the problems of our time." Because Bataille's provocations refuse the judgment of the reader and pre-empt those of the critic, however, his communication is "without reciprocity."[10]

Thus the lauded modernism of this edifying narrative—its mixture of drama and explication—leads to an uncomfortable meeting of subjective and objective understanding. The contradiction inherent in Sartre's assessment, which privileges one side of Bataille's activity while rejecting the other, is never confronted. Nor need it be, given a critical approach that argues for form but dismisses content. How this reading mirrors larger controversies within modern thought, including a collision between phenomenology and the social sciences, will now be considered.

Bataille allegedly disrupts communciation by displacing his irritation from the limitation of words onto his reader. Unable to articulate an expérience intérieure, he proposes explanations that claim a rigorous and scientific foundation. The substance of his vacillations between discourse and silence, according to Sartre, communicate the abiding need for religion in modern society, which must confront the irreconcilable: "God is silence, this I cannot deny—yet, everything in me seeks God and I cannot forget it."[11]

Pascal's legacy, shared by Bataille and all who testify to the absurdity of the human condition, is a historical consciousness that individuals make themselves. In rejecting metaphysics, they acknowledge that the *"déchirure"* is not given but produced. The fundamental contradictions of the absurd may momentarily be suspended in an instant of evanescent unity, but never dialectically overcome. The heroic stance of the expérience is, therefore, to tolerate ambiguity without expecting its resolution.

The tragic vision of modernity found in Bataille, Kierkegaard, and Jaspers is not necessarily sustained through common philosophical categories. Indeed, Bataille is reproached for abandoning the rigors of discourse for the "lived experience" of Heidegger without adhering to the obligations that project implied. But philosophy exacts its revenge: when one tries to seize Bataille's ideas, devoid of sequence or coherent argument, "they melt like snow."[12] Neither a philosopher nor a scientist, the author of *L'Expérience* borrows from both disciplines. His failure is most salient, Sartre claims, in the "scientism" tainting all his major propositions.

A prime example is the theory of the subject introduced through the expérience. Characterized as an *ipséité,* the self is at once autonomous, individual, different—irreducibly unique—but constrained by the collectivity on which it depends for a sense of totality. Bataille pursues two approaches to this dualism. He seeks to know himself through a "method" analogous to that of the *cogito* and through which he discovers his irreplaceable individuality. Suddenly, however, he comes out of himself in order to consider this individuality "with the eyes . . . of the scientist, as if it were a *thing* of this world."[13] Had Bataille restricted himself to internal discoveries, Sartre insists, he would have understood (1) that the givens of science do not partake of the certainty of the *cogito* and must be considered simply *probable;* (2) that within the domain of reality, contradiction is supplanted by the sense that appearance is the absolute reality; (3) that the *déchirure* of the self is, in its being, temporal: "Time in the expérience intérieure is not made of instants."[14]

Sartre's position is unambiguous: the subject cannot leave the domain of the expérience intérieure to examine itself from without. This leads to a serious confrontation with Bataille's definition of the outward movement of the *ipse* as *communication.* The permanent contradiction of the subject is that its identity cannot be limited to a "simple juxtaposition" because, as Sartre concurs, "individuals do not exist first, in order to then communicate, but communication constitutes them in their very being."[15] Moreover, the larger units so constituted produce a mode of understanding that transcends the isolated subject. Sartre cites Bataille: " 'In this way, knowledge appears as an unstable biological link, though no less real than that of the cells of a tissue. The exchange between two people is in fact capable of surviving a momentary separation.' "[16] Bataille underscores the opposing aspects of all organizations whose components are relatively autonomous, but whose whole is greater than the sum of its parts. Sartre does not immediately contest the structuring process; it is the ability of any one *ipse* to apprehend the form of these volatile totalities from without which he denies. Only God, Sartre reminds us, is in such a position.

Bataille's propositions ought to be inverted. Sartre regards the autonomy of the self as the only real certainty, since dependence on the larger configuration is illusory: "For if I am conscious of my dependency, then it becomes the object, and consciousness is independent."[17] Moreover, if this logic is applied to cosmic, and not just human, relations, then subjects must be considered as "things." This is a predictable position for Bataille, given, Sartre notes, his participation "in that strange and famous Collège de sociologie where each member, by means of a burgeoning science, pursued extrascientific activities. *That is where M. Bataille learned to treat man as a thing.*"[18] Sartre's criticism is not limited to the alleged inadequacies of Bataille's *modus operandi,* but extends to the very premises of sociological investigation, since his approach resembles that of "the sociologist who establishes a law by induction, based on the subject's observations of others, and then uses analogical reasoning to place himself under the law he has just established."[19]

Sartre's more immediate target, however, is Bataille's speculations on communication as a collective experience. What Bataille calls communication is what takes place among others, with the subject as only a spectator. Bataille was faced with a similar attack in the polemics of the collège. At issue was the nature of a *sociologie sacrée* actually generated by the "sociologist." Kojève, as Caillois recalls, reproached Bataille for wanting to play the sorcerer's apprentice: "Bataille did little to conceal his intention to recreate a virulent and devastating version of the sacred, whose epidemic contagion would touch and exalt even he who had sown its first seed."[20]

From Sartre's perspective, the position of the sociologist is a paradigm of humanity's dilemma; but what he labels absurd, Bataille considers tragicomic, to which one's only viable response is laughter. *Le rire* is that sovereign experience found at the confluence of collective and individual sensations Bataille names communication: a mode of intimacy leading not simply to approbation but to fusion. Laughter is touted as an alternative to the escapism endemic to Western culture, where the individual's sense of insufficiency is assuaged by activity rather than collective ecstasy. While Sartre invalidates the claims made for laughter, he appreciates the desire it represents for totality condensed within an instant and compares it to "the intuitive instant of Cartesian reason, the ecstatic instant of the mystic, the anguished and eternal instant of Proustian reminiscences."[21] Yet Sartre trivializes the loss of self implied by communication by dating it to the frivolous generation of 1925, whose experimentation with drugs and eroticism played out "a hatred of the project." By extension, he dismisses the notion of dépense.

In this useless and painful sacrifice of self, M. Bataille sees the extreme of
generosity: it is a disinterested gift. And, precisely because it is gratuitous,
it could not be accomplished à froid; it appears as the culmination of a
Bacchic inebriation. Sociology once more provides us with the appropriate images: what we perceive behind the icy exhortations of this solitary
figure is the nostalgia for one of those primitive festivals where an entire
tribe is entranced, laughs and dances and couples off randomly; one of
those festivals that are consumation and consumption, and where each
one, in the frenzy of the amok, in joy, mutilates himself, gaily destroying
a year's worth of patiently amassed riches and where one loses oneself,
tearing apart like a piece of cloth, slowly sacrificing oneself and singing,
without God, without hope, stimulated by wine and cries of rutting in the
extreme of generosity, kills oneself for nothing [pour rien]. Whence the
refusal of asceticism. . . . In order for sacrifice to be complete, it must
entail the consumption of the total man, with his laughter, passions, and
sexual excesses.[22]

The invitation to sacrifice is met with Sartre's challenge, "Is it sincere?
For after all, M. Bataille writes, he occupies a position at the Bibliothèque
Nationale, he reads, he makes love, he eats."[23]

Relentlessly, Sartre insists on defining man as project, "not out of fear
or cowardice, as Bataille accuses, but ontologically so." For if the goal of the
expérience intérieure is to provide access to states of trance and ecstasy, what,
demands Sartre, remains beyond a search that purports to be the antithesis of
a project if such joys "do not enter the path of new enterprises to contribute to
the formation of a new humanity that exceeds itself toward new goals?"[24]

The validation of the expérience relies on the degree of the author's
anguish to which it attests. In this "gratuitous affirmation of the metaphysical
value of suffering"[25] Bataille is Dionysian. Unlike its Nietzschean precedent,
however, the expérience intérieure betrays its commitment to material forces
and seeks transcendence through a "new species of mysticism" equated with
"ek-stase, that is, a move away from oneself [toward] the intuitive pleasure of
the transcendent."[26]

The steps leading Sartre to this accusation retrace Bataille's own search
for the unknown as "a pure hypostasized Nothingness," which, occasionally,
he names "God."[27] Bataille is indicted for being an embarrassed Christian.
"With the words 'nothingness' and 'non-savoir,' which denudes, he has
simply concocted for us a good little pantheistic ecstasy."[28] Not just any
pantheism, but a black one.

Sartre feels that the expérience itself leads Bataille to scientism because
he will not recognize that it alone offers real opposition to pantheism.
Restricted to the cogito, "there is no longer any question of losing oneself . . .
no more night, no more abyss . . . he illuminates and sees only that which he
lights up, and it is he who decides the meaning of things."[29] Durkheim's

sociology is pronounced dead and Bataille is immolated on his altar of
alleged scientism: "unfortunately for our author, social facts are not things,
they have meaning and, as such, they revert to the being from whom these
significations come into the world, to man, who cannot at the same time be
the knowing subject-scientist and the object of science."[30] Sartre imputes
Bataille's despair to the inability of all humans to judge themselves. In this
context, the mystic's experience is not exceptional.

Because this immanence is intolerable for Bataille, Sartre accuses him of
looking toward sociology for a specious transcendence. Here it must be
noted that Sartre's rebukes are generalized; any effort to leave immanence is
considered a move toward transcendence, and all science that persists in
looking at life from without is responsible for the "dissolution of individ-
ualities." Moreover, science betrays the potential revelations of the expérience since it is precisely when the specter of death is perceived that "Bataille
arranges things so that I see myself through the eyes of another." Quoting
Bataille on the *ipse,* Sartre completes its portrait: "What you are is contingent
upon the activity that links the innumerable elements of which you are
composed . . . they are contagions of energy, of movement, of heat, or
transfers of elements which internally constitute the life of your organic
being. Life is never situated on a particular point: it passes rapidly from one to
the next . . . like a sort of electric current."[31]

The similarities with Durkheim's own organic analogies are indeed
striking, and the evolution of his rhetoric indicates that it subsequently
enlisted images derived from thermodynamics and electricity. One study of
Suicide notes the prevalence of this terminology in the genesis and operation
of collective ideas and sentiments: "For each people there was a collective
force of a determinate amount of energy, impelling men to self-destruction
and such forces 'determine our behavior from without, just like physico-
chemical forces' and their strength can be measured 'as one does the strength
of electric currents.' "[32]

However debatable the value of this imagery may be, Sartre does not
limit his condemnation to Durkheim and Bataille. Earlier, he criticized
Bataille for appropriating terms from philosophy for an emotionally intense
discourse. Moreover, he denounces the attempt to integrate a meditation on
the expérience which draws on sociology. At stake are the possibilities of the
subject, here determined within the disciplines of philosophy and the
emergent social sciences. Historically, one can attribute Sartre's adherence to
individual understanding to his confrontation with the "mass" culture of
Fascism. But Durkheim's collective is not Le Bon's crowd.[33] It must be
located within the critique of rationality and utilitarianism where the general
economy is also situated.

The mainstays of the utilitarian system of social theory—atomism,
rationality, empiricism, and randomness of ends—were discussed in Chap-

ter 1 as they appeared within economics. Durkheim's sociological collec-
tivism aims to challenge the atomistic tendency dominating Western European intellectual tradition since the Reformation. The individualist fears the
assimilation of the individual to a larger whole, thereby sacrificing freedom of conscience and effacing his or her difference from others. The
individualistic elements of European culture generally emphasized the
discreteness of personality and of goals among those who make up a society.
Moreover, the historical trend has been to concentrate the means-end
relationship in the *unit* act of one particular type, the "rational norm of
efficiency."[34]

Durkheim's early work posed a challenge to what Parsons calls the
"causal individualism" of positivistic social theory.[35] Without a reiteration of
the problems raised by this initial phase, it is important to note that most
references to Durkheimian theory in the literature of sociology is arrested at
the stage of a career that the Anglo-American bias toward individualism and
positivism labels idealistic. In an effort to dispel this prejudice, while
validating the strong points of Durkheim's later epistemology, Parsons
assesses the foundations for the concept of social solidarity this way: "This
vast complex of action in the pursuit of individual interest takes place within
the framework of a body of rules, independent of the immediate individual
motives of the contracting parties. This fact the individualists have either not
recognized at all, or have not done justice to. It is the central empirical insight
from which Durkheim's theoretical development starts, and which he never
lost."[36]

From this starting point Durkheim formulated his most decisive attack
on utilitarian individualism, citing its inability to account for the normative
order of society. He then sought an explanation in terms exterior to the
individual. Herein lies the genesis of the famous criterion of "exteriority,"
the distinguishing mark of social facts so vehemently denounced by Sartre.
Parsons explains Durkheim's understanding of social facts as *choses:* social
phenomena are part of the external world of observation, but human
conduct is also to be understood in terms of forces that cannot be altered in
conformity with private wishes or sentiments. Durkheim's *choses* are antithetical to the wants of the utilitarians: they are given, not spontaneous;
exterior, not subjective. Durkheim's assertion that society as an organic unity
engenders its own reality finds this confirmation: "Atomistic theories are in
fact empirically inadequate."[37]

One must also consider that social facts are facts about psychic
realities that must be accorded the same status as natural things. The social
factor operates through the medium of the actor's objective knowledge of it;
social facts are *choses* insofar as they belong to the external world and
constrain the actor.

The final phase of Durkheim's work, relating to questions of religion and epistemology, is the one referred to in this study because it marks the decisive breakdown of positivistic methodology. Parsons credits the theory of religion with demonstrating the direct expression of "ultimate-value attitudes" in religious ideas and rituals.[38] Moreover, Durkheim prepared the way for a "voluntaristic" theory of social action by insisting on the necessity of will and effort in the fulfillment of ritual functions.

Sartre, however, equates the will to move beyond the self or the revelations of the expérience intérieure with a will to power and absolute knowledge. Thus, when Bataille tries to assess the impact of the order of constraints demonstrated by Durkheim, Sartre claims those "limits" must be understood from within. Onto the subjectivity of the individual, he is accused of imposing "the transcendent into the immanent."[39] The image decries an invasion, and its repetition throughout this essay constitutes the philosopher's defense against the meaningless forces of the sacred as the basis for sovereign communication.

Yet Sartre underestimates Bataille's agreement with him on the need to curb the tendency toward objectivism, the treatment of social facts "as if " they were things, by a study of the meaning of behavior, whether individual or collective. The two critics diverge again, however, at how to determine the significance of things. Sartre bases his critique on a phenomenological position that he feels Bataille, "an unfaithful disciple of Hegel," has betrayed.[40] In question is the commitment to study phenomena—the givens of consciousness—without seeking to explain either *from* whom or *for* whom they exist. The refusal to speculate further than "the thing itself " reveals within phenomenology "a disavowal of science" tantamount to a rejection of all explanation.[41] The phenomenological position is located "prior to scientific thematisation, where phenomenology unveils the fundamental style, or essence, of the consciousness of this given, which is intentionality."[42] This intentionality is determined by the psychological premise that consciousness is always consciousness of some *thing*. Thus for Sartre (for whom all knowledge is intentional), the fundamental contradiction of sovereignty is the desire to annul meaning by using discourse itself to cancel the tendency of words to impose unwanted associations. Moreover, it does so without appeal to an intelligible, transcendent order. Bataille is not merely careless in his confusion of realms; he believes his expérience attains communication through fusion: "with *non-savoir* as subject, and the *inconnu* as object, the subject-object dichotomy is overcome" (V, 21).

At the antipodes of Durkheim's study of social facts as things, phenomenology risks the extreme of subjectivism. The movement "outward" of the subject, however, comprehends both objects as well as the other, causing Husserl to wonder why it is that "I do not perceive the other as an object, but as an *alter ego?*"[43] By reasoning through analogy, the phenomenologist arrives at the following process, by which the relation to the other takes place:

> The projection onto the behavior of the other of my own actions implies that *autrui* be apprehended as an *ego;* which is to say, at the same time, I perceive myself as seen from without, or, as an other for an *alter ego,* since these "actions," to which I assimilate those of the other I observe, as a subject, I can only live them, not apprehend them.[44]

Thus, the fundamental condition for the appreciation of the other is posited: "that I not be for myself pure transparency." Otherwise, if the relation to the other is located exclusively at the level of transcendental consciousnesses, "it is clear that only a play of reciprocal destitution and degradation can be installed between these constituting consciousnesses." Sartre's analysis of the *pour-autrui,* which is carried out only in terms of consciousness, is cited as an illustration of what Merleau-Ponty called "the ridiculous solipsism among many," and what Lyotard summed up this way: "The presence of the other is translated through my shame, my fear, my pride, and my relations with others can only be of the nature of destitution: love, language, masochism, indifference, desire, hatred, Sadism."[45] Communication, Bataille insists, is disrupted by abuse or exploitation.

Sartre's position is not representative of all phenomenology. Merleau-Ponty explores the domain anterior to the thought of the other, a state of original undifferentiation within "an intersubjective world providing the terrain on which the social takes its meaning." Thus, prior to a *prise de conscience,* the social exists silently and as a solicitation. Love indicates that the adult can experience that condition of nondivision found in infancy. Again, Sartre provides a notable contrast to this "transitivism": "The essence of the relations among consciousnesses is not the *Mitstein,* but conflict."[46]

Underlying Sartre's criticisms of sociology is an ontology, a theory of behavior motivated by desire which serves as the basis for an existential psychoanalysis. Knowledge of the individual must be total: each desire (to eat, sleep, or create a work of art) expresses the entire human reality. Desire reveals the relation of the subject to the world and is manifested in the desire for some *thing.* The fundamental category of possession subsumes all others: to be or to do is to have: "one creates the object in order to enjoy a certain relation with it . . . this relation is reducible to *having.*" To possess an object is to be able to use it. Beyond the phase of usage, as in contemplation, the reaction to the object is without meaning, since to possess something is to appropriate it in this utilitarian fashion: "It is only when I go beyond *my* objects toward a goal, when I actually see them, that I can relish their possession."[47]

Possession, however, is also magical, since I *am* those things I possess, "but outside, facing me, I create them independent of me; that which I possess is myself, outside myself, beyond all subjectivity."[48] The consequences of this appropriation of the self by the objective order of things is devastating—the impossibility of possessing an object in this ontological sense incites the desire to destroy: "Destruction, perhaps more subtly than creation, realizes the desire for appropriation and even fusion."[49] Thus the object, a provocative reminder of its ultimate impenetrability, must be removed.

Sartre rereads the basic categories of being in light of this position: to *utilize* is understood as to *use,* in the sense of "wear down," "erode," or "destroy." To consume *(consommer)* is to annihilate, primarily through eating. One destroys the object of one's desire through incorporation, an assimilation of the other into the self.

In this context, the gift is regarded as a primitive mode of destruction, whose gesture defies the other as the first step toward subjugation: "The gift is a brief, sharp, *jouissance,* almost sexual: to give is to possessively enjoy the object one gives, it is an appropriative-destructive contact. . . . To give is to subordinate the other."[50] For Sartre generosity—the desire to give—is not irreducible. Rather, it conveys the desire for appropriation which, as a sentiment structured by the presence of the other, manifests this desire in the mode of destruction. The challenge to existential psychoanalysis is to understand why, within the freedom provided each individual to determine its being, one chooses to destroy or to create as the way to possess the world.

The meaning attributed to gift-giving by Sartre is not conclusive for phenomenology, as Lefort's reading of *The Gift* indicates. The conscious determination of the subject versus the object is finally overcome through the mutual recognition of self and other, resulting in the constitution of a "collective" *cogito,* as considered in Chapter 1 of this study. Bataille best articulated the tension between the approaches highlighted by Sartre when he questioned the viability of his own proposal of a *sociologie sacrée:* "Why should I not draw together the allegedly scientific findings of sociology with the purely phenomenological givens of Hegel? It is possible that my undertaking is reducible to this confrontation" (I, 320).[51] Yet he does not want to underestimate the specificity of an approach that emphasizes that "*radical* heterogeneity established between the sacred and the profane by French sociology or in psychoanalysis between the conscious and the unconscious, [which] is a notion totally alien to Hegel" (II, 324).

Similar concerns were voiced by other participants in the collège. Leiris, for one, insisted that all members abide by the Durkheimian rules of method. These preoccupations among even amateur ethnologists mirror the issues of professional self-definition confronted by the very disciplines within which they sought to orient themselves: sociology and anthropology. Their conflicts should be compared to Lévi-Strauss's subsequent evaluation of the collège. Of particular relevance here is his view that the distinguishing mark of French sociology is its strong dependence on anthropology. In Great Britain or the United States the two disciplines seem to stem from different impulses and attract two distinct types of scholars. Sociology, because it appears to improve and strengthen the existing social order through its techniques, attracts those who accept the status quo, while "anthropology has often provided a haven for individuals poorly integrated into their own surroundings."[52] In contrast, French social philosophy, whose prototype is Montaigne, is nearly always linked to social criticism. For this reason, French sociology in the prewar period is credited for nurturing ideas in impressively diverse fields:

> This influence was so wide that it reached even the "avant-garde" in art and literature. In the years immediately preceding World War II, the "Collège de Sociologie" directed by Roger Caillois became a meeting place for sociologists on the one hand, and surrealist painters and poets on the other. The experience was a success. This close connection between sociology and every tendency or current having Man, and the study of Man at its center, is one of the more significant traits of the French school.[53]

With the specificity of sociology so undermined, Lévi-Strauss concludes that one does not need to be a sociologist in order to do sociology, because the position adopted by the observer, rather than the object itself, delineates the aims and limits of the field.

In a later article, Lévi-Strauss points out that the position of the observer is determined by the demand to understand the social fact *totally*, thereby implying a perspective both from "without, as a thing," and from a subjective viewpoint or "appreciation (conscious and unconscious) that would exist if we lived the fact as does the native."[54] He then identifies the necessary conditions for such a realization. First, the ethnographer must transpose the internal understanding within the terms of external apprehension; the entire process succeeds to the extent that the subject can "objectify itself indefinitely."[55] It is difficult, however, for the individual to shift perspectives without risking some misunderstanding. In the paradigmatic example of the ethnologist and the native, these obstructions to communication are overcome in the conjunction of unconscious categories with those of collective thought, in the mediation between self and other, between the subjective self and the objective self.

The relative success and failure of communication is caught within the play of the restricted and general economies of language. The human condition, according to Lévi-Strauss, is such that there exists an "inadequation" between signifier and signified beyond one's means to communicate and which scientific thought struggles to balance. The surplus is accommodated by those "floating signifiers" of everyday language (e.g., *truc* and *machin*), which bring to bear upon common experience the message implicit in the systems—constituted through art, magic, and religion—whose ambivalent concepts indicate the other means of symbolic thought to channel excess. Thus, following Mauss's precept that "all social phenomena can be assimilated to language," Lévi-Strauss sees in the antinomies subsumed by *mana* (i.e., force and action; quality and state; abstract and concrete; noun, verb, adjective; ubiquitous and local) the fact that it is at once all and none of the qualities imputed to it.[56] Rather, it is a simple form or a symbol in its purest state—a "zero symbolic value."[57]

If, instead of pursuing the purely structural implications of exchange, Mauss's explanation of *mana* is reinstated, then, claims Lévi-Strauss,

> one must admit that, as in the case of *hau, mana* is but the subjective reflection of an unperceived totality. Exchange is not a complicated edifice, constructed from the obligations to give, to receive, and to return, then cemented by mystical and emotional affect. It is a synthesis immediately given to and by symbolic thought which, as in exchange or any other form of communication, surmounts its inherent contradiction to perceive things like the elements of a dialogue, simultaneously passing below the relation of self and other, and destined by nature to pass from one to another.[58]

Knowledge, including scientific understanding, consists in the realignment of paradigmatic boundaries and configurations within this closed Totality.

Sartre assimilates Bataille's struggle with the anthropological limits of discourse to the "hatred" of language he shared with his contemporaries. Similarly, he demotes the experiences of *dépense* provided by French sociology to the spurious liberation of an adolescent bacchanale. He also does not recognize that the absence of "sincerity" in Bataille's lexicon indicates a larger concern with the issue of authority, its influence on the nature of linguistic categories, and the experiences between self and other it mediates. Indeed, Bataille's obedience to the Gnostic precept to challenge all limits by shifting away from subordination to superior principles in order to "confound the human spirit and idealism with something base" (I, 225) led to an odyssey of extreme adventures.[59]

Anguish and terror are the Scylla and Charybdis of the voyage through degradation, a descent to a hell that is not only Bataille's. The surrealists also understood that tampering with the fragile boundaries dividing the possible from the impossible could incur an invitation to madness and death—but their choice was to retreat. The volley of insults hurled between Bataille and Breton was traced to this fundamental divergence—what Bataille disdained

as the surrealist spiritualization of the *valeurs basses,* affiliating the unconscious, sexuality, and vulgar language with that which is most immaterial. In
contrast, his own pursuit is a *mise en question* of self, immersed in the crucible
of experience from which the subject emerges radically transformed.

The conventional disparity between true self and public persona is, for
Bataille, inadequate. The relation between author/subject and others which
he seeks to define assumes a self that has been deliberately revealed as the
locus of communication for and among others. The death of God suggests a
language and philosophy of transgression unexplored by Sartrean dialectics,
but that haunts Bataille and other moderns. Blanchot asserted that the
expérience intérieure is its own authority, that the loss of one deity need not
be replaced by another. With the burden of truth placed exclusively on the
experience, however, evaluation must take place from within, engaging the
author in an interminable analysis, conducted by a decentered, shifting ego:
"Each one of my sentences is the acceptation of a game. . . . Whether it pleases
me or not, I must recognize my role as author, weaving and unraveling the
texture of possible thoughts" (III, 536). The renewal of Mallarmé's *jeu* further
removes Bataille from the surrealists who, he contended, did not appreciate
that "a pure and simple suppression of limits is pure and simple ver-
balism . . . the given (expressed in laws) can only be overcome through a
game" (III, 536). Sartre sensed that the originality of Bataille's language
participated in a broader shift in the value ascribed to language—a
modification that was to mark the future function of literature and philosophy. Yet he could only relate the superficial resemblances of tone to a
surrealist disdain, and did not perceive that Bataille's innovations challenged
the delimitations of modernity for literature and literary theory.

The relation of Bataille to surrealism can be reassessed within
Blanchot's postwar retrospectives of the movement. His main purpose is to
cast doubt on their cultivated image of total negativity by claiming that the
surrealists ultimately affirm more than they destory. The main area touched
by this deceptive nihilism concerns the interactions among language,
thought, and experience. Thus the *écriture automatique* aggressively set against
stereotypical thought patterns should be regarded as an aspiration toward a
new mode of understanding "where language is not a discourse but reality
itself, without ceasing to be the specific reality of language, where man
reaches the absolute."[60]

The originality of the surrealist proposition is that this point is not to be
sought in a privileged, mystical state of transcendence but in a condition of
unlimited potential that is accessible to all and within the scope of everyday
life. Confident of the cohesion between thought and language, language and
experience, the surrealist faith was bolstered by the illusory spectacle of

automatic writing where, explains Blanchot, "by lifting the constraints of reflection, I allow my consciousness to erupt into language. Thus emptiness is filled and silence expressed."[61]

If the surrealists and Bataille share a common perspective on language, it is to be found in the impassioned rejection of utility and thus of the instrumentality of words. The surrealists also accompanied him in a joyous sacrifice of language when codified by the conventions of discourse. Unlike Bataille, however, they elevated automatic writing to the status of an absolute—language become subject: "Thanks to automatic writing, it [language] has benefited from the highest promotion. It is now meshed with 'thought.' "[62]

A dominant leitmotif of surrealist slogans was an unqualified liberty, and the apotheosis of automatic writing effected a liberation of words from their restricted usage. Blanchot stresses the analogy between language and economy, and how "liberty" functions within both orders: "When the surrealists speak of 'liberating' words, of treating them other than as minor auxiliaries, what they actually have in mind are veritable social demands. *There exist men and a class of men which others treat as instruments and elements of exchange:* in the two instances, liberty, and the possibility for man to be subject, are justly put into cause."[63]

Liberty in this context acquires a two-fold meaning, figuring in both personal freedom and the freedom of the word itself. The speaker/writer is not only liberated from "usage"; he or she also discovers the initiative of words. No longer dependent on the objects they were supposed to represent, words acquire a life of their own: "Sliding, playing, intermingling, in the words of Breton, they 'make love.' "[64]

In contrast with the surrealists' optimism and revelry, Bataille remains skeptical. The writer, he insists, can only escape the constraints imposed by the social conventions of language by a willed determination to sacrifice "all that language adds to the world" (*L'Erotisme,* 288). Unwittingly, the author adds to society's store of fixed meanings—a thesaurus of codified references that the writer's work helps to construct. The lack of explicit considerations of this sort among the surrealists, however, also dampens Blanchot's enthusiasm: "Surrealism appears to us as primarily an aesthetic and seems first of all concerned with words."[65] But even this criticism is subject to modification. In the postwar period in which Blanchot wrote, a general infatuation with existentialism underplayed the surrealists' involvement in politics. Blanchot, however, considers it as an outgrowth of their more enduring tenets, particularly the search for totality. What Sartre dismissed as scientism in the case of Bataille, Blanchot traces to the surrealist impetus to promote, by whatever means possible, the unification of experience; but "it is not clear whether this 'other' existence can be attained through analysis or investigative experiences, such as that of the unconscious and the dream, abnormal states, by recourse to a secret knowledge buried in history, or if it should be realized through a collective effort to change life and the course of things."[66]

What is beyond dispute is that the surrealist explorations into the paraliterary rendered the accepted notion of literature obsolete. The only stone of the literary edifice left unturned remained the assumption that poetry constitutes a superior mode of expression. Thus in the context of his own reflections on words, poetry, and writing in *L'Expérience intérieure* Bataille states: "I situate my efforts in the path of, and along side, those of the surrealists" (V, 193). There he determined communication resulted from the individual's sense of insufficiency; "there cannot be knowledge without community, nor an expérience without a community of those living it" (V, 37). Blanchot also locates the originality of surrealism in its exploration of a group experience distinguished from other cells, religious sects, seminars, or collèges organized around a particular tendency by the fact that its adherents sought to give a new meaning to "plurality."[67] Distorted by such terms as *collectivity, association,* or *religion,* surrealism is understood as an *affirmation* of the plural; it expands the horizons of possible relations and experiences between self and other through the *champs magnétiques* of meetings with the other. The decision to extricate this field of attraction thanks to automatic writing is qualified as "inaugural."[68] The continuity restored between emotions and verbalized transcription is extended to an intersubjective encounter among many: their common terrain is an unconscious that creates, as much as it reveals, the shared realities so discovered.

The surrealist experience thus fulfills Bataille's notion of a religion as an essentially social phenomenon that, as in the anthropological experience described by Lévi-Strauss, looks toward the "primitive" not as a model to be emulated, but as a confrontation with the otherwise inaccessible unconscious of Western culture. Bataille, however, is less sanguine than Blanchot regarding the efficacy of automatic writing to liberate those energies monopolized by concerns of daily survival. At the same time, by defining itself as a total negation of the values of the marketplace, surrealism cut its ties to a community by indulging in activities exclusively symbolic. The denial of material interest must account for the specific form in which interest is manifested in a capitalist society—that is, as personal interest. In this way, surrealism appears to Bataille as a weaker negation than communism, a fact recognized by Breton and one of the reasons for the latter's affiliation with the Party. Thus, for Bataille, surrealism can avoid the impression of impotence only by engaging in a communal existence, rediscovering deeper realities touched by what he calls religion, and constituting the most apt response to Sartre's accusation of a new mysticism.

Sartre broached his critique of *L'Expérience intérieure* by signaling a larger crisis affecting both the essay and literary criticism. His argument against

Bataille touches on the latter's disruption of the hierarchy of discourses, whereby the theory and practice of writing are meshed, effecting the sort of transgressions proclaimed by the surrealists but never fully realized. No reader of Bataille was more conscious of the heretical implications of his work than the author himself. This assertion will be verified according to insights provided by Bataille's own reading of Bataille.

BATAILLE READING BATAILLE

Aware of the disorienting complexities of his work, Bataille feared that the study of excess energy he placed at the basis of all disciplines, including art and poetry, was so global that "a book such as this one *[La Part maudite]*, being of interest to all, risks appealing to no one" (VII, 20). Other interventions of self-criticism or explanation further situate a work whose concrete existence—the very investment of energy into its production— contradicts the sovereign expenditure its theories advocate. Bataille confronts the paradox through the text's systematic integration of the signs by which the reader is to be guided, thus permitting the author to dictate criteria whose values are representative of the general economy. These indicators fall into three classes: the mode of explicit intervention and self-appraisal cited above; statements on poetry and literature, language, and communication (found primarily in *L'Expérience intérieure*) subsumed under the rubric *poetics;* and reflections on the social and historical dimensions of literature united under the title *La Littérature et le mal*. The multiple dimensions of Bataille's reading of Bataille exemplify the challenge of a general economy of writing: the collapse, within a single discourse, of theory and practice, demonstrating the sovereignty of communication grounded in dépense.

The importance of the first category of markers, the technique of direct address, is to focus on the unorthodox quality of Bataillian erudition. The shift of interest away from the sexual extravagances of the early writings to the heterogeneity of the corpus in its entirety underscores the transgressive power of Bataille's mixture of discourses. Initially, the text's defiance of classification may appear at odds with Bataille's self-imposed stipulation to situate himself, but a close examination of *La Part maudite* reveals no such sustained effort through the rules and methods of traditional scholarship.

The corollary to the general economy's disruption of classifications lies in the upset of the critic (reader)/author hierarchy. Strongly pronounced in Bataille's poetics, the shift between readers and writers compels the latter to usurp the privileges of the former and to investigate the specifics of the literary discourse within their own text. If literature is the experience of limits, authors are responsible for maintaining the text at the precarious edge of meaning, to which they were lured by the game of *non-sens* and where they are tempted by the void of silence.

These indicators also contradict the appropriative criticism exemplified by Sartre, who introduced a historical perspective in order to stress similarities among families of kindred spirits. Bataille's immediate response to him therefore focused on the reading process: "What I was trying to describe in *L'Expérience intérieure* is the movement of a thought which, losing all possibility of arrest, easily falls prey to criticism that believes it can stop it from without, since criticism itself is not caught within this movement" (VI, 199).

Sartre imputed the frustrations provoked by reading *L'Expérience* to the limits of literary criticism and called on psychoanalysis as a panacea. This position is consistent with his opinion that the only viable dimension of the work is the experience itself; the substantiating evidence of nondiscursive modes of communication drawn from French sociology are dismissed as scientism. But by pitting the subjectivism of phenomenology against the objective givens of anthropology, or the discourse of language against the *dépense* of communication, Sartre intensifies a conflict among disciplines to the detriment of the larger issues at stake.

An alternative to Sartre, demonstrated in the organization of this study, is to allow the internal movement toward a *vue d'ensemble* to emerge from the categories of the general economy. In its second phase, this analysis considers the consequences of the general economy for the evaluation of literature and writing, where communication through dépense, heterogeneity, and sovereignty is weighed against the discursive coherence produced by restricted exchanges. The dominant reference controlling these reflections on words and meaning, signs and society, continues to be economic, and how to see the incommensurable—the noneconomic— remains the central question.

Bataille's answer begins with the author who, implicated in a proprietary relationship with his work, must initiate its dismantling if he is to communicate the superiority of dépense over accumulation. Otherwise, the author as producer remains indistinguishable from the common capitalist who derives pleasure and meaning from the spectacle of possession. Unlike the chieftain who enters the dramatized destruction of potlatch assured of the benefits of his expenditure, the modern poet is likened to Sisyphus, eternally condemned to seek absolution for his role in the restricted economy: "The only means to expiate the sin of writing is to annihilate that which is written. But this can only be accomplished by the author; destruction only leaves the essential intact. I can, nevertheless, link negation so closely to affirmation that my pen effaces that which it has just written" (III, 336).

Poetry is valorized if it frees the immured poet from the citadel of personal appropriation and undoes the walls erected by individualism. Impediments to communication are then lifted because "poetic genius is not a verbal gift: rather, it is the intuition of ruins secretly expected, so that many things are undone, lose themselves, communicate" (V, 173).

Bataille originally published several brief narratives under the ambiguous title *Haine de la poésie*, ostensibly reinforcing his reservations concerning poetic discourse. When the same works were reissued under the new heading *L'Impossible* (III, 101), his explanatory comments reiterate that only violence and revolt impart a forceful significance to poetry determined within the "impossible." Although its meaning is never explicit, the impossible evokes this fundamental ambivalence:

> On the one hand, the possibility of violent pleasure, horror, and death—exactly that of poetry—and, in the opposite direction, that of science or of the real world of utility. Only utility—the real—has a serious nature. We are never in a position to prefer seduction: truth has its claims on us. Yet, we can and must respond to *something* that, not being God, is stronger than these claims: this is the *impossible,* to which we can accede only by forgetting the truth of these claims, only by accepting disappearance. [III, 102]

To make claims for poetry as a privileged device to penetrate the unknown—perhaps unknowable—only aggravates Bataille's discomfort with the status of the author. The poet who touches the frontiers of the possible through his transgression should neither act nor write in the name of an individual subjectivity: "To write is to seek chance, not that of an isolated author, but of anonymity" (III, 495). This notion is not to be confused with conventional images of poetic madness or artistic alienation in which the artist/poet offers him- or herself as a heroic example, the saint or seer of modern illuminations. In such instances, the personality of the artist tends to overshadow the dialectic between social constraints and the particularized dementia. Moreover, the ability of literature to recoup the energy and violence necessary for transgression at the individual level leads to a general denunciation of poetry: "I am no less opposed to poetic mysticism than was Hegel. Aesthetics, literature (literary dishonesty) depress me. I suffer from the preoccupation with individuality and the *mise en scène* of self (of which I myself have been guilty). I reject the vague, idealistic, elevated spirit that shirks humiliating truths" (V, 336).

The limit that the author chooses to respect or undermine is determined by a subject/object dichotomy overcome most effectively through self-effacement. Bataille therefore concurs with Sartre on the exemplary quality of Mallarmé's poetry, where the elements of the antinomy are subordinate to the power of the word: "Reader and author are mutually annulled, reciprocally effacing each other so that finally only the Verb exists" (IX, 301). Bataille qualifies this observation by extending the criterion to all literature.

But unlike Artaud and Blanchot, contemporaries who also perceive literature among absolutes such as madness and death, Bataille challenged the delimiting consequences of reason responsible for the modern fragmented subject.[69] His transgression constitutes an anthropology of the impossible whose method utilizes multiple discourses: Bataille speaks through the languages of mysticism, eroticism, economics, and sociology in order to investigate their modifications of the subject. The particular economies at play within these respective experiences, including the communication that attempts to bypass discourse, reveal the basis for the opposition between Bataille and Sartre on the question of subject-as-author.

The *cogito,* for Sartre, is the inviolable, atemporal, irreducible foundation. . . . For me, it exists only within a relation . . . *it is a network of communications, existing within time.* The atom refers to a wave: to language, words exchanged, books written and read. Sartre reduces a book to the intentions of an author, the author. *If, as it appears to me, a book is communication, the author is only a link among many different readings.* [VI, 408, emphasis added]

Sartre's *cogito* is an agent of volition whose individual project can be evaluated by an *engagement* in the direction of total liberty. When Sartre used this standard to judge the nature of evil in Baudelaire and Genet, Bataille responded with the intertextual dialogues found in *La Littérature et le mal,* where he proffers his definitive views on literature as well as the meticulous response demanded by the *nouveau mystique* attack.

Sartre's position outlines two basic conditions for evil. The first is dedicated to "evil for evil's sake" as the obvious contrary to all that is promoted as good in the universe. Yet it ultimately reveals a crippling dependence on the very structure it declares its adversary. The alternative "dizzying" version of evil equates liberty with an absolute. More than a secondary derivative, it asserts an uncompromising encounter with Nothingness. With all props removed, the Sartrean character acts out a project on a stage of eerie emptiness, furnished only by the awesome burden of responsibility. If hell for Sartre is others, Baudelaire's inferno is peopled by the very judges he set out to scandalize. The author of *The Flowers of Evil,* he contends, exists as the creation of those who condemn him.

The basic thrust of Sartre's argument was already clear in the discussion with Bataille on sin. There, dépense was defined as a transgression of the hegemonic values of productivity and accumulation. The difficulty arises from a moral imperative that strains toward the apex *(le sommet)* of expenditure; an ascent that defies correlation with the "good." The highpoint of the expérience intérieure is, therefore, communication characterized by excess and exuberance, an expenditure implying the violation of another's integrity.

If goodness is equated with preservation, however, then such communication is closer to the evil of destruction. The moral summit under question is attained at the limit of *le néant,* the goal of communication. Nothingness then implies a further paradox, for if the individual does not communicate, he/she will be engulfed by the emptiness of an isolated existence. To communicate, however, one must risk the loss of self by putting it into play with the other: to "sin" is to refuse this gift. The *mise en jeu* needs a heterogeneous contact, often sparked by an act of degradation that renders the other penetrable; the force of heterogeneity is gauged by the resistance to such violation. Sartre comments that Bataille has a curious way of retaining what he otherwise seems to reject, and he detects in this notion of sin an implicit set of values and definition of "good." Thus, in this 1944 encounter Sartre reasserts his earlier position: language alone cannot be faulted for producing the contradictions Bataille faces. "There is on the one hand the *exposé* you propose, and on the other, your concrete research *(l'expérience).* It is only the search that interests me" (VI, 345).

Language does betray experience when joy meets anguish to produce those ambivalent "irréconciliables" Sartre insists must be identified according to the law of noncontradiction. But, according to Bataille, if loss without any compensation is promoted as a "good" thing because it needs such a justification, then the notion of dépense cannot be expressed: "Language is inadequate because it is built out of propositions that impose identities; if, starting from the excess that we are, we are motivated toward dépense in order to spend, not gain, then we can no longer remain at the level of identity. *We must open these notions beyond themselves"* (VI, 350, emphasis added).

By divorcing the expérience from the issues raised by its discursive transcription, Sartre skirts the essential decision to renounce any attempt to leave the self and construct an economy of rational expenditure limited only to the necessary level of production of energy: to eliminate "pure waste, pure dépense, pure luxury, pure absurdity" or to maintain "dépense, luxury and waste, which have no reason for being other than themselves" (VI, 347).

Sartre condemns Baudelaire's choice of evil, comparing it to that of the eternally adolescent rebel unable or unwilling to assume the responsibility of adulthood. He links the decision to the avoidance of "a terrible freedom"; thus, "when poetry espouses evil as its goal, and the two sorts of limited responsibility meet, we possess a 'flower of evil' " (IX, 190). The limitation occurs because evil continues to render homage to good, without which it would cease to exist. Bataille points out that when Baudelaire embraced the passivity of poetic existence he faced an agonizing conflict awaiting all individuals torn between the search for sovereignty and the freedom of action.

> Poetry can verbally bring the established order to its knees, but it cannot replace it. When the horror of ineffectual freedom engages the strength of

the poet into political action, he abandons poetry. But from then on he assumes responsibility for the future order to come and the direction of activity; in short, the *major attitude,* and we cannot help but recognize that poetic existence, where we formerly perceived the possibility of a sovereign attitude, is in truth the *minor, inferior* attitude, that of a child or a gratuitous act. [IX, 191]

Bataille's own ambivalence toward poetry occasioned outbursts of frustration or provoked pessimism but rarely led to an apologetic stance. Yet in this particular polemic he defends it against critics who, like Sartre, fail to recognize the contradiction of literature and the arts in a culture dominated by the values of work, accumulation, utility, and the rationality of scientific modes of thought.

Historically, literature and fiction replace the "extreme states" that once possessed precise ends in other cultures. Robbed of this former significance because such goals are now pursued through direct action, "art represents a small domain of freedom outside the realm of action, *paying for its liberty through its renunciation of the real world.* This is a heavy price, and there are few writers who do not dream of recapturing lost reality: but for it, they must pay in the other direction, renouncing liberty and serving propaganda." (VI, 22).

Art accedes to a domain Bataille claims is resistant to the categories of project and freedom, "a world that I cannot reproach Sartre for ignoring. . . . This new reality is what my book hopes to discover" (IX, 193). To do so, he situates the meaning, or more accurately, the *non-sens,* of the life of Baudelaire within a historical perspective obscured by Sartre's fixation on individual choice. Bataille's argument accounts for the nature of values espoused within an economy influenced by the same options and constraints that mark the individual's sense of possibilities. Baudelaire's predilection for daydreaming inhibits his capacity to work and earn money, and as such is a personal trait—but it is also tied to the desire for poetry. According to the *Ecrits intimes,* ' "each minute, we are crushed by the idea and sensation of time. And there exists only two options to escape from this nightmare in order to forget: pleasure or work. *Pleasure wastes. Work fortifies.* Let us choose' " (cited by Bataille, IX, 203, emphasis added).

By means of his poetry, Baudelaire lived through the impossible solicitation paraphrased by Bataille in a secular manner: "There exists in all men, at all moments, the pull in two directions: one toward work (God), the other toward dépense (Satan)" (IX, 203). Unable to escape the double bind, Baudelaire refused work and avoided pleasure. What Sartre insists on calling an individual deviation toward the negative, Bataille designates a transgression. To judge Baudelaire—or, more importantly, his evil flowers—is to recognize the historical exigencies to which they respond. Bataille countered Sartre's demotion of the "unequaled tension" (IX, 205) to the particulars of the poet's biography by looking at the material conflict as imposed from without. Society, like the individual, is also required to choose between a concern for the future and the demands of the present. While the primary commitment of the group is undoubtedly future-oriented, it nonetheless concedes to the present a "part" over which no decision is absolute.

Archaic society's preservation of the part maudite under the name of the sacred, however, has been displaced by the positivism of the market. Observing the capitalist expansion of French society, Baudelaire turned to the romantics and their reaction to the demise of aristocratic values of *l'ancien régime.* Such a response was itself trapped by "a naive exaltation of the past opposed to the present" (IX, 206). To the bourgeois apotheosis of work, the romantics opposed the impassioned, rebellious individual, characterized by Bataille as

> the product of bourgeois society. . . . The poetic, titanic form of individualism is to utilitarian calculation only an antibourgeois allure of bourgeois individualism. The rending negation of self, the nostalgia for what one does not have, expressed the malaise of the bourgeoisie which, entering history while aligning itself to the refusal of responsibility, expressed the opposite of what it really was, but managed so as not to suffer the consequences and even to profit from it. [IX, 207]

Only when the fevered romantic reaction had passed could literature extricate itself from moral compromise. Baudelaire was no radical, emphasizes Bataille, yet his refusal to subordinate the present to the future is more profound for denying the opposite affirmation. This brand of evil is less an active pursuit than a prevailing influence charming the poet into an effortless collusion to nurture his evil flowers. The fascination with evil nonetheless modifies the boundaries of poetry: when no longer subject to external constraints, it yields to the enticement of the impossible. The consequences of this pressure and the willed passivity it entails transcend the curiosity exerted by the individual poet. The poems alone arouse interest in a life otherwise fated to obscurity.

Bataille's reading of Baudelaire demonstrates the need to move literary criticism beyond existential concerns to "the primacy of the economy."[70] Whether this realization occurs at the level of a work's production or reception, Bataille's fundamental premise will be confirmed: "These considerations place economics at the basis of poetry. The question that appears at all times relates to the vulgar and material concern; given present resources, should I spend or accumulate" (IX, 203).

Baudelaire's deliberations with the arithmetic of morality set the terms for his readers. Bataille's circuitous argument is explained by the difficulty of distinguishing the significance of categories when employed by Sartre or himself. Central to the debate, for instance, is the concept of evil, examined either as the inevitable complement to good within a hierarchical duality, or, as Sartre contends, as an absolute that breaks with the compromised usage of the first concept. The economic strategy favored by Bataille exposes the consequences of the ubiquitous dualities of which good and evil is but one instance. Their internal economy is such that they preclude ambivalence and install an order based on identities—the manipulation of these antinomies is usually restricted to a simple inversion. Their participation within more than one cultural system, however, musters ideological implications as a result of correlations—often only implicit—with other dualisms. Thus the good/evil, production/expenditure, rationality/irrationality antinomies must be examined in relation to the capitalist/worker, adult/adolescent couples that inform Sartre's condemnation of Baudelaire.[71] This explains Bataille's acknowledgment that within the existing order, the poet's revolt can be considered only a "minor" infraction contained by the father's house.

Thus, initially, the negativity of the poet's refusal to work is evaluated against the values promoted within the "inevitable realm of rational utility." In its next phase, however, the economic analysis situates the work of the poet within the perspectives opened by dépense, heterogeneity, and sovereignty, revealing a dimension of communication *other* than that of restricted exchanges. The reinscription of these categories within a general economy that equates communication with the affirmation of giving is the issue central to the polemic between Sartre and Bataille in their respective readings of Genet.

Ironically, the resemblance between the two critics is striking: Sartre talks of Genet's search for sovereignty and sacred sacrifice within an experience of evil. Yet Bataille regrets that Sartre's faults have never been more pronounced, since he is still indifferent to "those discrete ravishments, subject to chance, that traverse life and provide it with furtive illuminations" (IX, 288). One source of closure is the economy of the monadlike entity adapted to the productive activities of the secular life. Rational man, working man, talking man is shut off from the "surreptitious flashes"—those emotions of sensuality and the festival, drama, love, and death—that induce communication. Impenetrable to others, each person is also a stranger to the universe; "he belongs to objects, to instruments, to meals, to newspapers, which lock him into a *particularity* ignorant of the rest" (VI, 304).

The Sartrean subject's encounter with the other as a field of possibilities is reduced to the objectivication of one subject through the glance *le regard* of the other. His "chosen" search for sovereignty perpetuates the classical model where the slave became the thing of the master, and the disdain for mutuality exhibited by the sovereign sundered the bonds of communication: "This infraction by the sovereign of the common rule installed the isolation of men; at first their separation could be reunited, though rarely, and then eventually, never" (V, 153).

Sovereignty, Bataille insisted, is the opposite of a thing. Neither *chose* nor object, it eludes apprehension with each renewed effort to grasp it. When encountered in the violent rupture with the universe of objects, sovereignty becomes sacred. Genet violates these precepts by denying the inevitable restrictions transgression implies: "It is to the extent that he abandons himself *without limit* to evil, that communication escapes him" (IX, 315).

At best, Genet is credited with dedicating literature to the pursuit of evil, yet he remains bound to a notion of sovereignty which is subordinate to the greater benefit of the "saint." Bataille points out that Sartre's title is not only an affront to genuine disinterestedness, but a misreading of Genet's deep fascination with royalty and its accompanying titles. Coveting the external trappings of feudal glamor and aristocratic sovereignty, Genet's imposture of sovereign communication affects his style. As a writer, he is at no loss to exercise the full range of his seductive charms, and Bataille compares the brilliant images and baroque constructions to the glitter of hard, cold, sparkling jewels.

> Genet's indifference to communication is the source for one certain fact: his narratives are interesting, but they do not *impassion* the reader. Nothing is colder, less touching, beneath the ostentatious display of words, than the celebrated passage recounting the death of Hercamone . . . I do not doubt that this sort of provocation will continue to seduce and fascinate, but the effect of the seduction is *subordinated* to an external success. [IX, 305]

Determined to acquire external signs of recognition and without debasing the hierarchy of good and evil, Genet managed to shock a relatively unmenaced bourgeois reader. Neither reader nor author was compelled to face a sovereign form of writing whose raison d'être can be traced to the desire "to modify the relations that exist between a man and his fellow beings" (II, 143). Among Bataille's remonstrances to Genet is an eloquent appeal to restore to literature its capacity to cross the abyss separating reader from writer.

> In the depression that results from these insufficient exchanges, where a glassy partition is upheld which separates us readers from an author, I nonetheless hold on to this certainty: humanity is not constituted of isolated beings, but made up of communications among them; we are never given, even to ourselves, except in a network of communications with others: we bathe in communication, we can be reduced to this incessant communication, whose absence we feel in the very depths of our solitude. [IX, 310]

Aware that Genet's mode of sovereignty is regressive, Sartre documents its consequences for his fictional as well as lived relations, but does not speculate on possible modification. In Genet, the condemnation of the consumer society motivates the extremes of his experience as both criminal and saint. But the limited effects of an inversion that leaves intact the hierarchy maintaining its poles is confirmed by Sartre's observation that "Extreme Evil is modeled on Sovereign Good."[72] When evil proves impossible, the criminal is converted to a saint. Their common ascetic impulse "to consume without producing" renders the transmutation feasible. Motivating the renunciation is the desire for sacrifice, a gift "made to nobody."[73] Finally, Sartre completes his portrait with pity for a hero "who will never know the joys of receiving or of sharing."[74]

Sartre himself does not endorse sovereignty and looks to the alternative productivity of the Soviet Union. The apotheosis of labor witnessed there, however, qualifies his endorsement, since the glory showered on the proletariat has spawned its own mythology. To claim that production encourages generosity, for instance, would be inconsistent with his earlier assertion that it is reducible to other motives such as appropriation. One does not produce "in order to give" but, more likely, to possess.[75]

After deriding the "antlike" activity of the Soviets, Sartre nonetheless exhorts readers to found a new society where "workers and militants will help with the birth of a producing community . . . And draw up a table of new values."[76]

The general economy is never claimed as the foundation for a new order. Rather, it constitutes a point of view discernible within those moments of furtive illuminations when "language is cried, a cruel spasm, mad laughter, and where harmony is born from the shared awareness of the impenetrability of ourselves and the world" (IX, 310).

Optical metaphors, however, do not accommodate the active participation of the Bataillian subject in a sovereign experience threatening to the economy of the *cogito*. Motivated by a sense of insufficiency, this individual discovers that the "essential is the instant of violent contact when life slides from one to the other, in a sensation of dreamlike subversion. This same feeling is experienced in tears. On another level, to look at a person laughing can be a form of erotic encounter" (V, 390).

Bataille situates the instant within history; similarly, sovereignty is determined from without, by an economy that endows it with a meaning to which "the givens of the internal life cannot be opposed."[77] In the same vein, Bataille locates the goal of a sovereign writing within the history of his "tumultuous" generation, which appreciated that literature was "suffocating in its limits" (IX, 171). The reflections of *La Littérature et le mal* are those of a mature man for whom age has only sharpened the passions of the youth convinced that literature bears within it the hope of revolution. Its confines are coextensive with social constraints: "It is not a question of verbal limits, but of real, social limits" (II, 73). The transfer of the transgressive tactics of the general economy to literature first modified the function of the author as sociological institution. Bataille's final position was to concede: "Whether it pleases me or not, I must recognize my role as author, weaving and unraveling the texture of possible thoughts" (III, 536).

The purpose of this chapter has been to show that Bataille's situating of his own text among intertexts must be appreciated as the historical complement to the differentiating process. In this proposed reading of Bataille reading Bataille, the process of autocriticism serves to gauge the taboos and transgressions of the dense historical fabric of which the author is a product. In Bataille's image, he is the obsessive spider playing out the strategem of his web, spinning and unwinding the many threads in which he is enmeshed.

CHAPTER

6

READING BATAILLE IN HISTORY

When the problem of connecting isolated phenomena has become a
problem of categories, by the same dialectical process every problem of
categories becomes transformed into a historical problem.

Georg Lukács

Upon failing to "disestablish"[1] the author, Bataille concludes his literary meditations with a seriousness commensurate with the holistic goals
of the general economy. To write, he asserts, is to reorient human relations.
In this radical mode, literature will be evaluated against the example of
authors who, "in their capacity as great anthropologists, have known how
to invest their work with an entire conception of man, culture, and nature."[2]
According to Bataille, the discontinuities among these three orders are
breached by dépense. As a limit-term, it subverts the categories of the
restricted economy—exchange, gift, waste—with the sovereign force of the
general economy.[3] By resisting any one meaning it refutes all and announces
Bataille's most extreme position.

> The fundamental right of man is to signify *nothing*. This is the opposite of
> nihilism, for it is meaning that mutilates and fragments. The right not to
> signify is nonetheless the one least recognized, most openly ignored. As
> reason extended its domain, the part of *non-sens* was diminished.
> Fragmented man is, at the moment, the only one whose rights are
> recognized. The rights of total man are declared here for the first time. [VI,
> 429, emphasis added]

The strategy of dépense is to discredit the isolating effects of language while
heralding the continuum of communication. For the first time claims are
made for a subject conceived outside the bounds of discourse, thus situating
this anthropology in a countercurrent to the triumph of modern linguistics.
Refusing both economic man and his ideological analog, *homo significans,*

138

Bataille declares: "If one were to ascribe me a place within the history of thought, it would be, I believe, for having discerned the effects within our lives of the dissolution of discursive reality . . . " (V, 231).

The risk of such a notion is evident in the tension it sparks between nostalgia and critical thought. Dépense evokes a paradigm attributed to non-Western, traditional cultures whose radical otherness exhibits qualities "lost" in the transition from the archaic to the modern. Whether the reference is to a state of original undifferentiation, symbolic exchange, fusion, collective consciousness, or totality, the common sentiment yearns for the vitality of an experience now warped or degraded by economism. The communication projected by Bataille annuls the values reinforcing hierarchical discriminations without flattening the intensity of dépense. The response to nostalgia is, therefore, twofold. The heuristic contribution of anthropological data must be safeguarded from ideological appropriation. Yet it is precisely the sense of deprivation motivating nostalgia which draws individuals together and constitutes the impetus for collective criticism of the status quo.

A culture traditionally compensates for the inadequacies of social discourse through symbolic modes of representation. Yet the reductionist economy evidenced in univocal language is demonstrably at work in other systems as well. When it touches the limits of understanding, dépense challenges language to reproduce the ambivalence of experiences informed by images of death. Unable to prove the force of dépense, Bataille reveals its active effects, demonstrating that what language cannot say often can be seen. This technique underscores the importance of the eye, "capable of a seduction that, at the limit, touches horror . . . "(I, 187).

Dépense implies an economy witnessed both among primitives and in one's backyard. Indeed, an early essay, "Le Langage des fleurs" (I, 173–78), points out that one must consider the "aspect" of a thing even if its significance defies language. One cannot neglect the "ineffable, real presence" of what is revealed by "the configuration of the color of the corolla, and that which the stains of pollen or the freshness of the pistil betray . . . " (I, 173). Moreover, this dimension becomes an integral factor of philosophical analysis, wary of "natural" truths reproduced through conventions such as the one associating a beautiful girl or a rose with love. The underlying assumption of the rhetorical device is that flowers are in fact beautiful, unlike their often hideous reality. Bataille points out the banality of his own contention that the odor of death emanates from the red rose of love. Moreover, desire has nothing to do with *this* ideal beauty, erected as a limit or *categorical imperative:* rather, one must be able to see in the flower an ignoble and brilliant sacrilege (I, 176).

The interpretation then shifts to the plant's botanical hierarchy, where one extreme reaches to the sky and the other digs its roots into the earth. By moving from high to low, this reading exposes the moral correlations inherited from idealism, so that what is low is literally grounded in what is closest to the earth, or, less euphemistically, dirt. More difficult to demonstrate is the opposition that meets in the flower and that takes on "an exceptionally dramatic significance" (I, 178). Bataille dismisses philosophers who deride as absurd the substitution of natural forms for abstractions; the real issue is the possibility of an anthropological materialism likely to upset the preeminence of that which is imposed as "high, noble, and sacred" (I, 178).

The point at which the hierarchy collapses and no term is dialectically sublated by another reveals the material foundation of the general economy. That this perceived ambivalence entails a qualitative difference other than an inversion of idealism becomes evident when it touches on prejudices transcending the immediate biases of philosophy. This is best illustrated in Bataille's relation to Hegel. Despite their rapprochement over the importance each philosopher grants to death, the latter is situated within the mainstream of the Judeo-Christian ethos, with its emphasis on liberty, history, and individuality. Moreover, Hegelian anthropology posits a spiritual being contained by the dialectic which reveals truth through the Idea. To Hegel's categories one could oppose Bataille's: limits to liberty; the instant to History; the collectivity to the individual. Yet these antinomies are themselves questioned by the general economy, which refuses to impose closure through active transgression; which posits an instant whose significance is determined by the economy; and which conceives the collectivity as the vehicle to heighten, not diminish, the potential of the individual.

The testing of Western ethnocentrism through the notion of dépense encounters its greatest difficulties, however, when trying to define the general economy against the restricted economy in terms of surplus or excess. The lesson of *La Part maudite* is that the bias of rationality arbitrarily subordinates sacrifice and festivals to the concerns of subsistence, thereby impeding an appreciation of the inextricability of the material and the symbolic. Within the subsystems of contemporary culture, each is dependent upon the values emanating from the primary locus of production—the economy. The innovation of the general economy is not simply to have revised the Marxist concept of the economy as a "determinant in the last instance" by examining the effects of the superstructure on the base. Nor is it to have expanded the purview of economics to include marginal phenomena. Rather, it rethinks the relation of the part to the whole so that the part maudite be conceived as coeval with the rational, and not as a secondary, superfluous, gratuitous (i.e., symbolic) epiphenomenon. Durkheim showed that the collective generates an economy of energy distinguished from the restricted one by its heterogeneity and by its inaccessibility through a logic of accumulation or simple juxtaposition.

Recent readings of Bataille, especially those of the *Tel Quel* group, have praised the tactical advances offered by this notion of economy for the production of culture, especially texts. Still stronger claims for it are made by Derrida, who situates Bataille "economically" in relation to Hegel and, through him, to the key concepts of Western metaphysics. Praise for a discourse declared one of the most audacious on record is justified by the exemplary "deconstructive" operation Bataille carries out under the aegis of sovereignty.[4] By not stopping at the first stage of that process—the inversion of the hierarchically organized binary oppositions—Bataille devises a constellation of figures guided by the general economy. The resulting "Hegelianism without reserve" proposes no new concepts but a reinscription of inherited ones within a syntax whose particular economy provides all the "difference." Because Derrida states that his major texts constitute a reading of Bataille, we are better able to evaluate the fate of the general economy within that area of contemporary critical thought which questions the nature and place of writing in our culture.[5]

The underlying economy of language surfaces most explicitly in the formulation of the Derridean notion of *différance* qualified as *the* concept of economy: "because there is no economy without *différance* it constitutes the most general structure of economy, so long as one understands by this notion *something other* than the classical economy of metaphysics or the classical metaphysics of economy."[6] *Economy* in this context refers to the production of values within language as determined by a system of differentiation, but Derrida also evokes the prejudice of economy as economizing: the minimum expenditure for maximum gain, or in this case, the capacity of a finite set of phonemes to generate unlimited combinations. At stake is the efficacy of communication, best assured by a one-to-one relationship between signifier and signified, sign and meaning. From this perspective, writing may appear to be the technical "supplement" to the spoken word, but its economy is not distinguished from that of speaking. Both are subject to the regimen of "logocentrism," characterized by the binary reasoning transmitted from Plato to computer science. The viability of Plato's logic depends on a domesticated linguistic system whose reductionism, Derrida contends, is inscribed in the *telos* of language itself: "Thus language is language only to the extent that is can analyze and master *polysémie*. . . . An unmastered dissemination is not even a *polysémie*, it belongs outside of language."[7]

Thus *différance* (spelled with a silent *a* rather than a second *e*) must be appreciated as bringing into play a plurality of meanings. One falls under the heading of *temporisation* and is etymologically derived from the Latin *differe,* "the action to postpone, to take into account time and forces in an operation that implies an economic calculation, a delay, postponement, reserve, representation, recourse to a detour, suspension of the fulfillment of a desire." The second, more common set of associations elicited by *différance* refers to its spatial dimension and is similar to the current use of *difference* as that which is not similar, which is perceived as other. Unable to play on this multiple potential, *difference* in its restricted use must be replaced with *différance* whose doubled value is "immediately and irreducibly polysemic, and this is not insignificant for the economy of the discourse which I attempt to maintain."[8]

The reworking of the Saussurean notion of difference is subsumed by the Derridean deconstruction of semiology through grammatology. Difference in its restricted economy refers to the diacriticity of the sign, dispossessed of any absolute worth, and dependent upon the surrounding elements within a system for its acquired value. Whereas Saussure's innovation was to stress the relativity of such value, Derrida faults it for remaining ultimately bound to a "theological" presence, albeit temporarily deferred. By extension, a critique of structuralism is outlined in the lecture on *différance* where oblique references are made to the "limits" of a period which would be revealed through the history of this notion. Neither a word nor a concept, *différance* is proposed as a cancellation or annulment of the original presence that aims to control or master the entire field of language; an omniscient presence that only temporarily relinquishes domination through the sign as its mediator. Thus the economy of the classical sign is based on a deferred presence, which is always regained. Herein lies the model of the restricted economy recognizable in all instances where the sign is found.

> The sign is thus a deferred presence. Whether it be a case of verbal or written signs, or monetary signs, of electoral delegation or political representation, the circulation of signs defers the moment when we encounter the thing itself, acquire it, consume it, or spend it, touch it, see it, or intuit its very presence.[9]

Thus, the poststructuralist literary theories of Derrida must be appreciated within the larger framework suggested by the deconstruction of the logocentric prejudice, examined in this study as the assimilation of reason to rationality. The issue of metaphor, for instance, is inseparable from an economy of the "proper," *le nom propre,* momentarily ellipsed by rhetorical devices but to which meaning finally returns.[10] The presence of metaphor in philosophical texts is, then, a question for metaphysics, that "white mythology which unites and reflects the culture of the West: the white man takes his own Indo-European mythology, his logos, that is to say, *mythos* of his own idiom, for the universal form of what he insists on calling Reason."[11] In Derrida's texts, reason emerges as a figure of domination, the instrument of repression, the means whereby one triumphs over many, pluralism gives way to monism, and the restricted economy overpowers the general.

The drama of Western logic and the delusion of its *mythos* crystallize in the figure of the *pharmakon,* purged from the Platonic text for being an "unstable ambivalence" whose contagion cannot be inserted within a fixed pair.[12] In him, contraries meet, collide, and ricochet off each other, only to enter into other temporary couplings: "It is from this game or movement that the oppositions or differences are *stopped* by Plato. . . . The *pharmakon*, without actually being something himself, always exceeds them."[13] To release the polysemic potential of the *pharmakon* requires a return to those texts where the reductionism adduced to Platonic logic is seen as stemming from within the structure the myths inherited from other cultures, as well as from without, i.e., from the language and logic Plato imposed on them in his rewriting. The interest of the Platonic text lies in its depiction of the moment at which these crucial decisions were made and which continue to haunt his "pharmacie": "It is in the back room, in the penumbra of the pharmacy, before the oppositions between conscious and unconscious, liberty and constraint, voluntary and involuntary, discourse and language, that these textual operations are produced. . . . "[14]

Yet it would be a capitulation to the power of logocentrism to concede that the *pharmakon* has been definitely expunged. Therefore, the inverted logos/*pharmakon* hierarchy is reinscribed within a cosmos of conflicting economies that signal the "eruption" of the *pharmakon*. These doublings indicate deconstruction's painstaking avoidance of dramatic metaphors, which would imply a decisive break or displacement with an initial framework. Instead, the aggressive tendency of one economy to undermine the other is shifted to the role of the reader/writer/critic, called on to liberate the textual element by manipulating threads otherwise tied by classical constraints. The final goal is to unleash the force of *écriture* which usurps meaning, signification, or form as the object of critical attention. Once the infinite play of *différance* is set into motion, the reader follows the dissemination of words throughout the text, a multidimensional system calling on others, present or absent, for its effect. Moreover, by reconstructing the anagrammatic *écriture* escaping authorial intentionality, Derrida uncovers the operations determining a text.

The appearance of *différance* or the *pharmakon* within a Derridean text signals the withdrawal from decisions leading to fixed dualities. As such, these *indécidables* encompass both economies without ever subsuming or dialectically overcoming one or the other.[15] Moreover, their "false" verbal, nominal, or semantic properties do not allow them to be retrieved by the philosophical dyads, although they may inhabit them as "a disorganizing agent."[16] Derrida describes their irreducibility as they erupt from the second phase of the deconstructive strategy at its point of "greatest obscurity,"[17] and their capacity to challenge the economy of the conceptual apparatus of philosophy is considered this way:

> How does one conceive *at the same time différance* as economic detour which aims to recapture the pleasure or presence calculatedly deferred (consciously or unconsciously) and on the other hand, *différance* as a relation to the impossible use of energy, an expenditure "without reserve," and, as in

the death instinct, to all appearances, an interruption of all economy. It is obvious that one *cannot* think together the economic and the non-economic.[18]

Clearly fearful that the *indécidables* could not resist philosophical mastery, that their instability would finally yield to the hierarchical structure of other oppositions, Derrida gauges the efficacy of deconstruction by its ability to maintain their condition of indefinite suspension. Meaning, never in complete abeyance, derives from a doubling of its possible registers. Thus the textural sovereignty of *différance*, *supplément,* and *pharmakon* admits contradiction as well as noncontradiction, touching both the conscious mind and the unconscious, by folding the text into a representation of writing itself.

On the consequences of sovereignty for writing, Derrida notes that it does not create another discourse: "Far from suppressing the dialectical synthesis, sovereignty enlists it in the sacrifice of meaning. . . . Poetry and ecstasy are that which *in every discourse* can open onto the absolute loss of meaning, to the depths of absence of knowledge or game, to the loss of consciousness by which it is awakened with a toss of dice."[19] He is also careful to warn that, despite the neutralization of the binary oppositions of metaphysics which sovereignty effects, the practice of writing is not itself "content to neutralize within discourse classical oppositions, but it transgresses within *l'expérience* the law of interdictions which are integral to the production of a discourse, and even the process of neutralization." More appropriately, he compares Bataille's sovereignty to a holocaust or potlatch of signs "that burns, consumes, and wastes words in the gay affirmation of death: a sacrifice and a challenge."[20]

Indeed, comparisons with Bataille's text are instructive, given that it is distinguished by the motor force of an excess traditionally refused by philosophy: death, dirt, eroticism, and an economy of expenditure are ejected as heterogeneous, foreign bodies. The writing thus produced qualifies as sovereign, according to Derrida, because it obliterates the classical distinction between form and content, a criterion generally reserved for poetry. One must, therefore, examine the nature of the writing which emerges from the economic reworkings of language by means of deconstruction. What are the consequences of the exhaustion of the text and its encouragement of something other? This textuality of Derrida's writing is contingent upon the neutralization of hierarchical dualities but should not, he warns, delimit the ensuing text's possibilities. Thus a process of displacement inheres in deconstruction, signaled by its indefatigable resistance of any one signifier as the privileged sign of ontotheological presence. *Ecriture* engenders the signifying practice of a chain never resting on a monovalent signified, and the work in question is executed by the *indécidables* "without dialectical relief, without any respite . . . and consistent with the obligation to avoid choice, decision, or appropriation."[21]

Derrida further explores the occultation of *dépense* and the general economy within the tradition of Western metaphysics consolidated through the *line:* "The enigmatic model of the *line* is thus the very thing that philosophy could not see when it had its eyes open on the interior of its own history."[22] The result is neither the loss nor the absence, but the *repression* of multidimensional symbolic thought, "solidary" with traditional concepts of time, organization of the world, and language. The linearity of the symbol is specifically Western because it is correlated with structural changes in the economy, technological advances, and ideology: "This solidarity appears in the process of thesaurization, capitalization, sedentarization, hierarchization, and the formation of ideology by the class that writes or rather commands the scribes."[23] Consequently, the deconstruction of philosophy is inseparable from a meditation on writing which, under the pressure of linearity, is subject to "successivity, to the order of logical time, or to the irreversible temporality of sound."[24] The alternative economy exhibited in *écriture* necessarily defies inscription within given concepts, prompting Derrida to state: "I have tried to describe and explain how writing bears in itself its own process of effacement and cancellation, all the while marking the remainder *[le reste]* of this annulment, following a logic which it is extremely difficult to summarize."[25]

At the "macro" level, the general economy destabilizes the hierarchy of discourses by its violation of disciplinary frontiers, including a transgression of the critic's domain. The force Derrida ascribes to *écriture* circulates among these multiple languages primarily to investigate their interfaces or *entre,* which, such as *le tympan* or *l'hymen,* constitute permeable but inviolate barriers marking both the limit of and passage to the most intimate recesses of the body of knowledge.[26]

Thus it is possible to appreciate the paradox of *écriture,* which counters the reductionism of language by means of the ambivalent, nondiscursive force of the general economy. The production of texts resistant to one-dimensional meanings attempts to compensate for the truncated, discontinuous experience of Western culture. Writing assuages the nostalgia for the encounter with the other by replacing intersubjectivity with intertextuality, and the text opens onto the critical space where something other awaits to be expended.[27]

The sovereignty of *écriture* perceived by Derrida in Bataille's text differs from the subordination of the logos to meaning, to mastery, and to presence, through its operation or science that places concepts in relation to an absolute *non-savoir* he insists will not be determined or circumscribed by "the history of knowledge as a figure restricted by the dialectic, but [which is recognized] as the absolute excess of every *episteme,* of all philosophy and of all science."[28] This science must think its relationship to logocentrism in terms consistent with the particular materialism of the general economy. The awkward maneuvers required to situate heterogeneity offer the best illustration of the dilemma replicated in the deconstruction of idealism. Commenting on the absence of Marx and Engels in his own text, Derrida substitutes for them a general economy "starting from Bataille."[29] To the extent that matter is designated a radical alterity, Derridean *écriture* can be qualified as materialist. Yet this concept of matter is marked by both a reversal and a positive displacement. As a final qualification, matter must be situated as "the absolute *dehors* of any opposition. . . . "[30]

Bataille's earliest statements on materialism appeared in *Documents* (I, 179–80) as a diatribe against the tradition that locates "dead" matter within a conventional hierarchy established by implicit idealism. The revitalization of this materialism through dépense stipulates that matter can be defined only by "a *nonlogical difference* that in relation to the economy of the universe, represents that which *crime* represents in relation to the law" (I, 319).

To differentiate heterogeneity as the transgressive *force* of dépense from its manifestation as the *things* of gift-exchange is Bataille's project in exploring potlatch. Derrida, however, does not locate this tension within history, fearing to demote the two economies to the position of any other philosophical pair. Rather, he attributes to them the opening of that historical space delimited by the concepts of reason, presence, and meaning which Western civilization claims as its privileged domain. Thus, it is when the ancient religions of fire and sun produce a *reste* and the "instant of consumation" is put into orbit that Derrida marks "the origin of history, the beginning of the decline, the setting of the sun, and the passage to Western subjectivity."[31] The resistance to such submission is concentrated in the figure of a *brule-tout* or *holocauste,* whose dedication to sacrifice must nonetheless be contemplated within the "double register" of the logic of a "calculable calculation."

> If you wish to burn all, you must also consume the conflagration, and avoid keeping it alive like a precious presence. One must therefore extinguish it, keep it in order to lose it (really) or lose it to keep it (really). The two procedures are inseparable and one can read them in either direction, from right to left or left to right, the sublating of one must consider the other.[32]

At stake here, as Derrida points out, is the ontological status of the gift, sacrifice, or total destruction. The "eruptive" event of the don is located at the origin of *logic* rather than in terms of being, in order to recognize that even when one gives without exchange or return, the don is kept and imposes a debt, since the other must receive it, recognize it: "Exchange has been initiated even if the *contre-don* only gives the return of the don. I give to you without expecting anything in exchange, but even this renunciation, as soon as it appears, constitutes the strongest and most internal bond—the link of the *pour-soi* and of debt."[33]

To deconstruct the don is to free its *énergie folle* from the restricted economy of the dialectic impeding its conceptualization as a donation or pure gift; that dialectic is, like the constraints of exchange, a bondage to an other enforced through the law of the father. Invested with the mythological presence of origin, the authority of this primary signifier is consolidated within the etymological associations linking the father as chief, head, and capital, to the source of good(s) and the word. The decapitation of this phallic hegemony inaugurates the economy of the fetish, another *indécidable,* whose subversion of the economy of metaphysics is perceived by Derrida as most effective in the work of Genet:

> In spite of all the variations to which it can be subjected, the concept of the fetish carries an invariable predicate: it is a substitute—of the thing itself as a center and source of being, the origin of presence, the thing *par excellence,* God or the principal, the archon, that which occupies the function of center in a system, for example, the phallus in a certain fantasmatic organization.[34]

The strength of the fetish is that it can be linked to contrary phenomena, as when a pubic girdle confuses sexual differentiation by allowing one to suppose at the same time "that woman was castrated or that she was not. Moreover, it allows for the supposition of the castration of the male." Thus does the fetish exhibit a double economic resistance, guaranteed by an undecidable connection to contraries: "The economy of the fetish is more powerful than that of truth, which is decidable, or the thing itself, or of a discourse deciding on castration. The fetish is that which cannot be opposed."[35]

The force of the fetish does not succumb to the temptation to reduce the general economy to "a circulating economy."[36] Nor does it submit to a moral imperative, unlike the sovereignty by which Bataille condemns Genet's travesty of communication. Derrida explains the blind spot of the author of "Le Langage des fleurs" as a deficiency in a system that allows for slippage into the most "authoritarian predication".

> As an unstable, inaccessible limit, sovereignty in its entire system is always in the process of swinging toward metaphysics [truth, authenticity, propriety, mastery]. It can always be read in the code it reverses, which it not only upsets but must also overthrow. All that is needed for a metaphysical reading to take place is a simple nothing *[rien],* a linguistic or logical discursive nothing: the affect of an intolerable identification . . . provokes an interpretive decision.[37]

With the allegation that in Genet's work sovereignty is betrayed and communication fails, Bataille, according to Derrida, falls victim to both his own categories and Genet's text. The latter lays traps for the reader in the way a trick mirror forces unwelcome reflections; "it sets a stage that obliges the other to unmask himself—to say what he would not have wanted, should not have said. . . ."[38] What Bataille claims to observe, however, is an ersatz, the inauthentic production of a brilliant *metteur en scène* who provides sensations through procurement. What is it, challenges Derrida, that the author of *Story of the Eye* wishes *not* to see?

The deconstructive perspective highlights facile appropriations of sovereignty through the trompe l'oeil of false identities and specious claims to presence. Most susceptible is a concept of the gift bounded by the restricted economy of exchange. Derrida, however, insists that every sacrifice or expenditure expresses a remainder or *reste* that can never be entirely consumed, dialecticized, or transgressed. Vomit or excrement, for example, overflows any project of containment or circumscription, and such excess is responsible for defying the restricted economy of mimetic representation.[39] The radical implications of the general economy should, therefore, be considered this way:

> To "deconstruct" philosophy is also to analyze the structured genealogy
> of its concepts in the most faithful, internal manner; but at the same time
> from without, from a certain *unqualifiable, unnameable* exterior, in order to
> determine what this history has been able to dissimulate or prohibit,
> constituting itself as history through its repressive process.[40]

Derrida subsequently qualifies repression by insisting that it must be differentiated from the unthinkable or the suppressed. This issue becomes central to deconstruction when it must indicate its position in relation to the discourse of domination, whose claim on meaning reinforces the triumph of the restricted economy over *non-savoir*. Thus, one must consider whether the general economy constitutes the repressed, suppressed, or unthinkable of Western civilization. Moreover, is that broad spectrum of values, behavior and modes of thought known as occidental responsible for this *impensé*, or is it to be understood as the transgression of limits determined anthropologically, or else within history?[41]

The deficiencies of these unqualified notions is equally striking in intertextual confrontations, and the questions raised there regarding the position of one author, text, philosophy, to another. For the moment, we will therefore say that what Bataille appears to resist is Genet's calculated demonstration that even the author's privileged access to the reader through the text cannot overcome the failed communication characteristic of all intersubjective relations. Sartre regarded this provocation as indicative of Genet's originality; his text solicits the reader to do the work: "To read Genet is to make a pact with the Devil . . . Genet's poetry is a murder of prose; a deliberate damning of the reader."[42]

Bataille discredits Genet in the name of sovereignty and communication, signaling for Derrida his invocation of authority to justify his own concept of these categories. Genet "murders" prose to the extent that he undertakes a dematerialization of the thing. Not to be confused with an idealization of the real, Genet's naming process aims to "kill."[43] This breakdown of solidarity through language is explained by the sense of being an outsider to language. Thus, his own creation is not intended for communication; it is not a system of signs nor a discourse on the world. Rather, Genet offers the reader a simulation of his own universe, which "undermines the existing one with its fallacious sense of the referent as a name."[44] We are told that the author of *Notre Dame des fleurs* loathed flowers—he adores not the rose, but its name; the word as emblem is thus divested of the "aspect" Bataille pursued: "there is not a touch of sensuality in this universe."[45] According to Sartre, Genet's primary activity, naming, is his narcissistic and onanistic way of giving: "Being an ascetic and having almost no needs, he retains only the naming which symbolizes for him his virtual integration into the society of the Just. That is precisely what we have called generosity. . . . "[46]

Bataille suspected the lack of affect in Genet's writing to be symptomatic of his betrayal of all bonds, including the loyalty mandated by sovereignty for communication between author and reader. Sartre defended Genet's repudiation of reciprocity even as he acknowledged the suspicious quality of the emotions transmitted by a writer who conceives of treason as the greatest evil and, therefore, his goal. Only the sorrow evinced for a dead lover seems to engage Genet in a sustained relationship. The obsessive desire to possess an other through incorporation, however, must be worked out through writing. Identification of this sort refuses loss and cannot overcome its subservience to indefinite mourning.

In this way, the pattern of relationships between the writer, the text, and the reader observed in Genet, as refracted through his position toward giving, reveals the less visible connections between economy and writing. In *Glas,* for instance, Derrida claims to intone the death knell of grieving—*le deuil du deuil*—and proceeds with a ceremonial beheading of the pillars of Western culture.[47] The sacrifice to end all sacrifices is formalized in a textual game exhibiting neither loss nor gain. Deconstruction incessantly plays out the antinomies that insist on reconstituting themselves, a process graphically depicted by the two columns of the text. By refusing all repose to the undecidable excess, the circulating *reste,* the sovereign *écriture* is locked into an unending movement and condemns itself to the particular economy of an indeterminate sentence.[48]

Derrida's textual economy is thus consistent with his position that all phenomena, however heterogeneous, are susceptible to recuperation. This is the warning issued through his reading of Bataille: Sovereignty can be read within the discourse of the master as well as that of the slave, within the code it reverses, which it not only upsets but must also overthrow. His own strategic safeguards against the homogenizing forces of control are the undecidables, and, therefore, unnameables. Following Bataille's lead, I have contended that heterogeneity points to the displacements to which it is subject within a variety of categories, including the sacred, eroticism, poetry, death, and mysticism, and illustrates the extent to which every culture provides more or less adequate accommodations for destruction. Yet the rubric of dépense also contends that heterogeneous forces motivate the human need to give, as manifested in a deliberate engagement of the other in reciprocal recognition. In question here are the radical implications of the economy of an experience determined as incommensurate with the categories of language.

Sartre derided Bataille for situating laughter at the confluence of communal understanding and discursive knowledge, and labeled his a "jaundiced" laugh. Unlike Bergson's "white and inoffensive" version or Nietzsche's "lighter" one, Bataille's laughter is "bitter and insistent." Moreover, Sartre trivializes the issue of a laughing subject modified through the communication encountered at the heart of "a unanimous crowd" by pointing out that Bataille neither makes his reader laugh nor does he give evidence of having laughed when not alone. In sum, he questions, *of what* has Bataille gained an understanding?"[49]

Bataille need not have defended those moments of greatest intensity in his text if the heterogeneity of *le rire* did not call into question the very quality of the expérience intérieure. To what extent does this "anguished contemplation" need justification if, indeed, it precludes action and extends to the author's ability to fight?

Bataille's response traces the impulse for the experience to a general nostalgia for ecstatic states, even though its immediate historical context of the Second World War makes such nostalgia seem "suspicious and lugubrious," because it is of no "active" value (V, 540).[50] That war is rejected as a viable collective experience under any circumstances is evident in the portion of the response preoccupied with confirming laughter's qualifications. Replying to Sartre, Bataille points out that phenomenology cannot be called on to appreciate laughter since, like all experiences incurring dépense, it cannot be known from within.[51] Though Sartre may agree, the issue then becomes one of defining the objectivity of a phenomenon that transcends the individual but is not mediated by a thing or the codes of exchange. Laughter, Derrida acknowledges, exceeds the mastery of philosophical dyads. He should also have recognized, however, that it encapsulates the ambivalence of the general economy by drawing together subjects whose sense of insufficiency engages their will to wholeness in gratuitous effusion. Thus *le rire* must be appreciated as part of the general economy's tendency to start from such "givens" as sacrifice, war, and the economy of the festival in order to explore all those lived states that nonetheless move beyond their immediately objective status and qualify as communication. The demand for objectivity makes no concessions to science, but points to one of the few paths leading to that region of the soul where life is wedded to death in a celebration that escapes the traditional matings of philosophy.

Finally, laughter, like eroticism, is sovereign by dint of its impersonal force engaging energy into any experience of dépense, including writing. Thus the deconstruction of the body evidenced in the *Histoire de l'oeil* was a necessary precondition to a mode of communication that undermines the restricted economy of the subject as structured through discourse: "what appears most strange in these diverse physiological states is that communication is linked to them, just as it is in laughter, to the break with the categories of language" (V, 566).

In general, Sartre expresses strong reservations regarding the collective dimension of the expérience intérieure as a contribution to social solidarity. He is particularly skeptical toward laughter's political potential. Bataille described the initial movement of *le rire* as proceeding from high to low. In its second phase of reflux, emanating from the base, laughter's ascent toward the summit contests the symbolic representatives of sufficiency ensconced there. Sartre asks why one calls the wave *laughter* when *revolt* or *analysis* would be more appropriate to the seriousness of most revolutionaries? Any manifestation of negativity, he contends, will provoke a correspondingly positive reaction. Refuting him is the "nonpositive affirmation" of dépense, indicative of the movement outward toward the other prompted by a paired sense of insufficiency and energetic overflow, neither of which is satisfied through production, accumulation, or exchange.[52] Cognizant of the degree to which dépense entails the painful relinquishment of conventional sources of identity, Bataille insists that he is the first to have demonstrated "the connection between anguish and communication" (V, 542). Thus, a response to the double solicitation of the Bataillian anthropology must be an experience like the laughter Bakhtin praised, which "purifies from dogmatism, from the intolerant and the petrified, liberates from fanaticism and pedantry, from fear and intimidation, from didacticism, naiveté and illusion, from the single meaning, from the single level, from sentimentality." Because laughter does not permit seriousness to atrophy and to be torn away from the one being, it restores that "ambivalent wholeness" for which revolutions are made. Observes Bakhtin: "Such is the function of laughter in the historical development of culture and literature."[53]

Indeed, the purpose of this study has been to show that dépense, the cornerstone of a theory of general economy which assumes the experience of laughter,[54] continues to orient the most innovative departures of recent French critical thought. This persistence must not be read as a nostalgic leitmotif deploring the conquests of Western economism, but as a critique of the quality of exchange and communication within contemporary culture. The evaluations I have undertaken here follow the procedures indicated by Bataille, a writer acutely aware that the foundation of one thought is that of another. He compares ideas to bricks cemented in a wall so that only the blind would not perceive the connecting mortar. Moreover, the illusory freedom of the isolated brick is inevitably paid for, because it cannot see "the vague terrains and accumulated detritus to which it will be abandoned" (VII, 285).

The parable extends to writer and critic alike. The work of the mason who assembles is most necessary: all of the contiguous bricks of a book must be as visible as the new one. The reader finds a place within such a construct which, more than a cumulus of debris, is tantamount to a consciousness of self. Propelled by the desire for an impossibly "unlimited assemblage" which requires courage, given the temptation to abandon "the open and impersonal movement of thought for an isolated opinion" (VII, 285), the act of consciousness exercises thought with no other goal than the negation of individual perspectives.

Reading Bataille, and through him the history of critical thought during the last half-century, reveals a striving toward consciousness that grapples for its specificity within a culture of restricted exchanges and their possible alternatives. The modern discontent reasserts itself, as Mauss noted, with "the theme of the gift, of generosity and self-interest in giving." Its current reformulation within dépense precludes satisfaction through nostalgia, but it also recognizes that only the force that awakens from the slumber of reason will attain full consciousness.

In my reading of Bataille, I show that it is not possible to substantiate a new mode of rationality through the speculative theories or empirical research of any one work, even though I have pointed out inadequacies and contradictions when necessary. Furthermore, the readings of Sartre and Derrida indicate that the evaluation of the general economy, effected through the interplay between limits and transgressions determining the Bataillian anthropology, cannot be confined to the microcosm of textual comparisons indifferent to the broader perspectives of a historical analysis.

This historical contextualization of dépense requires that it be differentiated from the don so that it not appear as the simple inversion of, or substitution for, production and accumulation. Similarly, I distinguish it from the conspicuous waste of potlatch which reaffirms the existing social hierarchy. To break the hegemony of a certain concept of reason, dépense has to be situated in relation to models of refusal which unwittingly reproduce a regressive notion of sovereignty limited to sanctioned domains —poetry, art, religion—or a special category of person—the aristocrat, the criminal, the saint. The subtleties of differentiation are further strained by the development of the bourgeois-capitalism of the last century into a consumer society that ostensibly gratifies the desire for consumption, but effectively precludes expenditure as irreversible loss. I do, however, read dépense within the text of the don, by insisting on its implications as a collective mode of giving. Praise for the political repercussions of these notions was expressed most recently this way:

> The politics of the "gift" thereby *also* becomes a tactic of subversion. By the same token, what in the economy of the gift was a willed loss and an intentional waste is within the profit economy transformed into a transgression, standing as the figure for excess (spoilage), for contestation (the repudiation of profit), or for crime (violation of private property).[55]

The general economy of dépense continues to be a forceful notion because it encompasses not only extremes, but illuminates nondiscursive instants of communication as well. As such, these exchanges of energy contribute to the displacement or deconstruction of the "heliocentric concept of speech" characteristic of Western logocentrism.[56] The presuppositions of Platonic metaphysics are consolidated within a rhetorical repertoire of figures allying the "intelligible" sun of idealism with the father as source of reason, good(s), and the word.[57] This sun hides the other, anal, pineal sun of dépense Bataille allows to shine forth in the phantasms of his mythological anthropology. Whence the importance of a figure lauded as the sole image worthy of literary description—a glaring sun to which the eye, located at the summit of a giant burning head, turns: "this is the unpleasant light of the notion of dépense, glowing above the still empty notion, which is the consequence of a methodical analysis" (II, 25).

The tension between the two suns, and the appreciation of dépense at stake, can be taken as paradigmatic of the issues raised in wanting to situate the general economy. The conflict is found in the challenge Bataille forwarded to all his readers, including himself, but is most pertinent to the critic, called on to propose yet another reading. I see my contribution to the evaluation of the general economy in the emphasis I place on its very generality. The result is an anthropology whose heterodoxy is constituted through the categories of Bataille. I have used the data of anthropology as a vantage point from which to challenge certain assumptions of *la pensée bourgeoise,* convinced that this perspective could modify the categories of critical thought by animating them with the energy of expenditure. With the opening of the eye, however, the comfort of a conclusion is sacrificed to

Bataille's *impossible:* "And in this place of gathering, where violence reigns at the limit of that which escapes coherence, the one who reflects within coherence perceives that there is no longer a place for him" (VII, 285).

NOTES

INTRODUCTION

1.   While it is not possible to detail here the *Tel Quel* readings, it is important to note that their central focus, the revolutionary claims—poetic and political—they make for Bataille's text, can be assessed from the point of view of the general economy developed in this study. The essays of Barthes, Derrida, Foucault, Kristéva, and Sollers comprise a practice of reading and writing at odds with the view of criticism as secondary to the original work. In this they stress Bataille's transgressive mixture of disciplines and discourses. Whether this is the most effective means to implement and evaluate the general economy is further considered in the account of Derrida and Bataille in chapter 6. The reader is advised to consult the review itself, and the papers collected from the 1972 Cérisy Colloquium which offer an excellent overview of the slant taken by its contributors in *Bataille*. See also Michèle Richman, "Georges Bataille."

2.   Roland Barthes, "De l'oeuvre au texte," p. 155, emphasis added. All references are to the English edition cited in the Bibliography.

3.   Ibid., p. 157

4.   References to the collected works of Bataille are cited in the text as "(volume number in roman numeral, page number in arabic numeral)." The collected works are listed in the Bibliography.

5.   The inadequacy of available terms to describe the history of a work in relation to such moments of consciousness was pointed out by Edward Said, who underscores "the limits to employing the human life cycle as a model of literary history: anthropomorphic units of reality, such as work, author, generation, and so forth" ("Roads Taken and Not Taken in Contemporary Criticism," p. 345).

6.   An important aspect of the *Tel Quel* reading is that both Bataille and Artaud represent critical positions vis-à-vis surrealism. See chapter 2 of this study for a discussion of the Breton-Bataille polemic.

7.   The most recent challenge to Bataille's contention that dépense stems from within is forwarded by Jean Baudrillard: "Il faut défier les dieux par le sacrifice pour qu'ils répondent par la profusion. Autrement dit, la racine du sacrifice et de l'économie générale n'est jamais la pure et simple *dépense,* ou je ne sais quelle pulsion d'excès qui nous viendrait de la nature, mais un processus incessant de défi" ("Quand Bataille attaquait le principe métaphysique de l'économie," p. 5).

8.   Louis Dumont, "Une Science en devenir," p. 19. Unless indicated otherwise, all translations from the French are my own.

9.   Ibid.

10.   Marc Augé, *Pouvoirs de vie, pouvoirs de mort,* p. 12.

11.   For a comparison between anthropology and surrealism during the 1930s, see Robin Horton, "Lévy-Bruhl, Durkheim, and the Scientific Revolution."

12.   Roland Barthes rightly notes the similarities between economics and linguistics as they both assimilate other domains, but he does not stress their contest for hegemony:
Semiology, which we can canonically define as the science of signs, . . . has emerged from linguistics through its operational concepts. But linguistics itself, somewhat like economics (and the comparison is perhaps not insignificant), is, I believe, in the process of splitting apart. On the one hand, linguistics tends toward the formal pole and, like econometrics, it is thereby becoming more formalized; on the other hand, linguistics is assimilating contents that are more and more numerous and remote from its original field. Just as the object of economics today is everywhere, in the political, the social, the cultural, so the object of linguistics is limitless. "Lecture in Inauguration of the Chair of Literary Semiology, Collège de France, January 7, 1977," *October,* no. 8 [Spring 1979], p. 10).
For the influence of the notion of "economy" on the study of literature, see Marc Shell, *The Economy of Literature* (Baltimore: Johns Hopkins University Press, 1978).

CHAPTER 1

1.   See Jean Piel, introduction to Georges Bataille, *La Part maudite,* p. 25. All succeeding references are to the edition in the collected works.

2.   Marcel Mauss, *Sociologie et anthropologie* (Paris: Presses Universitaires de France, 1950). The chapter entitled "Essai sur le don: Forme et raison de l'échange dans les sociétés archaïques" is published in English as *The Gift: Forms and Functions of Exchange in Archaic Societies,* p. 66. All references are to the English translation.

3.   See Claude Lefort, "L'Echange et la lutte des hommes."

4.   Nicolas de Malebranche, cited in Claude Lévi-Strauss, "Introduction à l'oeuvre de Marcel Mauss," p. xxxiii.

5.   Emile Durkheim, *Les Formes élémentaires de la vie religieuse* (Paris: Presses Universitaires de France, 1915). All references are to the English translation, *Elementary Forms of the Religious Life.*

6.   Pierre Bourdieu, *Esquisse d'une théorie de la pratique,* p. 233.

7.   "Man's economy is, as a rule, submerged in his social relations. The change from this to a society which was, on the contrary, submerged in the economic system was an entirely novel development" Karl Polanyi, *Primitive, Archaic, and Modern Economies,* p. 65.

8.   Marshall Sahlins, *Culture and Practical Reason,* p. 216.

9.   Lévi-Strauss, "Marcel Mauss," p. xxxiii.

10.   For a good summary of the common sources for the notion of the "symbolic order" in Mauss and Lévi-Strauss, see Jacques Lacan, *Speech and Language in Psychoanalysis,* pp. 249-61. See also Jean Baudrillard, *L'Echange symbolique et la mort,* for an overview of the history of the notion of dépense in relation to the symbolic order as Baudrillard views it.

11.   For a discussion of "ontological transformation," see Bourdieu, *Esquisse d'une théorie,* p. 239.

12.   For an excellent and more detailed study of this question, see Rodolphe Gasché, "L'Echange héliocentrique," p. 73.

13.   Mauss, *Sociologie et anthropologie,* p. 41.

14.   Baudrillard wrongly accuses Bataille of having misconstrued Mauss on this issue: "Bataille a mal lu Mauss: le don unilatéral n'existe pas" ("Quand Bataille attaquait le principe métaphysique de l'économie," p. 5).

15. "The objects of bright pride" is a phrase used by William Reid to describe the artifacts of Northwest Coast Indian art; it is cited in Allen Wardwell, *Objects of Bright Pride: Northwest Coast Indian Art from the American Museum of Natural History* (New York: Center for Inter-American Relations and American Federation of Arts, 1978).

16. Pierre Clastres, "Echange et pouvoir," p. 54.

17. See Alfred Métraux, "Recontre avec les ethnologues," p. 678, for a summary of Bataille's first article on anthropology.

18. Edward Said, "Roads Taken and Not Taken in Contemporary Criticism," p. 345.

19. Contemporary readers of Mauss are aware that current perceptions of the "Essai sur le don" are highly mediated by Bataille. Cf. Pierre Birnbaum, "Du socialisme au don," p. 46; also, Marc Augé, *Pouvoirs de vie, pouvoirs de mort,* p. 15.

20. See Polanyi, *Primitive, Archaic, and Modern Economies,* chap. 1.

21. Ibid., p.4.

22. Ibid.

23. Ibid., p.xii.

24. Ibid., p.70.

25. Ibid.

26. Ibid., p.71.

27. Maurice Godelier, *Rationality and Irrationality in Economics,* passim, esp. pp. 16–17.

28. Ibid., p. 18.

29. "Economics, according to Robbins' famous formulation, taken over by Von Mises, Samuelson, Burling, etc., is 'the science which studies human behavior as a relationship between ends and scarce means which have alternative uses' "(Cited by Godelier, *Rationality and Irrationality in Economics, op. cit.,* p. 13. See also Edward E. Le Clair, Jr., and Harold K. Schneider, *Economic Anthropology,* p. 8. See also Marshall Sahlins, "Political Power and the Economy in Primitive Society," for a discussion of the common fallacy among economic anthropologists to consider the individual, rather than the collectivity, as the basic unit of analysis.

30. Talcott Parsons, *The Structure of Social Action,* 1, p. 58.

31. See Sahlins for a general refutation of the basic assumptions of classical economics as applied to archaic economies. In particular, he stresses his disagreement with the alleged "hedonism" of economic man, whose "unlimited wants" must be satisfied through "limited means" (*Stone Age Economics,* p. 13).

32. Thorstein Veblen, cited by Sahlins, in *Culture and Practical Reason.*

33. Godelier, *Rationality and Irrationality in Economics,* p. 13.

34. Georg Lukács, *History and Class Consciousness,* p. 229.

35. Ibid., pp. 223–55.

36. Ibid., p. 230.

37. Ibid., p. 83.

38. Ibid., p. 239.

39. For a critical review of the literature, see Godelier, *Rationality and Irrationality in Economics,* chap. 1.

40. See ibid., and Maurice Godelier, *Perspectives in Marxist Anthropology.*

41. See Raymond Queneau, "Premières confrontations avec Hegel," pp. 695–700. See also Mark Poster, *Existential Marxism in Postwar France,* pp. 8–17.

42. Another important difference between Marxism and the point of view developed here is the persistent belief in the "use value" of things separate from their exchange value. As stated by Lukács, "this rational objectification conceals above all the immediate—qualitative and material—character of things as things" (*History and Class Consciousness,* p. 92).

43. Cf. Sahlins's recent assessment of the contribution of historical materialism to the critique of *homo oeconomicus* as "the ideal offspring of a bourgeois-capitalist society convinced that human cultures are formulated out of practical activity and, behind that, utilitarian interest" is

equally damaging. He boldly states that the underlying "continuity" in the Marxist concept of "species being" is "the rationality of utilitarianism" (*Culture and Practical Reason,* p. 161).

44.   Lefort, "L'Echange et la lutte des hommes," p. 1400.
45.   Sahlins, *Stone Age Economics,* p. 175.
46.   Richard Titmuss, *The Gift Relationship,* p. 224.
47.   Ibid.
48.   Anthony Heath, *Rational Choice and Social Exchange,* p. 60.
49.   Claude Lévi-Strauss, *Les Structures élémentaires de la parenté.* (Paris: Presses Universitaires de France, 1949). All references are to the English translation by James Harle Bell, John Richard von Sturms, and Rodney Needham, *The Elementary Structures of Kinship,* p. 497.
50.   Ibid., p. 496.
51.   Ibid., p. 497.
52.   Lévi-Strauss, "Marcel Mauss," pp. xliv, xlvi, xlviii, xlix, 1.
53.   Ibid., p. xix.
54.   See Jean Baudrillard, *Pour une critique de l'économie politique du signe.*
55.   Sahlins, *Culture and Practical Reason,* p. 211.
56.   Lévi-Strauss, "Marcel Mauss," p. xxx.
57.   Norman O. Brown, *Life against Death,* p. 265.
58.   Ibid.
59.   Ibid., p. 269.
60.   Queneau, "Premières confrontations avec Hegel," p. 697.
61.   Brown, *Life against Death,* pp. 307–22.
62.   Lefort, "L'Echange et la lutte des hommes," p. 1415.
63.   Ibid.
64.   Ibid.
65.   Ibid.
66.   Durkheim, *Elementary Forms,* p. 242.
67.   Ibid., pp. 242–43.
68.   Ibid., p. 469.
69.   Ibid., p. 468.
70.   Ibid., p. 426.
71.   Ibid.
72.   Baudrillard, *L'Echange symbolique et la mort,* p. 63, n. 1.

CHAPTER 2

1.   This essential difference between archaic and modern societies is dealt with in Raymond Firth, *Primitive Polynesian Economy,* p. 337, where he stresses the absence of a system of *equivalence* (as opposed to a scale of relative values) within archaic exchange. Firth also indicates that "goods are related to one another by a process of tacit comparison in which measurement is given by the possibility of substitution and not by actual transfer against one another." Cf. Maurice Godelier, *Rationality and Irrationality in Economics,* as well as Jean-Joseph Goux's important work, *Freud, Marx: Economie et symbolique,* where he analyzes the process of substitutions in relation to symbolization and exchange.
2.   Pierre Bourdieu, *Esquisse d'une théorie de la pratique,* p. 229.
3.   Ibid., p. 228.
4.   Ibid., p. 242.
5.   Ibid., p. 228.
6.   For the purposes of this discussion, we accept Georg Lukács's definition of rationalism as follows: "a formal system whose unity derives from its orientation towards that aspect of the phenomena that can be grasped by the understanding, that is created by the

understanding and hence also subject to the control, the predictions and the calculations of the understanding" (*History and Class Consciousness,* p. 113).

7.　According to Karl Polanyi:

The economic rationalism to which we are heir posits a type of action as *sui generis* economic. In this perspective an actor—a single man, a family, a whole society—is seen facing a natural environment that is slow to yield its life-giving elements. Economic action—or, more precisely, *economizing action, the essence of rationality*—is, then, regarded as a manner of disposing of time and energy so that a maximum of goals are achieved out of this man-nature relationship. And the economy becomes the locus of such action. It is, of course, admitted that, in reality, the operation of this economy may be influenced in any number of ways by other factors of a non-economic character, be they political, military, artistic, or religious. But the essential core of utilitarian rationality remains as the model of the economy.

[*Primitive, Archaic, and Modern Economies,* p. 117, emphasis added]

8.　Lukács, *History and Class Consciousness,* pp. 113–14.

9.　See Bourdieu, *Esquisse d'une théorie,* pp. 227–43.

10.　Georges Bataille, "Le Sens moral de la sociologie," pp. 39–47.

11.　Ibid., p. 41.

12.　Ibid.

13.　Ibid., p. 45.

14.　Ibid., p. 46.

15.　Ibid.

16.　Emile Durkheim, *Elementary Forms of the Religious Life,* p. 243.

17.　Ibid., p. 57.

18.　Steven Lukes, *Emile Durkheim, His Life and Work,* p. 27.

19.　Durkheim, *Elementary Forms,* p. 469.

20.　Ibid., p. 243.

21.　This widespread thesis can be found in Robert Bréchon's study, *Le Surréalisme,* but is challenged by Jean-Louis Houdebine in "L'Ennemi du dedans: Bataille et le surréalisme: Eléments, prises de parti," *Tel Quel,* no. 52 (1972), pp. 49–73; reprinted in Cérisy Colloquium, *Bataille,* pp. 153–99.

22.　André Breton, *Manifestes du surréalisme,* pp. 76–77.

23.　See Jacques Ehrmann, "Le Dedans et le dehors," pp. 29–40, for an excellent discussion of these categories as they relate to the ideological function of "anthropological" literature.

24.　Lukács, *History and Class Consciousness,* p. 140.

25.　Georges Bataille, "Le Surréalisme en 1947," p. 272.

26.　André Breton, *Position politique du surréalisme,* p. 59.

27.　The term *collège* was provided by Jules Monnerot, and Denis Hollier explains its significance here through the notion of "elective affinities." See Hollier, ed., *Le Collège de sociologie,* p. 15.

28.　Bataille, cited in ibid., p. 36.

29.　Ibid.

30.　Ibid.

31.　Roger Caillois, "The Collège de sociologie," p. 63.

32.　Rodolphe Gasché, for one, values the heterological practice of Bataille's writing over his theoretical presentation of heterogeneity. See Gasché, "L'Almanach hétérologique," p. 3.

33.　Durkheim, *Elementary Forms,* p. 479.

34.　Emile Durkheim, *On Morality and Society,* p. 162.

35.　Durkheim, *Elementary Forms,* p. 241.

36.　Walter Benjamin, *Reflections,* p. 189.

37. Durkheim, *Elementary Forms,* p. 471. The entire passage revealing Durkheim's views on historical materialism reads as follows:

Therefore it is necessary to avoid seeing in this theory of religion a simple restatement of historical materialism: that would be misunderstanding our thought to an extreme degree. In showing that religion is something essentially social, we do not mean to say that it confines itself to translating into another language the material forms of society and its immediate vital necessities. It is true that we take it as evident that social life depends upon its material foundation and bears its mark, just as the mental life of an individual depends upon his nervous system and in fact his whole organism. But collective consciousness is something more than a mere epiphenomenon of its morphological basis, just as individual consciousness is something more than a simple efflorescence of the nervous system. In order that the former may appear, a synthesis *sui generis* of particular consciousnesses is required. Now this synthesis has the effect of disengaging a whole world of sentiments, ideas and images which, once born, obey laws all their own. They attract each other, repel each other, unite, divide themselves, and multiply, though these combinations are not commanded and necessitated by the condition of the underlying reality. The life thus brought into being even enjoys so great an independence that it sometimes indulges in manifestations with no purpose or utility of any sort, for the mere pleasure of affirming itself.

CHAPTER 3

1. See I, 275–375, for Bataille's contributions.

2. See Raymond Firth, *Primitive Polynesian Economy,* noting that different spheres of exchange remain discrete in archaic economies (food vs. bark-cloth vs. bonito hooks and canoes). Firth states: "As far as material goods are concerned there is no class or object which serves as a unit of measurement for all others, and there is no conversion of the worth of different classes of object into one another in a systematic way" (p. 339). Cf. Maurice Godelier, *Rationality and Irrationality in Economics,* p. 297.

3. Pierre Bourdieu, *Esquisse d'une théorie de la pratique,* p. 228.

4. Ibid.

5. Karl Polanyi, *Primitive, Archaic, and Modern Economies,* p. 72.

6. Bourdieu, *Esquisse d'une théorie,* p. 234.

7. Ibid.

8. Ibid.: "The theory of economic practices is only one particular case of a general theory of the economy of practices" (p. 235).

9. See I, 379–432.

10. Georges Bataille, "Le Sens moral de la sociologie," p. 45.

11. See Walter Benjamin, *Reflections,* p. 191.

12. See Raymond Quenecu, "Premières confrontations avec Hegel," pp. 675–700. See also Mark Poster, *Existential Marxism in Postwar France,* pp. 8–17.

13. Alexander Kojève, *Introduction à la lecture de Hegel,* p. 174.

14. Ibid., pp. 178–79.

15. Ibid., pp. 11, 21.

16. Georges Bataille, "Hegel, la mort, et le sacrifice," p. 33.

17. Ibid., p. 34.

18. Kojève, *La Lecture de Hegel,* p. 27.

19. Ibid.

20. Bataille, "Hegel," p. 38.
21. Ibid., pp. 29–30.
22. Ibid., p. 30.
23. Michel Foucault, "Préface à la transgression," p. 761.
24. Both *jouissance* and its verbal form, *jouir,* appear frequently in contemporary French critical theory bearing the Bataillian connotation of an experience irreducible to the sexuality condoned by the restricted economy. See, in particular, Roland Barthes, *Le Plaisir du texte,* (Collection *Tel Quel,* Paris: Editions du Seuil, 1973), p. 90. See also Michèle Richman, "Sex and Signs: The Language of French Feminist Criticism," *Language and Style* 13, no. 4 (Fall 1980): 62–80.
25. Georges Bataille, "Conférences sur le non-savoir," p. 5.
26. Ibid., p. 18.
27. Foucault, "Préface à la transgression," p. 752.
28. Ibid., p. 767.
29. See Norman O. Brown, *Life Against Death,* p. 280, for a discussion of this matter.
30. Claude Lévi-Strauss, *The Elementary Structures of Kinship,* p. 496.
31. Bataille's originality is best appreciated in comparison with the Anglo-American literary tradition. The latter can be summarily characterized by its myth of "nature" or "natural" sex, of which the most evident example is D. H. Lawrence. See Gilles Deleuze and Félix Guattari, *L'Anti-Oedipe.* Another writer in point is Henry Miller, undoubtedly a major challenge to American puritanism, but one who ultimately remains a "soft" pornographer: eroticism is good, healthy, animal-like sex and can easily be integrated into the total life experience of the free-wheeling bohemian. There is an optimism here, an implicit view of human nature that can be freed once and for all from social repressions.
32. See Julia Kristeva, "Le Sujet en procès," pp. 12–30, 17–38, for her analysis of Artaud's writings as an effort to subvert the "sujet unaire."
33. Susan Sontag, *Styles of Radical Will,* p. 55.
34. The world of pornography is highly conventionalized at the emotive level—the purpose of these ritualizations is to deflect any emotion that would hamper the sexual machinery. In other words, the price for having deviated from social norms at one level is paid for by recuperating sexual energy into conventions that are equally repressive.
35. The connection of communication/community is not automatic, and the problem of its evaluation is typical of that found in Bataille's work. Denis Hollier has articulated the issue in these terms:

> Au sujet de l'opposition communauté/communication, ce que je voudrais dire c'est qu'il n'est en fait jamais possible quand on parle de Bataille de s'asseoir sur un mot, même sur deux. Il y a ce mouvement constant du vocabulaire qui fait qu'à un certain moment il y a des mots qui prennent une valeur stratégique décisive et je crois que c'est peut-être une des études les plus intéressantes à faire sur Bataille et des plus urgentes à faire. . . . Il y a certainement des textes qui se prêtent á cette opposition de la communauté et de la communication. Mais il y en a d'autres où la communication est présentée du même côté que la communauté. [*Bataille* (Paris: U.G.E., 1973), pp. 103–4]

36. Jacques Derrida first pointed to the need for this revision of the *Aufhebung* in a Bataillian context: "One must interpret one stratum of Bataille's writing against another. Bataille can, therefore, only have recourse to an empty form of the *Aufhebung,* in an analogical manner, in order to accomplish what had never been done before; that is, to designate the transgressive relation which links the world of meaning to the world of non-meaning" ("De l'économie restreinte à l'économie générale," p. 406).
37. For an extended discussion of this issue, see Richman, "Sex and Signs."
38. All references are to the English translation by Joachim Neugroschel, *Story of the Eye.*
39. Roland Barthes, "La Métaphore de l'oeil."

162

40. Ibid., p. 776.

41. Ibid.

42. Emile Durkheim, *Elementary Forms of the Religious Life,* p. 269.

43. The works consulted that deal specifically with the *historical* transformation from symbol to sign include Julia Kristeva, "Du symbole au signe," *Tel Quel,* no. 34 (1968), pp. 34–31; Michel Foucault, *Les Mots et les choses;* Jean-Joseph Goux, *Freud, Marx: Economie et symbolique;* Jean Baudrillard, *Pour une critique de l'économie politique du signe;* and Stanley Diamond, *In Search of the Primitive.* The gist of this argument is stated by Diamond, "In the rationalized modern market each partial, impersonal exchange reduces the symbolic constitution to a calculation, a sign" (p. 133).

44. Jean Baudrillard, "Quand Bataille attaquait le principe métaphysique de l'économie," p. 5.

45. Foucault, *Les Mots et les choses,* p. 768.

46. Brown's *Life Against Death* has been cited at various moments in this study because of the striking parallels it offers with certain arguments of Bataille, in particular Brown's chapter on archaic exchange and the history of money, "Filthy Lucre." On the connection between taboo/transgression and Brown's concern with repression in the psychoanalytical sense, however, a strong divergence between the two appears; cf. pp. 297-98.

47. Barthes, "La Métaphore," p. 772.

CHAPTER 4

1. Bataille refers to "the indissociable system of prohibitions and privileges" (*L'Erotisme,* 219). Regarding the correlation between taboo/transgression and the power reserved to men, see Michèle Richman, "Eroticism in the Patriarchal Order," *Diacritics,* March 1976, p. 52.

2. Georges Bataille, "Du rapport entre le divin et le mal," p. 228.

3. Ibid., p.229.

4. Ibid.

5. Ibid., p. 230.

6. Ibid., p. 231.

7. Ibid., p. 232.

8. Ibid., p. 233.

9. Ibid., p. 234.

10. William James, *Varieties of Religious Experience,* cited in Mary Douglas, *Purity and Danger,* p. 194.

11. It is interesting to compare Bataille's critique of Hegel with the following passage from Maurice Godelier:

Or, il n'y a aucune raison de confondre ce principe de l'unité des contraires, principe qui est scientifique, avec le principe fondamental de la dialectique hégélienne qui est celui de l'identité des contraires qui n'a aucun fondement scientifique. Le principe de l'identité des contraires n'est très précisément que la condition nécessaire pour bâtir un système métaphysique clos, celui de l'idéalisme absolu qui part du postulat indémontré que l'"Esprit" est la seule réalité qui existe et qui se contredit elle-même en elle-même et reste identique à soi à travers ses contradictions puisque la matière est de la pensée en soi qui ne se pense pas et se contredit en tant que pensée, et que le logos est la pensée pour soi qui s'oppose à la pensée en soi, à la matière, et que l'unité de la pensée en soi et de la pensée pour soi est dans leur identité comme formes de l'Esprit Absolu.

12. On the convergence of Bataille's recourse to Gnostic sources with that of Artaud, it is interesting to compare Bataille's statements with Susan Sontag's introduction to *Antonin Artaud:*

Selected Writings, pp. xlv–viii. See also the excellent study by Denis Hollier, "Le Matérialisme dualiste de Georges Bataille."

13.   Douglas, *Purity and Danger,* p. 210.

14.   Henri Hubert et Marcel Mauss, "Essai sur la nature et la fonction du sacrifice."

15.   Henri Lefebvre, *Everyday Life in the Modern World,* pp. 36, 38.

16.   Roger Caillois, *L'Homme et le sacré,* pref. to the 1939 edition, p. 13. Caillois's ambivalence toward his own project is reflected in the concluding paragraph: "Je n'ai pas cru devoir éviter de porter la question sur le plan métaphysique . . . je ne pense pas que les dix dernières pages d'un livre puissent suffire à discréditer celles qui les précèdent, quand celles-ci ont été composées sans arrière-pensée, avec le seul souci de l'objectivité, en toute indépendance d'une conclusion qu'elles ne préparent que par la force des choses."

17.   Hollier, "Matérialisme dualiste," p. 45.

18.   Georges Bataille, "Discussion sur le péché," reprinted in VI, 315–59.

19.   Pierre Klossowski, *Un Si Funeste Désir,* p. 12. The complete passage reads: "Le sacrilège a pour lui une fonction 'ontologique'; dans l'acte profanateur du *nom le plus noble* de l'existence, se révèle sa présence. Ainsi Bataille, en dépit de son attitude athée demeure solidaire de toute la structure culturelle du christianisme."

CHAPTER 5

1.   Jean-Paul Sartre, "Un Nouveau Mystique," pp. 143–88.

2.   Ibid., p. 143.

3.   Ibid., p. 187.

4.   Ibid., p. 145.

5.   Ibid., p. 152.

6.   Ibid., pp. 146–47.

7.   Ibid., p. 146.

8.   Ibid., p. 144.

9.   Ibid., p. 147, emphasis added.

10.   Ibid., p. 152.

11.   Ibid., p. 154.

12.   Ibid., p. 156.

13.   Ibid., p. 162, emphasis added.

14.   Ibid., p. 163.

15.   Ibid.

16.   Ibid., p. 164.

17.   Ibid., p. 165.

18.   Ibid., pp. 165–66, emphasis added.

19.   Ibid., p. 165.

20.   Roger Caillois, cited in Denis Hollier, ed., *Le Collège de sociologie,* p. 37.

21.   Sartre, "Un Nouveau Mystique," p. 169.

22.   Ibid., p. 174.

23.   Ibid., p. 175.

24.   Ibid., p. 187.

25.   Ibid., p. 177.

26.   Ibid., p. 179.

27.   Ibid., p. 184.

28.   Ibid.

29.   Ibid., p. 185.

30.   Ibid., p. 186.

31.   Ibid., p. 161.
32.   See chapter 2, n. 8.
33.   For a discussion of these differences, see Steven Lukes, *Emile Durkheim, His Life and Work.*
34.   Talcott Parsons, *The Structure of Social Action,* 1: 56.
35.   Ibid., p. 316.
36.   Ibid., p. 314.
37.   Ibid., p. 354.
38.   Ibid., p. 440.
39.   Sartre, "Un Nouveau Mystique," p. 163.
40.   Ibid., p. 154.
41.   Jean-Paul Sartre, cited in Jean-François Lyotard, *La Phénoménologie,* p. 7.
42.   Ibid., p. 8.
43.   Edmund Husserl, cited in ibid., p. 81.
44.   Ibid.
45.   Ibid.
46.   Ibid., p. 82.
47.   Jean-Paul Sartre, *L'Etre et le néant,* p. 652.
48.   Ibid.
49.   Ibid., p. 653.
50.   Ibid., p. 656.
51.   Cf.: "The work of Durkheim, and even more so that of Mauss, have had a decisive influence on me, but I always kept my distance. Nonetheless, my ideas are based on a subjective experience. If, along with others, I founded the *Collège de Sociologie* in 1937, it was, I believe, because I had the intention of regaining a world from which I am too easily diverted, that of objectivity" (VII, 615).
52.   Claude Lévi-Strauss, "French Sociology," p. 505.
53.   Ibid., p. 508.
54.   Claude Lévi-Strauss, "Introduction à l'oeuvre de Marcel Mauss," p. xxviii.
55.   Ibid., p. xxix.
56.   Ibid., p. xlix.
57.   Ibid., p. l.
58.   Ibid., p. xlvi.
59.   In her explanation for Artaud's estrangement from Breton, Sontag touches on an essential element of Bataille's own criticism:
That Artaud found Breton's thinking shallow—that is, optimistic, aesthetic— follows from the fact that Breton did not have a Gnostic style or sensibility. Breton was attracted by the hope of reconciling the demands of individual freedom with the need to expand and balance the personality through generous, corporate emotions . . . the mark of Gnostic thinking is that it is enraged by *all* limits, even those that save. [Introduction to *Antonin Artaud: Selected Writings,* p. xlviii]
60.   Maurice Blanchot, "Réflexions sur le surréalisme," in *La Part du feu,* p. 93.
61.   Ibid., p. 94.
62.   Ibid.
63.   Ibid., p. 95, emphasis added.
64.   Ibid.
65.   Ibid., p. 97.
66.   Ibid., p. 99.
67.   Maurice Blanchot, *L'Entretien infini,* p. 600.
68.   Ibid., p. 602.
69.   See Michel Foucault, *Les Mots et les choses,* p. 395.
70.   See Georges Bataille, "De l'existentialisme au primat de l'économie," pp. 515–26.

71. Cf. Marshall Sahlins:

Thus does the economy, as the dominant institutional locus, produce not only objects for appropriate subjects, but subjects for appropriate objects. It throws a classification across the entire cultural superstructure, ordering the distinctions of other sectors by the oppositions of its own—precisely as it uses these distinctions for purposes of its own [gain]. . . The interest taken in such conceptual correspondences as worker/capitalist, youth/adult is in no way an idealism. Their recognition by the anthropologist or economist, like their existence in the society, reflects a real experience of that society—if always the only kind of real social experience, namely, that mediated symbolically. [*Culture and Practical Reason,* pp. 216–17]

72. Jean-Paul Sartre, *Saint Genet,* p. 162.

73. Ibid., p. 193.

74. Ibid., p. 579.

75. Ibid., p. 200.

76. Ibid., p. 202.

77. Georges Bataille, "De l'existentialisme au primat de l'économie," pt. 2, p. 135.

CHAPTER 6

1.   The move to disestablish the author within literary criticism is treated by Susan Sontag in her introduction to *Antonin Artaud: Selected Writings,* p. xvii.

2.   Gilles Deleuze, *Présentation de Sacher-Masoch,* p. 14.

3.   For an excellent discussion of limit-term and its relation to discontinuities, see Fredric Jameson, "Imaginary and Symbolic in Lacan," p. 390. Unlike the position taken here, Jean Duvignaud argues that dépense is restricted by the Maussian determination of the don, a phenomenon he claims has been erroneously interpreted through the economic categories of the Western marketplace. See Jean Duvignaud, *Le Don du rien: Essai d'anthropologie de la fête* (Paris: Stock, 1977), p. 152.

4.   See Jacques Derrida, "De l'économie restreinte à l'économie générale," p. 399.

5.   See Jacques Derrida: "Je me permets de rappeler ici que les textes auxquels vous avez fait référence (en particulier "La double séance," "La dissémination," "La mythologie blanche," mais aussi "La pharmacie de Platon" et quelques autres) se situent *expressément* par rapport à Bataille, proposent aussi explicitement une lecture de Bataille" (*Positions,* p. 89, n. 25). The reader is advised to consult the texts cited by Derrida as well as the interview itself.

6.   Ibid., p. 17.

7.   Jacques Derrida, "La Mythologie blanche," p. 32.

8.   Jacques Derrida, "La Différance," p. 46.

9.   Ibid., p. 47.

10.   The issue of *le propre* appears throughout Derrida's work, but its relevance to a discussion of economy and economic theory is most explicit in "La Mythologie blanche," p. 7.

11.   Ibid., p. 4.

12.   For the multiple meanings of *pharmakon* and its translations, see Jacques Derrida, "La Pharmacie de Platon," *Tel Quel,* no. 32 (1968), p. 7.

13.   Ibid., p. 24.

14.   Ibid.

15.   Derrida describes the *indécidables* as follows: "A configuration of concepts which I consider to be systematic and irreducible; thereafter each intervenes and is more marked, at decisive moments in the work [of a text]" (*Positions,* p. 12). Concerned with the impact of the *indécidables,* in particular, their history as signifiers, Edward Said comments:

I think I understand him to be saying that 'différance,' or some aspect of it, depends for its exact meaning on its use at a given moment in a text. Yet we are left wondering how something can be practical, contextural, systematic, recognizable, irreducible and, at the same time, not really a fixed doctrine, nor a concept, nor an idea in the old sense of those words. Can we remain poised indefinitely between an old and a new sense? Or will not this median undecidable word begin to corral more and more meanings for itself, just like the old words? ["The Problem of Textuality," p. 699]

16. Derrida, *Positions,* p. 58.

17. Derrida, "La Différance," p. 58.

18. Ibid.

19. Derrida, *L'Ecriture et la différence,* pp. 382–83.

20. Ibid., p. 403.

21. Derrida, *Positions,* p. 56.

22. Jacques Derrida, *Of Grammatology,* p. 86.

23. Ibid.

24. Ibid., p. 85.

25. Derrida, *Positions,* p. 92.

26. Jacques Derrida: "Le mot 'entre' n'a aucun sens plein en lui-meme. . . . Ce qui vaut pour 'hymen' vaut, *mutatis mutandis,* pour tous les signes qui, comme *pharmakon, supplément, différence* et quelques autres, ont une valeur double, contradictoire, indécidable qui tient toujours à leur syntaxe" ("La Double séance," p. 250).

27. Julia Kristeva, "Le Mot, le dialogue, le roman," p. 146.

28. Derrida, *L'Ecriture et la différence,* p. 394. Cf. Duvignaud's description of the impenetrability of "le don du rien" for Western logic: "On a tôt fait de parler d'un 'non-savoir' ou d'un 'irrationnel' mais il s'agit d'un autre savoir qui ne se déduit pas d'un concept ni d'un rite, qui ne résulte pas de l'accomplissement d'une gestuelle mythique" (*Le Don du rien,* p. 164).

29. Derrida, *Positions,* p. 87.

30. Ibid., p. 89.

31. Jacques Derrida, *Glas,* p. 268.

32. Ibid., p. 269.

33. Ibid., p. 270.

34. Ibid., p. 234.

35. Ibid., p. 253.

36. Ibid. "Donner veut-dire donner un anneau et donner un anneau veut-dire garder: garde le présent. . . Le mouvement annulaire re-streint l'économie générale (compte tenu, c'est-à-dire non tenu de la perte) en économie circulante" (p. 271).

37. Ibid., p. 248.

38. Derrida, *Glas,* p. 242.

39. See Jacques Derrida, "Economimesis."

40. Derrida, *Positions,* p. 15, emphasis added.

41. For the respective positions of Derrida and Foucault regarding the *impensé,* cf. Said: "If for Derrida the *impensé* in criticism which he has frequently attacked signifies a lazy, imprecise understanding of signs, language, and textuality, then for Foucault the *impensé* is what at a specific time and in a specific way cannot be thought because certain other things have been imposed instead" ("The Problem of Textuality," p. 704).

42. Jean-Paul Sartre, *Saint Genet,* pp. 518–19.

43. Ibid., p. 397.

44. Ibid., p. 393.

45. Ibid., p. 107.

46. Ibid., p. 579.

47. See Jacques Derrida, "Ja, ou le faux-bond," p. 99.

48.   Derrida distinguishes Bataille's notions, such as sovereignty, from those of classical concepts, by their force and intensity. What appears to be characteristic of *écriture* is precisely its flattened tonality, described by Geoffrey Hartman (in an ironic paraphrase of Bataille on Genet) this way: "a desacralizing and levelling effect which the generic neutrality of the word reinforces. Many readers are left cold, seduced, and angry" ("Monsieur Texte: On Jacques Derrida, His *Glas*, p. 781). On the consequences of the economy of undecidablity for Derrida's text, cf. Said:

> Yet his work embodies an extremely pronounced self-limitation, an ascesis of a very inhibiting and crippling sort. In it Derrida has chosen the lucidity of the undecidable in a text, so to speak, over the *identifiable power* of a text; as he once said, to opt for the sterile lucidity of the performative *double scene* in texts is perhaps to neglect the implemented, effective power of textual *statement*. ["The Problem of Textuality," p. 703]

49.   Sartre, "Un Nouveau Mystique," pp. 169–72.

50.   Because all work, if not all activity (including language), is construed as subject to the criterion of utility, Bataille determined sovereign dépense as the *absence* of goals and action, whence the tension evidenced here.

51.   See also Derrida, "[On ne trouve] nulle part dans la phénoménologie un concept qui permet de penser l'intensité ou la force" (*L'Ecriture et la différence*, p. 46).

52.   Michel Foucault, "Préface à la transgression," p. 756.

53.   Mikhail Bakhtin, *Rabelais and His World*, p. 123.

54.   See Duvignaud, who does not refer to Bataille when celebrating laughter, yet describes it this way: "Le rêve, la fête, le rire, le jeu, l'imaginaire sous tous leurs aspects constitueraient, dans les formes diverses de l'expérience collective, la part irrecupérable par toute organisation de quelque importance" (*Le Don du rien*, p. 277).

55.   Michel de Certeau, "On the Oppositional Practices of Everyday Life," *Social Text*, no. 3 (Fall 1980), p. 5.

56.   Derrida, *De la grammatologie*, p. 139; English translation, p. 91.

57.   Jacques Derrida: "L'unité configurative de ces significations—le pouvoir de la parole, la création de l'être et de la vie, le soleil (c'est-à-dire aussi bien, nous le verrons, l'oeil), le se-cacher—se conjugue dans ce qu'on pourrait appeler l'histoire de l'oeuf ou l'oeuf de l'histoire. Le monde est né d'un oeuf: le soleil, donc, fut d'abord porté dans la coquille d'un oeuf ("La Pharmacie de Platon," p. 22)". And in n. 17: "Le paragraphe qui se clôt ici aura marqué que cette pharmacie de Platon contient et commente tout le texte de Bataille, inscrivant dans l'histoire de l'oeuf le soleil de la part maudite." For a criticism of Bataille's use of sun imagery, cf. Baudrillard: "In this sense we can reproach Bataille for having "naturalized" Mauss, and for having made of symbolic exchange a sort of *natural* function of prodigality, *a contrario* of the principle of utility and of the economic order which it exhausts itself in transgressing, without ever losing sight of it" ("Quand Bataille attaquait le principe métaphysique de l'économie," p. 4).

SELECTED BIBLIOGRAPHY

For more comprehensive bibliographical listings on Bataille, see:
Critique, no. 195–96 (August-September 1963).
L'Arc, no. 32 (1967).
Hawley, Daniel. *Bibliographie annotée de la critique sur Georges Bataille de 1929 à 1975.* Geneva: Slatkine; Paris: Honoré Champion, 1976.
Richman, Michèle H. "Georges Bataille" (annotated bibliography). In *A Critical Bibliography of Twentieth-Century French Literature.* Edited by Richard A. Brooks. Vol. 6, 3 parts. *The Twentieth Century,* edited by Douglas Alden and Richard A. Brooks. Pt. 3, All Genres since 1940. Syracuse: Syracuse University Press, 1980. Pp. 1437–40.
Semiotexte, vol. 2, no. 2, 1976.

Artaud, Antonin: Selected Writings. Edited, with an introduction, by Susan Sontag. Translated by Helen Weaver. New York: Farrar, Straus & Giroux, 1976.
Arnaud, Alain, and Gisèle Excoffon-Lafargue. *Bataille.* Paris: Editions du Seuil, 1978.
Augé, Marc. *Pouvoirs de vie, pouvoirs de mort: Introduction à une anthropologie de la répression.* Collection Science. Paris: Flammarion, 1977.
Bakhtin, Mikhail. *Rabelais and His World.* Translated by Helene Iswolsky. Cambridge, Mass.: MIT Press, 1965.
Barthes, Roland. "La Métaphore de l'oeil." *Critique,* no. 195–96 (1962), pp. 770–77.
―――――. "De l'oeuvre au texte." *Revue d'esthétique,* 24 (1971), pp. 225–32. Translated by Stephen Heath in *Image, Music, Text.* New York: Hill & Wang, 1977, pp. 155–64.
Bataille, Georges. "La Morale de Miller." *Critique,* no. 1 (1946), pp. 3–17.
―――――. "Le Sens moral de la sociologie." *Critique,* no. 1 (1946), pp. 39–47.
―――――. "Le Surréalisme et sa différence avec l'existentialisme." *Critique,* no. 2 (1946), pp. 99–110.
―――――. "Du rapport entre le divin et le mal." *Critique,* no. 10 (1947), pp. 227–34.
―――――. "De l'existentialisme au primat de l'économie." *Critique,* no. 13/14 (1947), pp. 515–33.
―――――. "Le Surréalisme en 1947." *Critique,* no. 15/16 (1947), pp. 271–72.
―――――. "De l'existentialisme au primat de l'économie," pt. 2 *Critique,* no. 20 (1948), pp. 127–41.

————. "Hegel, la mort, et le sacrifice." *Deucalion,* no. 5, Etudes Hegeliennes (1955), pp. 21–43.

————. *L'Erotisme.* Paris: Editions de Minuit, 1957.

————. "Conférences sur le non-savoir." *Tel Quel,* no. 10 (1962), pp. 5–20.

————. *La Part maudite.* With an introduction by Jean Piel. Paris: Editions de Minuit, 1967.

————. *Story of the Eye.* Translated by Joachim Neugroschel. New York: Urizen Books, 1977.

————. "Discussion sur le péché." *Le Nouveau Commerce,* no. 20 (1971), pp. 140–51.

————. *Les Larmes d'Eros.* Introduction by Lo Duca. Rev. ed. Paris: Pauvert, 1981.
Complete works:

I. *Premiers Ecrits, 1922–1940. Histoire de l'oeil. L'Anus solaire. Sacrifices. Articles.* Edited by Denis Hollier. Paris: Gallimard, 1970.

II. *Ecrits posthumes, 1922–1940.* Edited by Denis Hollier. Paris: Gallimard, 1970.

III. *Oeuvres littéraires. Madame Edwarda. Le Petit. L'Archangélique. L'Impossible. La Scissiparité. L'Abbé C. L'Etre indifférencié n'est rien. Le Bleu du ciel.* Edited by Thadée Klossowski. Paris: Gallimard, 1971.

IV. *Oeuvres littéraires posthumes. Poèmes. Le Mort. Julie. La Maison brûlée. La Tombe de Louis XXX. Divinus Deus. Ebauches.* Edited by Thadée Klossowski. Paris: Gallimard, 1971.

V. *La Somme athéologique I L'Expérience intérieure. Méthode de méditation. Post-scriptum, 1953. Le Coupable. L' Alleluiah.* Edited by Paule Leduc. Paris: Gallimard, 1973.

VI. *La Somme athéologique II. Sur Nietzsche. Memorandum. Annexes.* Edited by Henri Ronse et Jean-Michel Rey. Paris: Gallimard, 1973.

VII. *L'Economie à la mesure de l'univers. La Part maudite. La Limite de l'utile* (fragments). *Théorie de la religion. Conférences,* 1947–48. Edited by Thadée Klossowski. Paris: Gallimard, 1976.

VIII. *L'Histoire de l'erotisme. Le surréalisme au jour le jour. Conférences,* 1951–53. *La Souveraineté.* Edited by Thadée Klossowski. Paris: Gallimard, 1976.

IX. *Lascaux ou la naissance de l'art. Manet. La Littérature et le mal.* Edited by Denis Hollier. Paris: Gallimard, 1979.

X. Forthcoming.

Baudrillard, Jean. *Pour une critique de l'economie politique du signe.* Collection Les Essais. Paris: Gallimard, 1972.

————. *Le Miroir de la production.* Paris: Casterman, 1973.

————. *L'Echange symbolique et la mort.* Paris: NRF Gallimard, 1976.

————. "Quand Bataille attaquait le principe métaphysique de l'économie." *La Quinzaine Littéraire,* June 1–15, 1976.

Benjamin, Walter. *Reflections: Essays, Aphorisms, Autobiographical Writings.* Edited, with an introduction, by Peter Demetz. Translated by Edmund Jephcott. New York: Harcourt, Brace, Jovanovich, 1979.

Birnbaum, Pierre. "Du socialisme au don." *L'Arc,* no. 48 (1972), pp. 41–54.

Blanchot, Maurice. *La Part du feu.* Paris: NRF Gallimard, 1949.

————. *L'Entretien infini.* Paris: Gallimard, 1969.

Bourdieu, Pierre. *Esquisse d'une théorie de la pratique.* Geneva and Paris: Droz, 1972.

Bréchon, Robert. *Le Surréalisme.* Collection U. Paris: Armand Colin, 1971.

Breton, André. *Position politique du surréalisme.* Paris: Editions de Sagittaire, 1935.

_____. *Manifestes du surréalisme.* Collection Idées. Paris: Gallimard, 1967.

Brown, Norman O. *Life Against Death: The Psychoanalytic Meaning of History.* Middletown: Wesleyan University Press, 1959.

Caillois, Roger. *L'Homme et le sacré.* Collection Idées. Paris: Gallimard, 1950.

_____. "The Collège de Sociologie: Paradox of an Active Sociology." *SubStance,* no. 11/12 (1975), pp. 61–64.

Cérisy Colloquium. *Bataille.* Collection 10/18. Paris: U.G.E., 1973.

Clark, Terry Nichols. *Prophets and Patrons: The French University and the Emergence of the* Social Sciences. Cambridge, Mass.: Harvard University Press, 1973.

Clastres, Pierre. "Echange et pouvoir: Philosophie de la chefferie indienne." *L'Homme* 2, 1 (1962): pp. 51–65.

Deleuze, Gilles. *Présentation de Sacher-Masoch.* Paris: Editions de Minuit, 1967.

_____, and Félix Guattari. *L'Anti-Oedipe: Capitalisme et schizophrénie.* Paris: Editions de Minuit, 1972.

Derrida, Jacques. *De la grammatologie.* Paris: Editions de Minuit, 1967.

_____. "De l'économie restreinte à l'économie générale: Un Hegelianisme sans réserve." In *L'Ecriture et la différence.* Paris: Editions du Seuil, 1967, pp. 369–408.

_____. "La Différance." In *Théorie d'ensemble.* Paris: Seuil, 1968, pp. 41–66.

_____. "La Pharmacie de Platon." *Tel Quel,* no. 32/33 (1968), pp. 3–48, 18–59.

_____. "La Mythologie blanche." *Poétique,* no. 5 (1971), pp. 1–52.

_____. *La dissémination.* Paris: Seuil, 1972.

_____. *Positions.* Paris: Editions de Minuit, 1972.

_____. *Glas.* Paris: Editions Galilée, 1974.

_____. "Economimesis." In *Mimesis des articulations.* Paris: Aubier-Flammarion, 1975, pp. 55–94.

_____. *Of Grammatology.* Translated by Gayatri Chakravorty Spivak. Baltimore: Johns Hopkins University Press, 1976.

_____. "Ja, ou le faux-bond." (Entretien, pt. 2). *Digraphe,* no. 11 (April 1977), pp. 84–121.

_____. *Writing and Difference.* Translated, with an introduction and additional notes, by Alan Bass. Chicago: University of Chicago Press, 1978, pp. 251–300.

Diamond, Stanley. *In Search of the Primitive. A Critique of Civilization.* New Brunswick, N.J.: Transaction Books, 1974.

Douglas, Mary. *Purity and Danger: An Analysis of Concepts of Pollution and Taboo.* Harmondsworth: Penguin, 1966.

Dubar, Claude. "Retour aux textes." *L'Arc,* no. 48 (1972), pp. 23–25.

Dumont, Louis. "Une Science en devenir." *L'Arc,* no. 48 (1972), pp. 8–22.

Duplessis, Yves. *Le Surréalisme.* Collection Que sais-je? Paris: Presses Universitaires de France, 1967.

Durkheim, Emile. *Elementary Forms of the Religious Life.* Translated by J. W. Swain. New York: Free Press, 1965.

_____. *On Morality and Society.* Edited, with an introduction, by Robert N. Bellah. Chicago: University of Chicago Press, 1973.

Ehrmann, Jacques. "Le Dedans et le dehors." *Poétique,* no. 9 (1972), pp. 29–40.

Firth, Raymond. *Primitive Polynesian Economy.* London: Routledge and Kegan Paul, 1939.

Foucault, Michel. "Préface à la transgression." *Critique,* no. 195/96 (1963), pp. 751–69.

―――. *Les Mots et les choses: Une Archéologie des sciences humaines.* Bibliothèque des Sciences Humaines. Paris: Gallimard, 1966.

―――. *L'Ordre du discours.* Paris: NRF Gallimard 1971.

―――. *Language, Counter-Memory, Practice: Selected Essays and Interviews.* Translated by D. F. Bouchard and S. Simon. Ithaca: Cornell University Press, 1977.

Gasché, Rodolphe. "L'Echange héliocentrique." *L'Arc,* no. 48 (1972), pp. 73–84.

―――. "L'Almanach hétérologique." *Nuova Corrente,* no. 66 (1975), pp. 3–60.

Gobeil, Madeleine. "Interview with Michel Leiris." *Sub-Stance,* no. 11-12 (1975), pp. 44–60.

Godelier, Maurice. *Rationality and Irrationality in Economics.* New York and London: Monthly Review Press, 1972.

―――. *Perspectives in Marxist Anthropology.* Translated by Robert Brain. Cambridge: Cambridge University Press, 1977.

Goux, Jean-Joseph. *Freud, Marx: Economie et symbolique.* Paris: Editions du Seuil, 1973.

Harari, Josué V., ed. *Textual Strategies: Perspectives in Post-Structuralist Criticism.* Ithaca: Cornell University Press, 1979.

Hartman, Geoffrey. "Monsieur Texte: On Jacques Derrida, His *Glas.*" *Georgia Review,* no. 29 (Winter 1975), pp. 759–97.

Hawley, Daniel. *L'Oeuvre insolite de Georges Bataille: Une Hiérophanie moderne.* Paris: Librairie H. Champion, 1978.

Heath, Anthony. *Rational Choice and Social Exchange: A Critique of Exchange Theory.* Themes in the Social Sciences. Cambridge: Cambridge University Press, 1976.

Herskovits, Melville J. *Economic Anthropology: The Economic Life of Primitive People.* New York: Norton, 1965.

de Heusch, Luc. *"Pourquoi l'épouser?" et autres essais.* Paris: Gallimard, 1971.

Hesnard, A. *De Freud à Lacan.* Paris: Editions ESF, 1970.

Hollier, Denis. "Le Matérialisme dualiste de Georges Bataille." *Tel Quel,* no. 25 (1967), pp. 41–54.

―――. "La Parution des *Oeuvres Complètes,*" *Le Monde des Livres,* no. 7910 (June 20, 1970).

―――. "Malaise dans la sociologie." *L'Arc,* no. 48 (1972), pp. 55–62.

―――, ed. *Panorama des sciences humaines.* Collection Point du jour. Paris: NRF Gallimard, 1973.

―――. *La Prise de la Concorde: Essais sur Georges Bataille.* Paris: Gallimard, 1974.

―――, ed. *Le Collège de sociologie.* Collection Idées. Paris: NRF Gallimard, 1979.

Horton, Robin. "Lévy-Bruhl, Durkheim, and the Scientific Revolution." In *Modes of Thought,* edited by Robin Horton and Ruth Finnegan. London: Faber & Faber, 1973, pp. 249–305.

Hubert, Henri, et Marcel Mauss. "Essai sur la nature et la fonction du sacrifice." In *Oeuvres de Marcel Mauss.* Vol. 1. Paris: Editions de Minuit, 1968.

Jameson, Fredric. "Imaginary and Symbolic in Lacan: Marxism, Psychoanalytic Criticism, and the Problem of the Subject." *Yale French Studies,* no. 55/56 (1977), pp. 338–95.

Klossowski, Pierre. *Sade, mon prochain.* Paris: Editions du Seuil, 1947.

―――. *Un Si Funeste Désir.* Paris: Gallimard, 1963.

Kojève, Alexandre. *Introduction à la lecture de Hegel.* Paris: Gallimard, 1947.

Kristeva, Julia. "Le Mot, le dialogue, le roman." In *Recherches pour une sémanalyse*. Paris: Editions du Seuil, 1969.

_____. "Le Sujet en procès." *Tel Quel*, nos. 52/53 (1973), pp. 12–30, 17–38.

Lacan, Jacques. *Speech and Language in Psychoanalysis*. Translated, with notes and commentary, by Anthony Wilden. Baltimore: Johns Hopkins University Press. (Originally published in 1968 as *The Language of the Self.*)

Le Clair, Edward E., Jr., and Harold K. Schneider. *Economic Anthropology*. New York: Holt, Rinehart and Winston, 1968.

Lefebvre, Henri. *Everyday Life in the Modern World*. New York: Harper & Row, 1971.

Lefort, Claude. "L'Echange et la lutte des hommes." *Temps Modernes,* no. 64 (February 1951), pp. 1400–17.

Lévi-Strauss, Claude. "Introduction à l'oeuvre de Marcel Mauss." In Marcel Mauss, *Sociologie et anthropologie*. Paris: Presses Universitaires de France, 1950, pp. ix–lii.

_____. *Elementary Structures of Kinship*. Ref. ed. Translated by James Harle Bell, John Richard von Sturmes and Rodney Needham. Boston: Beacon Press, 1969.

_____. "French Sociology." In *Twentieth-Century Sociology,* edited by Georges Gurvitch and Wilbert E. Moore. Freeport, N.Y.: Books for Libraries, 1971, pp. 503–37.

Limousin, Christian. *Bataille*. Collection Psychothèque. Paris: Editions Universitaires, 1974.

Lukács, Georg. *History and Class Consciousness; Studies in Marxist Dialectics*. Translated by Rodney Livingstone. Cambridge, Mass.: MIT Press, 1968.

Lukes, Steven. *Emile Durkheim, His Life and Work: A Historical and Critical Study*. Harmondsworth: Penguin, 1973.

Lyotard, Jean-Francois, *La Phénoménologie*. Collection Que sais-je? Paris: Presses Universitaires de France, 1969.

Malinowski, Bronislaw. *Argonauts of the Western Pacific*. New York: Dutton, 1922.

Marcuse, Herbert. *Eros and Civilization: A Philosophical Inquiry into Freud*. New York: Vintage, 1962.

Mauriac, Claude. "Georges Bataille." In *The New Literature*. Translated by S. Stone. New York: Braziller, 1959, pp. 91–102.

Mauss, Marcel. *The Gift: Forms and Functions of Exchange in Archaic Societies*. Translated by I. Cunnison. New York: Norton, 1967.

Merleau-Ponty, Maurice. "From Mauss to Lévi-Strauss." In *Signs*. Northwestern University Studies in Phenomenology and Existential Philosophy. Evanston: Northwestern University Press, 1964. pp. 114–25.

Métraux, Alfred. "Rencontre avec les ethnologues." *Critique,* no. 195/96 (1963), pp. 678–84.

Parsons, Talcott. *The Structure of Social Action*. 2 vols. New York: Free Press, 1937.

Peignot, Colette [Laure]. *Ecrits de Laure*. Edited, with an introduction, by J. Peignot and the Collectif Change. Paris: Pauvert, 1977.

Polanyi, Karl. *Primitive, Archaic, and Modern Economies*. Edited by George Dalton. Boston: Beacon Press, 1968.

Poster, Mark. *Existential Marxism in Postwar France: From Sartre to Althusser*. Princeton: Princeton University Press, 1975.

Queneau, Raymond. "Premières confrontations avec Hegel." *Critique,* no. 195/96 (1963), pp. 695–700.

Sahlins, Marshall. "Political Power and the Economy in Primitive Society." In *Essays in the Science of Culture,* edited by Gertrude E. Dole and Robert L. Carneiro. New York: Crowell, 1960.

_____. "Philosophie politique de l'Essai sur le don." *L'Homme* 8, no. 4 (1968); 5–17.

_____. *Stone Age Economics.* Chicago: Aldine, 1972.

_____. *Culture and Practical Reason.* Chicago: University of Chicago Press, 1976.

Said, Edward. "Roads Taken and Not Taken in Contemporary Criticism." *Contemporary Literature* 17, no. 13 (Summer 1976): 327–48.

_____. "The Problem of Textuality: Two Exemplary Positions." *Critical Inquiry,* no. 4 (Summer 1978): 673–714.

Sartre, Jean-Paul. *L'Etre et le néant.* Paris: Gallimard, 1943.

_____. "Un Nouveau Mystique." In *Situations I.* (Originally published in *Cahiers du sud.* Paris: Gallimard, 1947, pp. 260–62 [1943].)

_____. *Saint Genet: Actor and Martyr.* New York: New American Library, 1963.

Sasso, Robert. *Georges Bataille: Le système du non-savoir. Une Ontologie du jeu.* Paris: Editions de Minuit, 1978.

Sollers, Philippe. "De grandes irrégularités du langage." *Critique,* no. 195/96 (1962), pp. 796–801.

Sontag, Susan. "The Pornographic Imagination." In *Styles of Radical Will.* New York: Dell, 1966. pp. 35–73.

Titmuss, Richard M. *The Gift Relationship.* New York: Vintage, 1972.

INDEX

Anthropology, 5, 95, 153; Bataillian, 3, 22, 23, 66, 78, 86, 96, 130, 138, 153; Hegelian, 140; philosophical, 5

Antinomies: of Hegel, 104; of Kant, 104; subversion of, 71

Aufhebung: Bataille on, 71, 86, 108; Derrida on, 161 n.36

Bakhtin, Mikhail, 151

Barthes, Roland, on Bataille, 1, 2, 88, 89, 99

Bataille, Georges: on author, 128–29, 137, 138; on Bataille, 2, 127–37; on Baudelaire, 132–33; Breton's polemic with, 49–56 (*see also* Surrealism); on community, 44; on death, 67, 69; on Durkheim, 36; on Genet, 134, 135, 149; on Hegel, 67, 69, 103; on heterology, 42, 104; on *le jeu*, 74; on language, 69, 72, 98, 99, 124, 125; on laughter, 38, 67, 68, 113, 115, 150, 151; on Lévi-Strauss, 79; on literature, 73, 127–32; on *le mal*, 74, 75; on Marxism, 49; on Mauss, 16–23; on mysticism, 68 (*see also* Eroticism); on Nietzsche, 50, 51, 72, 73; on philosophy, 78; on poetry, 69–77; on sacrifice, 68, 71; on Sartre, 128–37, 150; Sartre on, 112–20 passim, 150, 151; on structuralism, 80; and surrealism, 49–56, 124–26; on theory of subject, 114, 151. Works: "Coincidences," 89, 92–93; *Contre-Attaque*, 65; *Critique*, 1; *La Critique sociale*, 61; "Divinus Deus," 82; *Documents*, 94; "Dossier de l'oeil pinéal," 92, 93; *L'Erotisme*, 64, 75, 77, 78, 80, 84, 85, 86, 89, 99, 100, 107, 108, 109, 110; "La Figure humaine," 94, 95; *L'Expérience intérieure*, 65, 66, 69, 70, 74, 77, 108 (*see also* Sartre, Jean-Paul); *Haine de la poésie (L'Impossible)*, 129; *Histoire de l'oeil*

(Story of the Eye), 88–99, 148, 151; *L'Impossible (Haine de la poésie)*, 129; "Le Langage des fleurs," 139, 147; *La Littérature et le mal*, 127, 130, 136; "Ma Mère," 82; *Madame Edwarda*, 108; *Méthode de méditation*, 74; "La Notion de dépense," 8, 33; *La Part maudite*, 2, 5, 8, 17, 18, 20, 25, 91, 92, 127, 140; *La Somme athéologique*, 76, 109; "La Structure psychologique du fascisme," 60; "Le Supplice," 108; "La Vieille taupe et le préfixe *sur* dans les mots *surhomme* et *surréaliste*," 49

Baudelaire, Charles, Sartre on, 130–31

Baudrillard, Jean, 31

Benjamin, Walter, 65

Blanchot, Maurice, 124, 126

Bourdieu, Pierre, 12, 62; on dualities, 42; on Lévi-Strauss, 42; "original undifferentiation" of, 41, 63; "praxeological model" of, 42. *See also* Totality

Breton, André, 52, 56; polemic with Bataille, 49–56. *See also* Surrealism

Brown, N. O., 32, 33, 39

Caillois, Roger, 58; on Bataille, 59

Categories: Bataille on, 44–45; bourgeois, 27; collective, 32; of general economy, 3, 4, 6; Marxist, 28; of Mauss, 5. *See also* Communication; *Dépense*; Heterogeneity; Sacred, the; Sovereignty; Surreal, the; Totality; Transgression

"Coincidences" (Bataille), 89, 92–93

Le Collège de sociologie, 58; Caillois on, 59; Lévi-Strauss on, 122; Sartre on, 115, 116

Communication, 21, 36; Bataille on, 68, 69; as collective experience, 117, 161 n.35; Lévi-Strauss on, 122–23; nondiscursive, 138, 139, 150, 151